The Domestic Politics
of German Unification

The Domestic Politics of German Unification

edited by

Christopher Anderson
Karl Kaltenthaler
Wolfgang Luthardt

Lynne Rienner Publishers ▪ Boulder & London

Published in the United States of America in 1993 by
Lynne Rienner Publishers, Inc.
1800 30th Street, Boulder, Colorado 80301

and in the United Kingdom by
Lynne Rienner Publishers, Inc.
3 Henrietta Street, Covent Garden, London WC2E 8LU

Library of Congress Cataloging-in-Publication Data
The Domestic politics of German unification / edited by Christopher
  Anderson, Karl Kaltenthaler, and Wolfgang Luthardt.
      p. cm.
    Includes bibliographical references and index.
    ISBN 1-55587-409-6 (alk. paper)
      1. Germany—Politics and government—1945–1990. 2. Political
  parties—Germany—History—20th century. 3. Germany—History—
  Unification, 1990. I. Anderson, Christopher, 1966– .
  II. Kaltenthaler, Karl, 1966– . III. Luthardt, Wolfgang.
  JN3971.A58D58 1993
  943.087'9—dc20   93-10015
                                                                        CIP

British Cataloguing in Publication Data
A Cataloguing in Publication record for this book
is available from the British Library.

Printed and bound in the United States of America

The paper used in this publication meets the requirements
of the American National Standard for Permanence of   ∞
Paper for Printed Library Materials Z39.48-1984.

Contents

Part 2 Political Institutions and Policy Choices: New Challenges

Tables and Figures

Tables

Figures

Acknowledgments

We gratefully acknowledge the German Academic Exchange Service (DAAD) for providing very generous financial support for the completion of this book. Working with such backing made our lives as editors a lot easier. We would also like to thank the Political Science Department at Washington University in St. Louis, which provided us with a home while we worked on this project. We appreciate in particular the support of the department's chairs, John Sprague and Robert Salisbury, as well as the clerical help provided by Janet Rensing—faxing was more fun when done with Janet's help.

Chris Anderson acknowledges the support of John Sprague and Karl Kaltenthaler, and of Russell Dalton of the University of California, Irvine, who graciously supplied helpful hints on publishing an edited volume on German politics. Thanks also to Kylie Jill Hansen, a special friend in the English Department at Washington University, for straightening out questions of prose and everyday life.

Karl Kaltenthaler acknowledges the support provided by a Fulbright Research Grant to the German Democratic Republic in 1989–1990, which facilitated his research on East German politics, and also furnished a unique opportunity to witness history in the making. Gerd Horsch, Günther Streibel, and Manfred Melzer were particularly helpful in explaining the politics of East Germany. Last, but by no means least, Karl Kaltenthaler thanks his wife, Florence Kot, for encouragement and support.

Wolfgang Luthardt thanks the German Academic Exchange Service (DAAD), in particular Wedigo de Vivanco and Heidrun Suhr in New York and Marianne Reichling and Gottfried Gögold in Bonn. Moreover, he thanks the director of the European Studies Program at Washington University, Paul Michael Lützeler; the Department of Political Science, especially Robert Salisbury, John Sprague, John Kautsky, Arnold Heidenheimer, and Victor LeVine; his coeditors; and Wilhelm Neuefeind of the Department of Economics. These institutions and colleagues made his time as a visiting associate professor at Washington University in 1990–1992 a pleasant and intellectually rewarding experience.

Finally, the editors would like to thank Martha Peacock of Lynne Rienner Publishers for her competent, quick, clever, and ever-friendly and cheerful help in turning this project into a finished book.

There is a museum in Berlin, next to where Checkpoint Charlie used to be. It documents the ingenuity and courage of people trying to flee the German Democratic Republic after the Wall was built in 1961. They swam rivers, built balloons to fly to the West, hid in secret compartments in automobiles, and used trucks to crash crossing-points. Many of them were imprisoned when their plans were discovered, and a number of them lost their lives.

The museum is a testament also to the human desire to live in freedom from an authoritarian regime. Not everyone tried to flee. In fact, most East German citizens decided to stay behind the Iron Curtain, and many sought to reform the Communist system from within—into a system in which democracy was real and not just a slogan. They formed discussion groups, they met secretly in churches, and they believed in the possibility of real reform. These individuals played a large part in the peaceful surrender of the old Communist regime.

This book is dedicated to the spirit of freedom embodied both by those trying to flee and by those who believed in the possibility of a peaceful transformation of the East German system.

Christopher Anderson
Karl Kaltenthaler
Wolfgang Luthardt

Introduction

Christopher Anderson
Karl Kaltenthaler
Wolfgang Luthardt

The unification of the two German states is easily one of the most significant events of the twentieth century, not only in German national history but also for world politics. Moreover, the unification process of East and West Germany has been at the heart of the recent wave of democratization that has swept Central and Eastern Europe. And although the formal incorporation of the old German Democratic Republic (East Germany) into the Federal Republic of Germany (West Germany) may seem to some to have accomplished the major task of German unification, in reality it was only the beginning of a new and difficult era of German politics: the German political system is now charged with rebuilding a democratic system and a viable economy in the eastern part of the country.

The Context of German Unification

When one considers the forty-five years between the partition of Germany in 1945 as a consequence of the Allied occupation of the country and its unification in 1990, it is difficult to overlook just how differently the two German states evolved. Both the Federal Republic of Germany (FRG) and the German Democratic Republic (GDR) were founded as separate political entities in 1949. But despite that common starting point, they developed along divergent lines politically, economically, and socially.[1]

The West German political system was based on the principles of liberal democracy. These principles provided the foundation of the Basic Law (*Grundgesetz*), West Germany's provisional constitution, which was originally meant to be in force only until eventual reunification with the eastern part of the country. The Federal Republic's political institutions resembled those of the Weimar Republic, but there were a number of important differences. Take, for example, the electoral system, an institutional feature that some scholars early on identified as one of the culprits for the demise of the

Weimar Republic:[2] Instead of pure proportional representation, a 5 percent hurdle was established in elections to the federal legislature and the *Länder* parliaments in order to guard against the fragmentation of political power that had plagued the Weimar Republic. And, as the name belies, the Federal Republic of Germany was designed as a federal state in which the individual states (*Länder*) maintained substantially more power than had been the case during the Weimar Republic. Important policy areas like education were turned over to the *Länder*, which were only required to follow broad guidelines from the federal government. The federal nature of West Germany was the result of a conscious effort to create a more decentralized German state that would incorporate checks and balances.

But the Federal Republic of Germany also presented a distinct break with Germany's past because both the West Germans and the Allies worked to instill democratic values in the West German populace. The attempt to de-Nazify and democratize the German polity profoundly shaped the nature of West German politics; to this day German political elites seem ever so anxious about the fragility of German democracy. This sensitivity to the extremes of the political right and left, partially a result of the Weimar period and partially conditioned by the Cold War, led West German political elites to develop institutional rules that substantially and effectively reduced the potential for a rise of extreme antidemocratic parties on both sides of the political spectrum. Despite what the bans on parties on the extreme left and right may indicate, democracy never faced a serious challenge during the course of the FRG's existence. Over the years, a remarkable record of solid democratic politics and stable political institutions imbued West Germans with faith in their "Bonn Democracy" and, as the opportunity arose, with the confidence that the political institutions of the Federal Republic would be suitable for a united Germany.

While the FRG maintained political stability similar to that of its liberal democratic neighbors in Western Europe, the GDR followed the pattern of its Soviet-bloc allies. The creation of the German "workers' and peasants' state" was a much more dramatic break with Germany's past than the creation of the FRG. East German political institutions were shaped by the Soviet model and were based on the Leninist principle of democratic centralism.

The East German state, although originally federally organized (it was centralized in 1952) and nominally a multiparty democracy, developed a much more centralized and controlled political system than its western counterpart. The authoritarian nature of the East German state, above all, differentiated it from the Federal Republic. No free elections were held from the founding of the GDR in October 1949 until March 1990 (they were originally scheduled for May but were moved up), just seven months before the unification of the two German states. The Socialist Unity Party (SED), which was formed as a result of the forced merger of the

Communist Party and the Social Democratic Party in 1946, was the central source of political power in the GDR. Yet the National Front, a vehicle used by the SED to include as many social and political groups as possible in a controlled political process, also included Christian Democratic, Liberal, National Democratic, and farmers' parties. The National Front, the Marxist-Leninist Free Confederation of German Trade Unions (FDGB), and the Freie Deutsche Jungend (FDJ—the youth organization of the SED), were all designed to add some semblance of political participation and pluralism and thus legitimacy to the GDR. Establishing legitimacy was particularly important in a state where many of its own citizens voted with their feet and risked fleeing to West Germany despite an intricate system of obstacles to leaving the country. The inability of East German political elites to convince their citizens that the GDR was a legitimate and viable counterpart to the Federal Republic only accelerated the rapid collapse of the GDR and the subsequent unification of the two German states. When Mikhail Gorbachev withdrew the Soviet blessing from the SED regime in October 1989, the SED lost its last hope of remaining legitimate in the eyes of the East German population.

The glaring discrepancies in living standards between the two Germanies were perhaps the most crucial factor undermining the legitimacy of the GDR. East Germans constantly saw just how well off their neighbors "over there" were because of their access to West German television. Although East Germany enjoyed a better standard of living than any other socialist country in the world, the SED regime was never able to quell the people's desire to achieve a life like that broadcast nightly by West German television.

Despite the GDR's inability to match the economic development of the FRG, East Germany did make some startling economic achievements, given its rather daunting handicaps. It must be remembered that the Soviet occupation zone of Germany had been more badly damaged by Allied bombing than the western portions of the country. Moreover, the Soviets had stripped the eastern part of Germany of up to 30 percent of its industrial plants and equipment and shipped them back to the Soviet Union in lieu of reparations. The GDR was also handicapped by the westward flight of many of Germany's top scientists and technicians from the advancing Red Army. Perhaps the most serious obstacle facing the economic development of the GDR was its inclusion in the Soviet economic orbit. This not only precluded the GDR from receiving Marshall Plan aid but also meant that the GDR's trading partners were the underdeveloped economies of Eastern and Central Europe. A lack of natural resources also forced the GDR to rely on fuel supplies from its often unreliable eastern neighbors.

Despite these economic handicaps, the GDR maintained impressive rates of economic growth and developed the most technologically advanced economy in Eastern and Central Europe. This relatively impressive economic record was achieved while the GDR adhered to the Soviet-Stalinist economic model. East Germany never experimented with "goulash communism," as did the Hungarians, or turned to the West as did the Romanians and Yugoslavs. The German Democratic Republic, as Erich Honecker, leader of the SED from 1971 to 1989, would sometimes arrogantly claim, was an economic success within the Council for Mutual Economic Assistance (COMECON) because of the East Germans' discipline and hard work.

But if the East Germans had reason to be proud, their western neighbors in the Federal Republic had perhaps even more reason to be self-congratulatory. West Germany rose from a bombed-out shell of the western portion of the German Reich into the world's third-largest economy. The West German economic miracle was a product of hard work, careful postwar planning, and the fortune of being part of a vibrant Atlantic economy. The West German economic model, referred to as the social market economy because of its combination of the principles of laissez-faire capitalism with those of the welfare state, became the envy not only of other European states but also of developing countries outside Europe. The size and might of the West German economy turned the FRG into a model for others to emulate; they also gave West Germany the power to influence economic and political relations between European states and allowed it to play a more significant role in shaping the events in the wider world economy.

It was the Federal Republic's firm roots in Western Europe, more specifically in the European Community (EC), that provided the basis of its economic miracle. West Germany's ties to the advanced industrialized states of the Atlantic economy provided markets and resources for its export-oriented economic growth. West Germany's firm commitment to the EC helped placate those who feared the reemergence of a strong and confident Germany. But it was West Germany's membership in the NATO alliance that did the most to convince edgy Europeans that a strong Germany was an asset and not a threat to European security. The Federal Republic's commitments to its European and Atlantic allies lifted it out of political isolation and made it a respected member of the world community.

While the Federal Republic of Germany benefited from its membership in the EC and NATO, the German Democratic Republic had to bear the weight of being entangled in the economic and military alliances of the Soviet bloc. The GDR's membership in COMECON and the Warsaw Pact cut it off from the nurturing ties of the West and made it the front line of the Cold War. The GDR also bore the brunt of a diplomatic campaign on the part of West Germany, based on the Hallstein Doctrine, which announced that any state that recognized the GDR would automatically lose the diplomatic recognition of West Germany. This policy was the product of Chancellor Konrad Adenauer's foreign policy during the 1950s and 1960s of moving the Federal Republic firmly into the Western camp while trying to isolate the GDR and demonstrate the FRG's resolve to stand up to the Soviet Union. When the Christian Democratic Union/Christian Social Union–Social Democratic Party(CDU/CSU-SPD) grand coalition collapsed in 1969 and was replaced by the Social Democratic Party-Free Democratic Party (SPD-FDP) coalition, the West German policy of trying to isolate the GDR gave way to Willy Brandt's policy of *Ostpolitik*. (*Ostpolitik* was the policy of opening to the East to relieve tensions between West Germany and its eastern neighbors, particularly the GDR and Poland.)

This opening to the GDR led to the *Grundlagenvertrag,* or basic treaty, of 1972, which provided de facto recognition of the GDR as a separate state but never offered the GDR de jure recognition. It served as the basis for inter-German relations from 1972 until unification, a period in which East-West relations in general moved from détente to renewed tensions and finally to the demise of the Cold War. But despite the ups and downs in superpower relations, inter-German relations remained relatively consistent throughout the 1970s and 1980s, even gaining ground during the very tense early 1980s. Meanwhile, the SED leadership was wary of its lack of legitimacy among its own population and feared that a substantial rapprochement with the Federal Republic would threaten the SED's ability to control the East German population. Due to the economic slowdown and subsequent austerity measures introduced by the East German government in 1982, East Germans became increasingly aware during the course of the 1980s that the SED regime denied them the quality of life that their West German neighbors took for granted.

However, instead of following the direction of the Soviet Union and its policies of glasnost and perestroika in order to bolster the East German economy and gain popularity, the SED leadership chose to remain recalcitrant and rejected Soviet-style reform. Erich Honecker's regime adopted a pose of defiance in the face of Soviet liberalization, even going so far as to ban Soviet periodicals it found too politically provocative. When asked by Western journalists in 1987 why the GDR had not embarked on the path of reform mapped out by the Soviet Union, Kurt Hager, an SED politburo member, countered with "Why do we need to change our wallpaper every time our neighbor does?" Such statements only heightened the tension between Soviet and East German leaders.

Reform in the Soviet Union was not the only cause for tension between the SED and the Soviet leadership. In the spring of 1989, Mikhail Gorbachev announced the end of the Brezhnev doctrine and endorsed the profound reforms that were under way in Hungary and Poland, including the Hungarian leadership's decision to dismantle the border between Hungary and Austria on May 2, 1989. When this became known in East Germany, thousands of East Germans traveled to Hungary with the intention of escaping to the Federal Republic via Austria. This sieve in the East German state's borders worsened as more and more East Germans began to fear that reform was not forthcoming from the SED and that the best option was to leave immediately or face a bleak future in the GDR.

In addition to the problem of the mass flight of GDR citizens to the West, Erich Honecker was also faced with rising discontent at home. During September 1989 East Germans took to the streets to demand reforms and freedom of travel. As these demonstrations increased in size and intensity, the GDR celebrated its fortieth anniversary, on October 7, 1989. Mikhail Gorbachev, who was to give a speech commemorating the founding of the GDR, used the celebration ceremony as an opportunity to warn Honecker that resisting reform would lead to his being overtaken by history. The speech set off a series of large-scale demonstrations in Berlin and Leipzig that continued throughout October 1989. Honecker remained obdurate and used the GDR's security police to quell the demonstrations. Realizing that Honecker's position on reform threatened to ignite violence, the SED politburo removed Honecker from office on October 18, 1989. Honecker's successor, Egon Krenz, grappled with ways to stem the swelling protests and continuing flow of East Germans to the West. When promises of reforms did not placate GDR citizens, Krenz took the radical step of opening the East German border for travel to the West.

When Günther Schabowski, member of the East German politburo and speaker for the government, announced at a press conference in East Berlin on the evening of November 9, 1989, that all East German citizens could travel without restriction to West Germany and West Berlin, he probably did not anticipate that this move would only accelerate the collapse of the SED regime and lead to the eventual unification of Germany. In fact, Schabowski's rather casual statements marked the beginning of a memorable night and the end of the infamous Berlin Wall. The decision to open the borders of the GDR was a desperate attempt by the SED leadership to bolster its own popularity and stop the demonstrations and continuing flight of its citizens. Instead of showing gratitude to the SED, citizens voted with their feet in the following weeks and months, leaving the GDR at a rate of 2,000 per day.

After November 9, 1989, the political hierarchy in the GDR started to crumble. On November 18, 1989, the East German People's Chamber, or Volkskammer, elected Hans Modrow, a representative of the reform-minded elements in the SED, to the then relatively powerless post of prime minister. Modrow managed to turn his office into a more influential instrument of political power after the Volkskammer on December 1 repealed the section of the constitution that provided for the "leadership role" of the Socialist Unity Party, and after the entire SED leadership resigned on December 3. Although his reformist credentials equipped Modrow with some, albeit a very limited, degree of legitimacy, he lacked the kind of legitimacy derived from free and democratic elections. When the power apparatus of the Communist system started to disintegrate further, the

Modrow government agreed to negotiate with the most prominent dissident groups and newly formed political parties in the form of "round table" (*Der Runde Tisch*) discussions. The round table held its first session on December 7 and continued to meet until March 12, 1990. The leadership's announcement in January 1990 that free elections would be held in May of that year represented a last-ditch effort to save the GDR as an independent state. But it came too late. The end of the GDR as a sovereign state came in sight: The GDR had little reason to exist separately from West Germany if it was not a socialist state.

The round table negotiations were a dynamic phenomenon that went through several phases.[3] First, they served to delegitimize and disarm the old power apparatus of the SED and the state security forces. Second, they led to the creation of a "government of national responsibility" (*Regierung der nationalen Verantwortung*) of which the round table was an integral part. And finally, this second phase led to a third stage in which the various contenders struggled for government control.

Initial plans for popular elections scheduled for May 1990 had to be shelved in favor of holding elections for a new East German Volkskammer on March 18, 1990, while the mass exodus of citizens to West Germany continued unabated and the political structure of the Communist state showed increased signs of deterioration. This transitional period between the fall of the Berlin Wall and the elections of March 18, 1990, was heavily influenced by a sense of power vacuum, with the formal instruments of power and the institutions of the old regime still in place but with no clearly identifiable political actors in charge. The Modrow government lacked democratic legitimacy; however, those forces with popular backing were not yet formally part of the institutionalized political process. The elections scheduled for March were designed to alleviate this problem and install legitimate political actors as representatives for the East German state, because the ongoing political process required actors that were able to conduct business on behalf of the East German state without the liabilities that had frustrated and inhibited the Modrow government.

The elections to the East German Volkskammer were the first and last free and democratic countrywide elections held in the GDR, and they were dominated by a single overarching issue: the pace of German unification. Along with the organizations that had been instrumental in bringing about the peaceful ouster of the Communists in 1989, a total of twenty-four parties competed in these elections. The most important parties were the newly founded left-leaning Social Democrats and the more conservative Alliance for Germany. The Social Democratic Party had been formed in October 1989 and had originally been called SDP, but it was then "adopted" and supported by its big brother from West Germany, the Social Democratic Party of Germany (SPD). The Alliance for Germany was designed by the West German electoral managers of Chancellor Helmut Kohl's Christian

Democratic Union (CDU). It consisted of the bigger Christian Democratic Union and two smaller parties, the German Social Union (DSU) and Democratic Awakening (DA). The Social Democratic Party had traditionally been strong in the eastern part of Germany before the Soviet occupation, and it had not had ties with the Communist regime. In that regard the Social Democrats were different from the CDU, which had once been a "puppet party" in the Communist-controlled National Front. In early March, the SPD was heavily favored to win the election contest. Instead, the resounding winner in the election was the Alliance for Germany, which had run on a platform of free-market economic reforms and, most important, unification as quickly as possible. The Social Democrats and the Communist SED (now renamed the Party of Democratic Socialism, or PDS) were trounced. These election results had important implications for the dynamics of the unification process because they installed the CDU politician Lothar de Maizière as the East German prime minister; he initially governed in a grand coalition with the Social Democrats.

On February 7, 1990, more than a month before the election, the West German government had offered East Germany immediate negotiations toward the creation of a monetary union and an economic community. It had been proposed that the East German Ost Mark be replaced by the West German Deutsche Mark on a yet-to-be-determined date. At the same time, the GDR was expected to create the conditions for the introduction of a market economy. The two German governments quickly took up this proposal after the election, because the East Germans seemed to have expressed their desire for a quick conclusion of the unification process and Chancellor Kohl had campaigned heavily on this issue. The core of the Economic, Monetary, and Social Union Treaty that was signed by the two Germanies on May 18, 1990, and went into effect on July 2 consisted of the introduction of the West German currency. The introduction of "good money" and the treaty in general had, and continue to have, significant implications for all aspects of the East German and West German societies and economies—implications that can hardly be overstated, as they have affected wages, salaries, prices of goods, inflation and credit, welfare benefits and pensions, aspects of economic cooperation in the European Community, taxation and public debts, and the structure of the economies.

The international attitude toward these proceedings encouraged the two German states to move toward unification. Negotiations known as the two-plus-four talks between the two German states and the four occupying powers were initiated to settle the unresolved issue of granting Germany full sovereignty. The Soviet Union, with some 300,000 troops stationed in the GDR and an historical distrust of Germany, was the potential major international obstacle to German unification. But with promises of sizable loans and payments for the resettlement of Soviet troops, the Federal

Republic was able to convince the Soviets to go along with German plans for unification. With the Soviets satisfied, and the Western powers willing to accept German unification, the road to unification was clear when the Allies granted full sovereignty to Germany just before formal unification.

Although the two-plus-four talks proceeded smoothly, monetary union turned out to be a disaster for the GDR economy. East Germans exchanged their worthless Ost Marks for the valuable D-Mark at a one-to-one rate, and then proceeded to buy only Western products. As the East German economy collapsed, the calls for immediate unification came not only from the CDU and its allies but also from the Social Democrats, who felt the Federal Republic had a responsibility to aid the East because of the effects of the monetary union.

The express desire of East German citizens to speed up the process of unification moved the debate about the process of formal political unification to the forefront. How was the political unity of the two Germanies to be accomplished? The political actors in Bonn and Berlin chose the quickest possible route to unification. On August 31, 1990, the two Germanies signed a second treaty, called a Unification Treaty, that stated in Article 1:

> Upon the accession of the German Democratic Republic to the Federal Republic of Germany in accordance with Article 23 of the Basic Law taking effect on 3 October 1990 the Länder of Brandenburg, Mecklenburg–Western Pomerania, Saxony, Saxony-Anhalt and Thuringia shall become Länder of the Federal Republic of Germany. The establishment of these Länder and their boundaries shall be governed by the provisions of the Constitutional Act of 22 July 1990 on the Establishment of Länder in the German Democratic Republic . . .

East Germany reestablished once-existing states and acceded to West Germany on October 3. Thus, the unification of Germany was formally completed less than eleven months after the fall of the Berlin Wall. Yet these new states did not have democratically elected governments. In order to institute such governments, state and local elections were held in all five new *Länder* and Berlin on October 14. Except for one state (Brandenburg), the CDU dominated the elections and won either an absolute majority (Saxony), or formed coalitions with the Free Democratic Party (FDP), its coalition partner in Bonn. Hence, the electoral success which the Christian Democrats had experienced in March was repeated at the state (*Länder*) level.

It became apparent in late summer of 1990 that the 1990 West German elections, which had initially been planned as the regular Bundestag elections for the old Federal Republic, would be the first free all-German elections since the 1932 Weimar Republic elections. It did not come as a surprise that the national elections held on December 2 were also dominated by the issue of unification and were seen by many as a referendum on the performance of the Kohl government during the unification process.

While the politics of unification were to a considerable extent driven by the political and economic collapse of East Germany, it is undeniable that the successful completion of the unification project in 1990 was the achievement of one politician: West Germany's Chancellor Helmut Kohl. Starting with his ten-point program of unification in November 1989, he quickly and firmly grasped the historical chance that was offered him as the chancellor of the democratic Germany. Thus he was able to transform the March GDR elections into a plebiscite on the speed of unification by personally campaigning in the East for the conservative Alliance for Germany; shortly thereafter he presided over the negotiations that led to the signing of the Economic, Monetary, and Social Union and the Unification treaties between the two German states.

Kohl's challenger for the chancellorship, the SPD's Oskar Lafontaine, argued time and again that the unification process was proceeding too rapidly, that it was fundamentally flawed and socially unjust to the citizens of East Germany, and that a socially and economically just unification process was being sacrificed for the sake of short-term political gain. Even though Lafontaine's points seem accurate after the fact, they did not discourage the German electorate, which confirmed Kohl in a resounding victory on December 2, 1990.

The Scope of the Book

This book addresses the domestic politics of German unification. It broadly examines the unification process and consequences, while focusing on the following questions: (1) How did the process of unification take place and how can it be understood? (2) What are the effects of unification, both short- and long-term, on the democratic process in Germany? (3) What are the consequences of unification for German political institutions? and (4) What are some concrete examples of policy problems facing the unified Germany? The scope of the book is meant to reach beyond the immediate effects of unification and look at some of the possible long-term consequences unification will have on German political life. The volume is limited mostly to domestic German politics, because we feel that the inclusion of various aspects of international politics would have left too little space for the discussion of the domestic aspects of unification.

Part 1 of the book examines the breakdown of the East German regime, the electoral politics of the unification year, political parties and their strategies, political elites, and the recent rise of right-wing extremism. This section delineates the unification process and explores the political dynamics of a year that led to the unification of the two Germanies less than eleven months after the fall of the Berlin Wall. Part 2 deals with the real and potential consequences of the unification for German political institutions. It considers the challenges and problems that the rapid unification brought with regard to the country's constitution, federalism, administrative structures, and policymaking processes.

The first section of the book opens with Gerhard Lehmbruch's chapter, examining the process of regime change in the GDR. The collapse of the SED regime is intriguing, not only because it represents the peaceful fall of an authoritarian regime, but also because it serves as an example of a state's transformation from Stalinist socialism to liberal democracy.

Gerhard Lehmbruch puts the process of regime change in the GDR in the broader perspective of regime change in general. Instead of focusing on a step-by-step description of the fall of the Communist regime and how this led to unification, Lehmbruch touches on a number of issues that are crucial for understanding this process. In addition, Lehmbruch explores potential long-term effects of the unification process on German political institutions and modes of politics.

Max Kaase examines the electoral politics and public opinion of the 1990 unification year in great detail. He places the March and December elections within the broader context of the Federal Republic's electoral history not only by focusing on the outcomes of the elections that were held during the year of unification, but also by investigating the social bases of political parties and the attitudes of Easterners and Westerners that drove the dynamics of these elections. His examination of public opinion in Germany during the unification year helps illuminate the trends for future German elections.

Peter Lösche's contribution to this volume concerns the financing of East German political parties during the campaign for the East German elections in March 1990. He argues that the West German parties did not, on the whole, take over their East German counterparts. The East German parties may have been strategically dependent on their West German partners, but their funds came mostly from the East German state. Thus, the image that West German parties bankrolled their sister organizations is, according to Lösche, misleading.

The immense importance of the March and December 1990 elections for the process of German unification is evident. Less evident are the consequences of unification on political elites in both parts of Germany. Christopher Anderson analyzes the social composition of the Bundestag from the founding of the Federal Republic until the unification of the two German states (1949–1990). He finds that, overall, there is a striking continuity in the types of people elected from both parts of the country to the new 1990 Bundestag despite the fact that the GDR survived as a separate socialist German state for forty years. However, Anderson also finds some noteworthy differences between the representatives from the East and the

West. He argues that this is probably a consequence of a host of factors, such as electoral rules, party infrastructure, and recruitment mechanisms.

The social composition of the Bundestag may have remained relatively constant following the first all-German elections, but the German electorate has become more volatile. Gerard Braunthal discusses the phenomenon of right-wing extremism in Germany. He argues that right-wing extremism has risen in Germany because of the social dislocation brought about by unification. The anxieties that have resulted from the economic uncertainties of life in a unified Germany as well as the end of the secure East German police state have prompted many youths to turn to neo-Fascist movements. Braunthal looks at the prospects of these movements and describes scenarios that could redress the problem of political extremism.

The second section of the volume deals with the profound effects of unification on Germany's political institutions: In the former GDR they have been dismantled on a massive scale, and the capacities of West German institutions have been severely tested. Wolfgang Seibel examines the transformation of these institutions in the new Germany. His chapter addresses three questions: How was the process of unification managed politically? What crucial institutional problems are likely to emerge and how will the German political system deal with them? How will the process of unification affect the general structure of the German polity? Seibel concludes that the unified Germany is not merely an expanded West Germany but a new Germany whose political institutions will have to adapt to the new social and political circumstances.

The inclusion of six new *Länder* into the federal structure of Germany has raised some very important constitutional questions that relate to the nature of the *Grundgesetz* and the nature of German federalism. Donald P. Kommers addresses the issue of the effects of unification on the German *Grundgesetz*. By choosing Article 23 of the *Grundgesetz* as the route to unification, Germans avoided a prolonged constitutional battle that would almost certainly have ensued from creating a new all-German constitution. But the constitutional issues of German unification have not yet been resolved. Many legal consequences of German unification remain highly contentious. Battle lines have been drawn between those trying to maintain the constitutional status quo and those who argue for changes in the German constitution because of their progressive agenda or because they feel that the *Grundgesetz* was indeed only meant to be a provisional document.

The federal structure of Germany has come under extreme pressure as a result of the accession of the new eastern *Länder* to the Federal Republic. West German federalism was already under considerable strain before unification because of the regional disparities in wealth and the system of financial equalization. The addition of five poor *Länder* has intensified these pressures. Arthur B. Gunlicks deals with the questions of German federalism that have arisen from unification. He argues that in the long run a change in the structure of German federalism is bound to occur because of financial burdens placed on the wealthier states by the poorer states. Unification has exacerbated an already contentious issue.

Other, less formal institutional patterns have been affected by the unification process as well. A good example is labor-employer relations, which are also in a state of flux. The addition of the economically decrepit former GDR to the FRG has put new demands on the corporatist structure of the German economy. M. Donald Hancock examines the reconstruction of organized labor and employer associations in the former GDR. He argues that the extension of West German organizational and programmatic patterns to the territory of the former GDR is likely to lead to an increased assertiveness on the part of organized labor. This is due not only to the increased numerical strength of the all-German unions but also to the ideological infusion resulting from several million East German workers joining the ranks of these unions.

Problems that have become all-German issues because of unification are treated by Karl Kaltenthaler in Chapter 10 and Lutz Reuter in Chapter 11. The years of neglect or mismanagement of important sectors of the East German infrastructure have left these sectors in shambles. The cost of rectifying these problems is staggering. The Federal Republic, a state that has traditionally maintained tight budgetary policies, faces a situation that strains its financial resources to their limits. The political consequences of rebuilding the East German infrastructure will have long-term implications for policymaking in unified Germany.

One of the most pressing policy problems in the former East Germany is the environment. The East German environment has been ravaged by years of abuse due to the economic myopia of the SED regime. Karl Kaltenthaler asks how the new Germany can deal with the legacy of East German environmental policy. He argues that it was the SED regime's mania for economic growth that has left the former GDR with such serious environmental problems. This situation will be partially remedied by closing many of the polluting factories in the East that cannot compete economically. The transfer of West German policymaking institutions will also aid in alleviating this situation. Part of the problem with East German institutions of environmental protection was their lack of clearly defined policy responsibilities and their subservience to economic planning. As with many other policy problems in the former GDR, environmental problems will require a huge financial commitment.

Lutz Reuter examines how the Germans are reconciling their differing systems of education and are creating an educational system in which all credentials have equal value. This issue, like the issue of constitutional change, has resurrected old political debates between those who want to maintain the status quo and those who want to reform the entire system of

German education. The controversy arises mainly between those who want to make the German educational system more equitable and those who believe that the West German system has been very successful. As in the case of the environment, the funds to rectify the crumbling East German education system are hard to come by, which in itself complicates an already contentious political issue.

The concluding chapter draws on the contributions in the book and spells out some of the major themes that underlie the current domestic politics of Germany. The dominant undercurrents of German politics that influence party strategies, electoral behavior, and policymaking are the economic situation—particularly in the East—and the legacy of the past.

In this book we have tried to tie together various important aspects of the politics of German unification to create a more comprehensive picture of its process and consequences. In order to make sense of German politics in the future, we need to understand the politics of the past and the present. A large part of that past and present is directly, or indirectly, tied to the domestic politics of German unification.

Notes

1. For a good introduction to the politics of West Germany, see Russell Dalton (1993), *Politics in Germany,* 2nd ed. (New York: HarperCollins). For a critical introduction to the politics of East Germany, see David Childs (1988), *The GDR: Moscow's German Ally,* 2nd ed. (London: Hyman).

2. See, e.g., Ferdinand A. Hermens [1941] (1971), *Democracy or Anarchy? A Study of Proportional Representation* (New York: Johnson Reprint Corporation).

3. Thaysen, Uwe (1990), *Der Runde Tisch. Oder: Wer Was das Volk? Der Weg der DDR in die Demokratie.* Opladen: Westdeutscher Verlag.

Part 1
The Process and Politics of Unification

Chapter 1

The Process of Regime Change in East Germany

Gerhard Lehmbruch

In recent years, students of comparative politics have repeatedly undertaken cross-national studies of processes of political regime change. In particular, there have been studies of the breakdown of European democracies between the two world wars and of the more recent developments in regions where military and/or authoritarian dictatorships gave way to democracy. What distinguishes the regime changes in Eastern Europe is not simply that we still lack much of the historical information that usually becomes available as time passes. In the research just mentioned, regime change became the object of inquiry only after it was completed, through the installation of a new political order. The collapse of the Communist regimes in Eastern Europe is different, because these countries have reached only a transitional stage of democratic institution building. This process is far from complete, and much uncertainty about the final shape of the new democratic regimes remains.

There is, of course, one important distinction between East Germany and most other East European countries (the Baltic states excepted): The fundamental pattern of statehood survived the establishment of a new democratic framework. Hence, in these countries the problem of the national state is not an issue, and considerable institutional continuity can be expected once the cycle of regime change is completed. In the case of the GDR, the range of analytical uncertainty is much greater. Of course, the GDR did not survive as a separate state and has surrendered its political identity in a united Germany. But I want to warn against imagining the united Germany simply as some kind of spatial extension of the old FRG. Some in western Germany have even begun to wonder whether the history of their state, as it has developed over forty years, is now over.

To be sure, as some political leaders in Bonn like to stress, the former GDR is only the size of one major West German *Land.* Yet the concept of "reunification" implicit in this argument neglects an important issue. The national unity to which it refers, Bismarck's German state, lasted only

17

eighty years, from 1867 (when the North German Confederation was established) to 1947 (when effective four-power rule over the occupied Reich ended). Since then forty-some years have passed, more than half the lifespan of the former Reich, and in this period both parts of Germany developed very distinctive political and social institutions. Although policymakers in the Federal Republic are determined to tear down the East German institutional framework, it cannot simply be replaced by the West German model. Most of its important elements have been introduced in the East, but others will require a difficult process of adaptation. A protracted, probably laborious, and painful process of building new institutions is inevitable. There are good reasons to believe that this will also strongly affect the nature of the Federal Republic. The united Germany confronts economic problems and cultural tensions that pose entirely new challenges for the political system.

I begin with an analysis of some of the fault-lines in the power structure of Honecker's GDR that finally led to its collapse. Subsequently, I examine this process as it unfolded, first as an internal crisis, and then as it was precipitated by the irruption of the West German party system into the political system of the GDR. I argue that this led to a new, and different, type of predominance of party politics over economics, which carries with it implications that are still difficult to fully anticipate. Finally, I outline some of the formidable problems of institutional reconstruction in a united Germany.

The Disintegration of the GDR: Causes and Origins

It is clear that the crisis would not have evolved as fast as it did had Gorbachev not abandoned Honecker to his fate. But for the purposes of this chapter, I take the important role of the Soviet Union as a given. My question is rather why Honecker did not survive the change of Soviet policy. What were the internal weaknesses of the system, and how did the domestic process of change unfold?

Under the leadership of Honecker, the GDR had achieved a certain stability and, as it appeared to many observers, some legitimacy in the eyes of its citizens. This legitimacy certainly had weaknesses, and they mirrored some of the weaknesses of legitimacy of the West German state. To the attentive observer, the GDR lacked the kind of popular support that accompanies the concept of nation in many Western countries. But it is doubtful whether the situation was fundamentally different in the Federal Republic. West Germans were, and are, aware of a German cultural identity, but that identity is not coterminous with their state. Traditional identification with the nation-state has not survived the catastrophe of the Nazi imperial rule; it has been asserted that some kind of "constitutional patriotism" has developed instead. I am not very happy with this notion. Unlike Americans, West Germans have a very prosaic relationship with the constitutional order. They seem to be comfortable with the broad institutional framework, including the economic and social institutions, as they have developed. This feeling of comfort is of course supported by the perception of a collective success story, and that goes somewhat beyond mere economic prosperity. However, if one can speak of an "institutional patriotism" in West Germany, it probably still depends upon the performance of that institutional framework.

The limited legitimacy that Honecker's government achieved was not altogether dissimilar in nature. In relation to the other "real-socialist" countries, the GDR for some time appeared quite efficient in economic terms. It seemed well administered, and as a welfare state it aimed to give its citizens a feeling of economic security. Unlike the West German variety of welfare state, the system shielded the individual against all the risks that characterize a market economy and society. Many East Germans found at least some comfort in these social institutions.

One fundamental difference in the political culture was the very limited range of opportunities for autonomous choice in shaping one's personal life, for example, in choosing a career. Social opportunity depended upon strict conformity with the official value system administered by an authoritarian and bureaucratic party apparatus. Emigration to the West, a security valve as well as an economic liability during the 1950s, was precluded by the existence of the Wall and its rigid custody, at enormous and probably quite disproportionate economic costs. The alternative, pretty much tolerated by the regime, was retreat into *Biedermeier*-like depoliticized private niches and a quietist mentality. The "Prussian path to socialism" (as it apparently was once called in Poland) emphasized order and passive compliance.

The almost complete lack of opportunities for meaningful participation, that is, participation that increased choice, was the most distinctive mark of the GDR's institutional framework. In contrast, in West Germany the participatory revolution of the late 1960s and early 1970s had resulted in the emergence of a remarkably strong and self-conscious, sometimes quite rebellious, individualist grass-roots culture. Nevertheless, these Western experiences crept into the GDR, and some individuals and small groups deliberately accepted considerable personal hardships and discrimination for their growing willingness to voice dissent. It appears that these contrasting attitudes fueled the crisis of the regime. Whereas the refractory minorities played an active and decisive role in finally and successfully challenging the bureaucratic party rule, the predominant mode of passive compliance probably explains much of the sudden collapse of allegiance to the GDR as a state and the complete inability of the regime to mobilize even a minimum of popular support.

Moreover, the institutions of the security-oriented welfare state themselves had some important built-in weaknesses. Honecker's official doctrine was the "unity of social and economic policy," or a deliberate subordination of economics to party politics and its aim of social redistribution. Growth depended on an equally deliberate neglect of social realities. The subordination of economics was most evident in the technique of subsidizing basic consumption. To be sure, a policy of cheap rents was popular and contributed to the perception of guaranteed social security. Between 1970 and 1988 the index of rent costs fell slightly, whereas it more than doubled in the Federal Republic. The distortion of economic incentives became more visible in the pricing of food and other basic consumer goods. For example, hogs were fed with subsidized bread because it cost less than grain. To give another example: A maker of wooden ladders sold his product to the local "trade organization" store for 6 Marks, where it then had to be resold to the consumers for half that sum. In 1988 subsidies amounted to 25 percent of the total consumption. On the other hand, taxes on higher quality and imported consumer goods were high, constituting 22 percent of total consumption. This system inevitably led to considerable inefficiencies.

Overcentralization of economic management in huge, monopolistic, industrial units (*Kombinate*) and the rigidities of economic planning further impaired the efficiency of the GDR economy. Differences in labor productivity are difficult to assess, but according to reasonable estimates the GDR's production was at best half that of the West German economy. If East Germany wanted to maintain growth and still subsidize consumption, it could do so only by recklessly neglecting the environment. Per capita energy consumption in the GDR in 1970 was 110 percent of that in the FRG. In 1988 that proportion had increased to 124 percent. Most of this energy was wasted and contributed to an incredible degree of air pollution in the heavily industrialized southern part of the country, as well as devastating large territories by open strip-mining of lignite, the GDR's only domestic source of fuel (see also Chapter 10).

Although the pattern of economic governance resulted in an economic leadership position for the GDR within Eastern Europe, it became self-defeating in the long run by accumulating deficits. The situation was made worse by the impact of the oil shocks, to which the GDR adapted only with difficulty. From the mid-1970s onward, the East German GNP grew more slowly than that of the Federal Republic. Because of the increased availability of West German television in most East German territory, the lag in economic performance behind West Germany could not go unnoticed by the public. Between 1970 and 1988, the percentage of East German households owning a car grew from 16 to 52, whereas the percentage grew from 51 to 97 in the Federal Republic. The proportion of households with telephones grew from 6 to 9 percent in the East during that time, whereas it grew from 20 to 98 percent in the West. The latter figure illustrates how the GDR lost ground in technologically advanced industries and in building the technical infrastructure of the emerging information society. The widespread perception of relative deprivation resulting from such observations undermined the eventual impact of the GDR's economic leadership role in Eastern Europe. More specifically, this perception had to impair the legitimacy of a regime that emphasized performance so strongly.

Finally, regional disparities created additional tensions. East Berlin, treated as a showcase for the republic, received disproportionate shares of state subsidies and manpower, which was in short supply, in particular in the construction sector. The resulting resentments boiled over in the fall of 1989. It is no accident that the revolution took off in Leipzig, the industrial heart of Saxony that particularly suffered from the environmental irresponsibility of the leadership.

Social Forces and Motivational Syndromes
in the East German Revolution

The situation described so far resulted in two characteristically different protest syndromes: One protest syndrome was related to participation and the other was related to opportunity and performance. On the one hand, participation-oriented critics focused on human rights and increasingly cited the Helsinki documents; on the other hand they also focused on environmental policy. The activists who initiated and led the protest movements were mostly people with a high degree of formal education who were employed in the service sector. Their social profile and political agenda resembled that of the Green and alternative movements in West Germany and other West European countries. They came from quite diverse ideological backgrounds, from young Protestant activists to Communist Party members outside the formal apparatus as well as those who had defected from the party ranks. The opposition was most active in the large cities, especially in the south. But, according to the available accounts, blue-collar workers were conspicuously missing from the active participants.

Opposition groups began to meet mainly in Protestant churches and parish houses, and Protestant ministers were represented among their spokesmen in disproportionate numbers. This peculiar feature distinguished the GDR opposition from that in other East European countries. It appears somewhat paradoxical, given that the GDR was anything but a Christian country. Only a minority of the children were baptized, and in most parts of the republic only a minority attended Sunday morning services. It is probable that a large portion of those who participated in the regular Friday evening prayers in Leipzig's St. Nicolai Church, particularly visible manifestations of opposition as the revolution unfolded, were not religious at all.

Two factors contributed to the prominent role of Protestant communities. First, the churches, after having resisted attempts to be made political instruments of the regime, were virtually the only autonomous institutions in East German society. Their ministers belonged to the only profession with rhetorical skills that did not depend on the state for a living. Second, the clergy had developed a new political and spiritual outlook, a new social activism that differed remarkably from older traditions of German Lutheranism. Accepting the situation of a *Kirche im Sozialismus* (church in a socialist society), they adopted an attitude of critical loyalty to the GDR, but remained aloof from a ruling party that continued to profess doctrinaire atheism and often discriminated against Christians in the educational system and with regard to careers. Not that the Protestant churches unanimously supported the opposition. In fact, some bishops tried to keep good relations with the regime. And in contrast to Poland, the Catholic church, which in eastern Germany is strongly rooted in some southwestern regions and is noted for the conservative orientation of its clergy, maintained a skeptical and apolitical distance from the democracy movement.

The most striking features of the East German revolution, its high discipline, strict avoidance of violence, and a pronounced moralism, were largely due to the moderating influence of the Protestant activists. After the collapse of Communist Party rule, Protestant ministers often served as mediators and helped manage the transition process. In many places they played leading roles in the round tables that served as provisional revolutionary authorities.

As indicated above, the participation-related protest orientation of these minorities can be contrasted with another, more opportunity- and performance-related orientation. Some observers denounced the appetite for Western consumer goods as the main motive behind the desire for political change. To be sure, this cultural pattern cannot be entirely denied. There was certainly considerable resentment against techniques of (often petty) political control that quite simply ignored citizens' desire for personal autonomy and denied them individual opportunity unregulated by an overprotective and paternalist bureaucracy. The sealing of the borders with the West symbolized this denial of individual choice.

After the 1988 Vienna conference recommended freedom of travel, and the GDR government dragged its feet in implementing the recommendations (in contrast to Hungary and Bulgaria), a wave of discontent instilled by the opportunity- and performance-orientation arose. It quickly moved toward a peripety when many hundreds of asylum-seeking East German tourists invaded the West German embassies in Budapest, Prague, and Warsaw. In the resulting diplomatic crisis, the authorities in East

Berlin found themselves largely isolated, in particular after the Communist reform government in Budapest unilaterally decided to open the borders for west-bound GDR citizens. Honecker's overriding objective of preserving a working modus vivendi with Bonn, and his anxiety not to compromise the celebrations planned for the fortieth anniversary of the GDR, let him yield on the departure of hundreds of refugees through the West German embassy in Prague. East Berlin accepted the face-saving proposal of West Germany's foreign minister Hans-Dietrich Genscher to route the trains with these people through the GDR and to discharge them from their citizenship on East German territory.

This move, however, turned out to be a fatal mistake. Riots erupted in some towns through which the trains were expected to pass. To make things worse, many loyal party activists lost their confidence in the leadership. In their view, the authority of the state they were supposed to represent was now seriously compromised by a gerontocracy no longer able to direct events. Within the SED, party members increasingly doubted whether the party could continue to govern without a radical change of leadership, as a precondition for further-reaching economic and political reforms.

Other developments contributed to this mood of dissatisfaction among the party faithful as well. The Helsinki process had led to increasing unrest among writers and artists loyal to the SED. A series of discussions between representatives of the West German Social Democrats and the SED had resulted in a 1987 document that outlined the fundamental differences in the positions of both parties and called for a dialogue in a "culture of controversy" (*Streitkultur*). This paper was very reluctantly endorsed by the politburo (and, incidently, by the SPD *Präsidium*), and it provoked a critical discussion within the SED about the capacity of the party to reform itself. Further erosion of the confidence in the party leaders had resulted from the accession of Solidarnosč to political power in Poland, and from what was seen as the "revolution from above" taking place in the Soviet Union. Gorbachev's remark about history punishing those who are too late, made at the fortieth anniversary of the GDR on October 7, 1989, sounded like a final condemnation.

In an attempt to preserve the socialist system, the party finally toppled its old leadership group. This was the immediate consequence of mass demonstrations, particularly in Leipzig and other southern cities. At that time the demonstrators were led by activists who represented the participation-oriented rather than the performance- and opportunity-oriented protest syndrome. They emphasized this through slogans such as "We are going to stay here" (*wir bleiben hier*) and "We are the people" (*wir sind das Volk*), apparently referring to the people in East Germany. This implicitly affirmed a separate political existence for the GDR and its supposedly less materialist culture, and perhaps even affirmed that some kind of socialism should be preserved. It was, using a term coined to characterize trends in Western electorates, a "post-materialist" orientation.

After the ouster of the old leadership, any remaining confidence broke down with the disclosures of the extraordinary privileges the members of the politburo enjoyed and the practices of corruption from which they had benefited. An interim leadership under Honecker's former "crown prince," Egon Krenz, proved unable to redress the situation. Finally, the direction of the SED was seized by newcomers who were not visibly compromised by the events of the past and much less affected by the bureaucratic authoritarianism of the traditional party apparatus. However, considerable effort was necessary to rid the party of the demoralized old personnel. The move to rebaptize the Socialist Unity Party (SED) as the Party of Democratic Socialism (PDS), which was meant to symbolize the (probably quite sincere) reorientation, could not overcome the strong resentments, even of the democratic left, against an organization that in the past had stood for very different values.

The Irruption of the West German Party System

Given the weak collective identity of the GDR that I have discussed above, it was long thought virtually certain that the GDR would not survive long as an autonomous state without the political support of the Soviet Union. When this support dwindled, the question was no longer whether both German states would be united, but rather when and how. Reunification had, of course, been a ritually proclaimed objective of the West German authorities, but it had not been considered likely to happen in the foreseeable future. West German public opinion was neither prepared for nor particularly enthusiastic about it.

On November 9, in a surprising move, the interim SED leadership opened the borders of the GDR. If, as is likely, this was an attempt to meet the demand of performance- and opportunity-oriented protestors, the move overshot its goal. Less than two weeks later, the participation-oriented demonstrators at Leipzig found themselves outnumbered, and the slogan "We are the people" was superseded by "We are *one* people." Predictions that the stream of emigrants to West Germany would soon decrease proved wrong, and a sense of demoralization continued to spread.

It became apparent after the installation of Prime Minister Modrow's government on November 17 that its support was rapidly eroding. Political leaders in both parts of Germany who perceived a heightening political and economic crisis became increasingly convinced that it would be difficult to check the spread of panic and the further exodus without a strong engagement from the Federal Republic. A realistic analysis might have led them to conclude that economic reason dictated a longer transition period with an autonomous GDR currency and trade regime (certainly the opinion of a majority of economic experts). But such a transition period would require a massive program of economic assistance and the mobilization of broad popular support and consensus for such a policy among West Germans.

The highly competitive West German party system was not at all prepared for such a task. Political leaders in the Federal Republic were focusing on the next *Land* elections, to be held in the spring, and on the federal elections scheduled for the end of 1990. Reactions to the critical situation in the GDR were subordinate to these dominant strategic concerns. It was, for example, taboo within the governing coalition to even discuss an eventual postponement of the business tax cuts that had been promised. The competitive logic of the West German party system had still further–reaching consequences.

On October 7, 1989, a small group of intellectuals, the majority of them Protestant ministers, met in a village north of Berlin to found a Social Democratic Party (SDP) in the GDR. Until then, opposition activists had preferred to act in grass-roots–oriented movements rather than establish political parties. The founders had no contacts with West German Social Democrats (SPD), who initially reacted with irritation. But then some of the leaders of the West German party discovered some interesting electoral aspects in the East German initiative. Historically, social democracy had been strong in large parts of East Germany, and many speculated that in the free elections originally scheduled for May 1990 some form of democratic socialism might be quite popular with the voters. An outcome favorable for the East German SDP might perhaps help the SPD in the forthcoming West German elections.

Chancellor Kohl also discovered some electorally promising perspectives in the new situation, and his highly developed power instinct led him to grasp them quickly. When he submitted a ten-point program toward reunification to the Bundestag in a surprise move on November 27, it was clearly meant as a domestic electoral ploy: The program had been prepared in the "kitchen cabinet" of the chancellor's office, and neither the cabinet nor even Foreign Minister Hans-Dietrich Genscher (a member of the Free Democratic Party) had been informed in advance. Obviously, Kohl saw a unique opportunity to bolster his weakened position in the public debate and, in particular, to effectively reclaim the leadership role in a field that so long had been dominated by his coalition partner and rival Genscher.

These short-term electoral calculations were soon reinforced by more long-term strategic considerations. The West German Social Democrats and, following them, the Christian Democrats, began to speculate that the East German election might turn out to be what voting researchers call a "realigning" or "critical" election. The SPD hoped that this might give them the leadership position in a united Germany. And the CDU, in turn, feared the definitive loss of its *strukturelle Mehrheitsfähigkeit* (a "structurally determined capacity to win a majority"), a concept that reflects the idea that German voting behavior is strongly determined by the social context.

As a consequence, the SPD "adopted" the East German Social Democrats as its counterpart in the East. The CDU initially had considerable problems finding a partner in the GDR. The history of the East German party system proved a burden for the CDU that the SPD did not have to share. The basic patterns of the party system in both German states date back to 1945 and 1946. Under four-power occupation rule, a largely identical party system emerged, with CDU, SPD, Liberals, and Communists being licensed by all four powers in their respective occupation zones. In 1946, the Soviets put strong pressure on the East German Social Democrats to merge with the Communist Party, and the Soviets helped the Communists transform the new SED into a Stalinist organization in which Social Democratic traditions did not survive. Hence, the Social Democrats could claim that they had not been compromised by the SED regime.

The situation was different for the CDU and the Liberals. After World War II they found the links with their West German counterparts cut, and under initially strong pressure, they joined the "bloc" (or pseudo-coalition) system installed by the Soviets and dominated by the SED. Over many years they remained captive but loyal partners to the Communist regime, and they played no role in the opposition movement that emerged with Gorbachev's perestroika. Only in the final crisis of Honecker's rule did some of their minor representatives distance themselves from the regime. Therefore, they encountered strong distrust from West Germany's Christian Democrats, some of whom recommended supporting new conservative parties without such a compromising past. Finally, however, a more realistic position prevailed. After all, the former "bloc CDU" had an established organization with considerable resources, and West Germans decided to create the Alliance for Germany, in which the East German CDU was joined by two smaller, newly founded, conservative organizations.

As a further consequence, the first competitive election campaign in the GDR in forty-four years was not only sponsored but literally overwhelmed by the strategies and the electoral techniques of the West German political parties and transformed into a sort of "proxy war" between them. The results of the ballot (advanced to March 18) were correspondingly interpreted as a remarkable success for Chancellor Kohl. I would not deny that. But it also seems that they demonstrated the remarkable strength of old East German parties with an established organization, not only the former "bloc party" CDU, but also the Party of Democratic Socialism (PDS), the successor to the SED. The modest results of the participation-oriented tickets confirmed that, in spite of their leading role in the revolution, these were movements of the urban intelligentsia without a mass following. The Social Democrats appeared as the real losers after they had appeared as the favorites in the first opinion surveys. It now became clear that the tradition of the labor movement as it existed before 1933 had been eradicated by forty years of bureaucratic socialism. The blue-collar voters clearly preferred the bread-and-butter appeal of the Christian Democrats. Moreover, the public-sector employees (who in West Germany constitute an important segment of the Social Democratic constituency) apparently felt that the PDS was more likely to defend their endangered jobs than the Social Democrats with their rigid demarcation from former Communists.

The strong engagement of the West German parties in the East German elections does not necessarily signify that the competitive patterns of party politics prevailing in the Federal Republic will also be reproduced in the GDR. The Social Democrats, after some hesitations, did join a grand coalition led by the CDU. Prime Minister de Maizière and other Christian Democratic leaders also seemed quite concerned about preserving a considerable amount of autonomy from the Bonn government.

But this strong engagement of the West German parties in the electoral campaign of the GDR had consequences that went far beyond the conquest of power positions in the political arena. Not only did the West German party system dominate the GDR elections, but it transferred its competitive logic to economic decisionmaking. The routine pattern of economic policy in West Germany is embedded in a policy network in which top bureaucrats from the Ministry of Economics and the Bundesbank occupy a central position, and the business community and experts from mainstream economics play an important consultative role. Yet, in the first months of 1990, this network was largely circumvented. Fundamental problems in the economic and monetary union with the GDR were discussed and decided in the party arena without regard to the strong objections coming from the central bank and a number of economic think tanks and expert bodies. It appears that party leaders felt so much pressure, both from what they believed to be at stake in the electoral campaign, and from the perception of the crisis that went along with the increasing stream of immigrants from the GDR, that conventional notions of economic rationality were deliberately set aside. At that time, even top business leaders reacted quite helplessly to what they described as the unexpected precedence of politics over economics. The Bundesbank managed rather late, and to a very limited degree, to have its views on the projected monetary union taken into consideration. (It has been rumored that its president, Karl-Otto Pöhl, first got the news from a taxi driver and reacted with the exclamation: "But, that's incredible!")

The Implications of Unification for Economic Policy

I have discussed the unification process in some detail because the politically motivated and overly hasty decisions on monetary and economic union will have important and lasting implications for the economic development of a united Germany. After Honecker's fall, unification was first envisaged as the eventual outcome of a gradual, confederative process. The GDR would be transformed into a pluralist political system with a market economy, but for some still indeterminate time it would retain its political autonomy, just like other East European countries. Step by step, close economic and political links would then be established. Finally, a constituent assembly would deliberate on a new constitution, as provided for in the last article (§146) of Bonn's Basic Law. Such a text might then be adopted either by a vote of the assembly or by a popular referendum. Article 146 did not require that this form of unification be preceded by a confederation. But it would be logical for a federative process to conclude with deliberations on a new constitution.

In the first months of 1990, many political leaders in both Germanies became increasingly convinced that the process of unification had to be accelerated because of the disintegration of political authority in the GDR, and that it would be much too laborious to go through a confederative stage. At this point, a constitutional alternative to Article 146 emerged in the discussion. Article 23 of the Basic Law permitted the GDR to join the FRG by a unilateral decision, much faster than if it first set up a preceding constituent assembly. It turned out that the parties of the governing coalition in Bonn preferred this solution (for reasons to be discussed later). Both scenarios, however, have had different implications for economic policy.

Political leaders in Bonn and the Modrow government agreed in principle that introducing the legal framework of a decentralized market economy in the GDR would be an essential condition for the economic viability of a confederation. The Bonn government emphasized this point because it refused to bail out the ailing state enterprises and believed that an economic recovery of the former GDR should be mainly the work of West German private businesses. The two governments also decided to reform banking and credit, reduce the huge money supply, discontinue subsidized consumption, and free prices. Currency convertibility was also to be established as soon as feasible. Many experts were originally inclined to maintain controls on transborder trade because of the low productivity of the East German economy, and believed that the exchange rate of the East German Ost Mark to the West German Deutsche Mark would have to remain fixed. Some even argued that keeping the Ost Mark undervalued would assist the industrial recovery.

After the opening of the borders, however, the increasing emigration from the GDR presented decisionmakers with a major uncertainty: Sticking to a gradual, confederative process would become difficult if they did not limit the stream of emigrants. Restoring confidence, however, would have required a combined effort from the major players in both German states, which was made increasingly difficult by the overwhelmingly competitive logic of the West German party system. On the one hand, Chancellor Kohl apparently wished to destabilize Modrow's caretaker government for electoral reasons. On the other hand, the introduction of the Deutsche Mark had become a central pledge in the East German electoral campaign with enormous symbolic appeal.

The consequences of the speedy economic integration are controversial. It is obvious that monetary and economic union exposed the East German economy to competitive pressures that many industries did not survive. Some of the consequences will be offset by growth in other sectors, particularly in services. This might eventually yield as many as half a million new jobs. But this number will largely be offset by layoffs in the manufacturing and public sectors. Half of the 800,000 jobs in agriculture may become redundant; otherwise, low productivity would put a united Germany at a severe disadvantage measured against the other European Community countries. All in all, most experts project net unemployment figures somewhere between one and two million, equaling between 15 and 25 percent of the working East German population.

Those who expect new growth to take off soon contest these figures. First, they argue that the low productivity of the former GDR economy results from organizational weaknesses inherited from the centralized command economy. Training business cadres and executives in management and marketing skills should therefore boost the productivity of East German industry. Second, the relatively high qualification of the East German work force and the low level of wages should be attractive to investors. It is said that "capital sits in the starting pits," and that the slowness of the changes in the legal framework created uncertainty and temporarily discouraged investment.

These arguments are not quite convincing. On the basis of newspaper information about West German business firms preparing to invest in East Germany, a significant pattern can be discerned. Most of these initiatives have been found in distribution and financial services. Given the scarcity of capital resources in eastern Germany, and the absence of a banking system, the strong engagement of West German banks and insurance companies makes economic sense as far as financial and credit markets are concerned.

However, the already visible large-scale penetration of West German business into consumer markets necessarily comes at the expense of East German consumer goods industries (textiles, for example, seem to be in a hopeless competitive position). Agriculture is in an even worse position, as temporary protection is categorically excluded by West German policymakers because it runs counter to the principles of a market economy. It is uncertain whether the chemical industry, once a key industrial sector in this part of Germany, will be able to survive. One can also doubt whether the often predicted rebirth of small business in East Germany will have enough economic importance to compensate for layoffs. Manufacturing sectors also face enormous handicaps. Investment projects in the once important manufacturing industries of the former GDR appear to be largely limited to some exceptional sectors, including automobiles (in which this expansion seems part of the global strategy of firms like Volkswagen); telecommunications (in which Siemens and Alcatel can count on the postal service as their most important customer); and some smaller, technologically advanced firms in fields such as machine-tool engineering. Even in these areas, many jobs will certainly become redundant.

Thus, the odds in this scenario are that considerable regional disparities in industrial structure will result from the rash economic and monetary union. They could prove extremely difficult to correct in the future. The transport and communication infrastructure of the East German economy is in dismal shape. For telecommunications alone, public expenditure required to modernize the former GDR system to the level now attained in West Germany is estimated at about twenty billion dollars. And while this could be done in a relatively short time, rebuilding the roads and the railway system will require a much greater effort. These conditions are likely to discourage many potential investors. Because the East German markets are open to West German industries, only distribution and service networks are needed. "Agglomeration effects" will play strongly in favor of the urban regions of West Germany, where investors find much more favorable conditions. In the aggregate, German unity may indeed stimulate considerable economic growth, but its distribution may be extremely unequal.

Initially, wages will naturally be lower in the East, but the institutional framework of industrial relations in a united Germany will push for very fast wage increases, at least for those who happen to have jobs. Western Germany has a segmented labor market that makes the high-wage economy coexist with relatively high unemployment. This pattern could well extend to East Germany. For the privileged holders of jobs, the standard of living may rise, even if not to West German levels. As in West Germany, unemployment could become politically neutralized as it hits more marginal segments of the working class. Women, in particular, will eventually be the big losers in a free labor market. The very generous provisions for maternity leave and similar benefits (which are probably taboo for political reasons) will disappear with the planned economy.

The emergence of an economic cleavage between a prosperous West Germany and an East German "rust belt" is thus quite possible. Unification is likely to stimulate additional economic growth in West Germany and in some privileged parts of the East, particularly in the region around Berlin. But there is a strong possibility that the rural north and the industrial regions in the south and southwest of the former GDR will decline in relative and, as far as employment is concerned, in absolute terms. In a worst-case scenario (which, I am afraid, cannot be ruled out) Leipzig would become Germany's Liverpool, and Mecklenburg its Mezzogiorno. Internal migration from East to West would then naturally increase once more and further aggravate the existing disparities.

To what degree this scenario will become reality is, of course, a question of policy choices. A massive redistribution of public resources in favor of East Germany, in particular for investment in the basic infrastructure and for an environmental cleanup, could help to avoid the worst case. The CDU/CSU-FDP government, however, seems to consider economic reconstruction of the former GDR essentially a task that should be left to the private sector. This is probably consistent with the mood that prevails in the West German electorate. Recent state election results seem to indicate a growing resentment against East Germans, which could turn into a significant backlash if unification is viewed as imposing an undue burden on the West German taxpayer. The competitive party system is certainly not geared toward engineering a national consensus on redistribution efforts. Political realities may even prevent a further increase in public sector borrowing, the device that is apparently reaching its limits in Bonn at the moment.

Problems of Institutional Reconstruction:
Past, Present, and Future

The scenario just outlined may seem unduly pessimistic and may underestimate the dynamics of a market economy once it unfolds in a society whose potential for development was artificially blocked. But for growth to happen, and to happen without distributional disparities, an appropriate institutional framework must exist. The more optimistic scenarios sometimes developed in the West German discussion neglect the institutional rigidities inherited from history and the huge and complex problems of institutional reconstruction that are involved in the unification process.

It is a serious misconception to liken this task to the recovery of West Germany after World War II. Although the foundations of the West German state and its economy were profoundly shaken, reconstruction started at that time from a relatively similar situation for all actors involved, and developed on the basis of a homogeneous institutional heritage. But Germany now faces the task of merging two systems with highly complex and very different institutions. This has, to my knowledge, no real historical precedent and is therefore a unique and gigantic experiment in social engineering. German unification under Bismarck's leadership took place under quite different conditions because the basic institutional frameworks of Prussia and the other German states were relatively similar, even though Prussia may have developed further in some respects. A somewhat closer parallel may be the unification of Italy in 1861, when Piedmont occupied Naples and Sicily after Giuseppe Garibaldi had led the revolution there (whereupon Garibaldi exiled himself on the island of Caprera). The resulting cultural schism in the Italian polity has often been discussed, as have the economic consequences that are known as the "Mezzogiorno question." Another relevant case is the period of Reconstruction in the United States after the Civil War. Perhaps some analogous problems of institution building can also be found in the creation of Yugoslavia after the peace treaties of Saint-Germain and Trianon.

However, in all these cases unification took place in largely rural and small-town societies, with traditional social hierarchies and economies in an early stage of development. In the German case we are dealing with two urbanized, highly industrialized, and complex societies, and two very different versions of the modern welfare state. That poses incomparable challenges in particular for the institutions of social welfare and for those of the legal-administrative order. These challenges are probably at the same time rendered more complex, but perhaps also somewhat alleviated, by the German federal heritage.

Unification challenges not only East German institutions but also some institutional features of the Federal Republic. This explains the passions that erupted in the discussions over Articles 23 and 146 of the Basic Law as alternative constitutional routes to German unity. Accession of the GDR on the basis of Article 23 did, in principle, reaffirm the institutional identity of the FRG, whereas a constituent assembly established by Article 146, although it might have taken the Basic Law as the basis for discussion, would have symbolically put that identity into question. And as long as speculation persisted that the left might win the East German elections, there was also authentic fear that the procedure might be used to introduce some radical and even socialist features into a new German constitution. Under the procedures of Article 23, constitutional amendments that eventually become necessary require a majority of two-thirds in the Bundestag and in the Federal Council (representing the *Länder*), whereas under Article 146 a new constitution could have been ratified by a simple majority of the assembly.

Obviously, the procedures of Article 23 prevailed. This should, however, not simply be seen as the victory of one party over another. In reality, this result was very much in accordance with a traditional feature of German politics, namely the preference for bargaining among important collective actors when it comes to fundamental decisions of constitutional character. In particular, the states (*Länder*) have always asserted their ability to block attempts aimed at severely curtailing their role. Even where the West German institutional framework has been adapted, decisions had to be made in a bargaining process (unlike the decisions on monetary and economic union taken in early 1990). In this political tradition, unification took the form of an accession, the terms of which were negotiated between both German states.

However, the problem with this process was that the negotiations took place between unequal partners. The GDR's desperate economic situation made it difficult for even its freely elected democratic government to defend East German interests. There was also considerable inequality in bargaining resources such as legal expertise. The democratic parties of the GDR had no specialists in constitutional law, and even their leadership had less experience in negotiation. This disparity affected all domains open to discussion, from social policy to the organization of the administration. And the five East German *Länder,* abolished in 1952 and restored in 1990, had so few financial and administrative resources that they were powerless hostages of the federal government. *Wer zahlt, schafft an*—the one who pays the piper calls the tune.

With regard to the institutions of social welfare, there was considerable agreement about a "social union" that would accompany the monetary and economic union. Essentially, the West German system of social insurance, in particular of old-age pensions, has been introduced in the East. Average pensions will be lower than in the West, but this might be acceptable on the condition that basic costs of living also remain lower, something which is likely in the foreseeable future but not guaranteed.

Problems may arise in some sectors in which the East German welfare state was clearly more egalitarian, whereas its West German counterpart preserved status privileges from the old German prewar period. Among these, the most conspicuous case is the public health sector: It seems rather problematic to transfer the highly fragmented and not particularly efficient West German health insurance system to the East. Some large West German associations of insurance funds for privileged status groups of wage earners (*Ersatzkassen*) lobbied hard for such a transformation, proba- bly out of fear that maintenance of a unified structure in the East might in the long run make this model attractive for the rest of Germany. With regard to medical institutions, West German medical lobbies want to do away with the East German system of local public health centers (*Polikliniken*), a form of medical practice that they have fought in the past and had outlawed in the Federal Republic.

Another field in which status-related concerns of West German interest groups are at issue is education. Whereas some fundamental organizational patterns of the East German system (in particular the "unitary school" and the principle of "polytechnic instruction") were originally very much influ- enced by egalitarian reformers,[1] West Germany's educational system is organized along status lines. Although this system has become highly dys- functional and can no longer guarantee either social privilege or excellence, lobbies like the conservative association of high school teachers

(*Philologenverband*) would like to see the East German *Einheitsschule* (unitary school) replaced by the FRG's three-tier system with its status-oriented differentiations (see Chapter 11).

Institutional problems of social welfare and education are probably minor compared to those related to the legal system and to administrative and judicial institutions. Cross-national research on the West German political system often, and justly, emphasizes the highly legalist character of the West German administrative culture and the crucial importance of the judiciary for the resolution of social conflict. Now this legalist political-administrative system must merge with one in which lawyers are in very short supply and furthermore have received a very different education and have undergone a different institutional socialization process. Important elements of the former German commercial law were still on the books in the GDR and therefore offered themselves as a possible common framework in the economic domain. However, these laws have been replaced by West German statutes, with which East German lawyers and judges are not familiar. The situation grows more complex for penal law and also for the organization of criminal justice. Not only are there few judges, but they also come from a very different legal culture. It is difficult to see how this situation can be managed. Finally, administrative law and an administrative judiciary, both essential elements of West German political organization, were completely unknown in East Germany.

The GDR did not have the institution of civil service that is so powerful in the West. In 1919 and again in 1949, the bureaucracy managed to have a guarantee of the institution, and of the "acquired rights" of civil servants, written into the constitutions. It is doubtful whether the extension of civil servant status to professors, teachers, mailmen, and railway engineers is functionally justified. Under the procedures of Article 23, the constitutional guarantee of the civil service necessitates its reintroduction in East Germany. However, most GDR bureaucrats would not, in theory, be permitted to serve as civil servants in the Federal Republic under the interpretation of the "duty of political allegiance" contained in traditional German civil service law, as it has been confirmed in the famous "radicals decree" of 1972 and continues to be upheld by the West German courts. Of course one could argue that the public sector in the GDR was heavily overstaffed, and that much of its bureaucracy should be laid off. But the question remains: Which principles should govern the reorganization of the public sector? Since 2.3 million out of 16 million inhabitants of the former GDR were members of the SED, it is difficult to see how Germany could be politically and culturally integrated without a new culture of tolerance superseding the ideological schisms of the Cold War. This would require the equivalent of an ideological peace treaty. But here, again, the competitive logic of the West German party system, and a mood of vengeance now spreading in East Germany, may make such tolerance impossible.

Federalism, an institutional feature strongly rooted in German history, might, under certain conditions, help to counteract some of the trends outlined in my scenario. Before formal unification was accomplished, the GDR returned to the federal structure it had until the early 1950s. That is, the five *Länder* created in 1946 by the Soviet military administration and abolished in 1952 in favor of a strictly centralist reorganization, were restored. Their accession to the federal structure of the Basic Law poses some quite intricate problems, in particular for the system of revenue sharing. It is difficult to see how this system can persist in its present form, and it is equally difficult to see how a consensus can be found about a workable alternative. A parafiscal institution run jointly by the federal and the West German state governments (and mostly funded by borrowing) has been set up. But this could probably only be a transitory solution.

In spite of these difficulties, the insertion of East Germany into the federal framework had broad support on both sides. In the past, the federal structure of West Germany has eased the regional disparities that existed after the war. Moreover, it has played an important role in the resolution of political and social conflicts by allowing for a limited degree of diversity, in particular in the field of education. When it comes to economic and fiscal policy, West Germans have had a strong preference for homogeneity of welfare and state subsidies and have therefore opted for coordination in a system of "interlocking politics" (*Politikverflechtung*). This system has accommodated a diversity of interests within a bargaining structure that became legitimate even though it was complex and cumbersome. Thus, the federal framework should, at least in theory, help to disaggregate some of the problems and conflicts that are likely to arise from unification and help to solve them.[2] Again, however, the enormous disparity in wealth creates a structural asymmetry that puts the East German state in a strongly inferior bargaining position. Because its administrative structures will have to be reconstructed practically from scratch, the institutions of the eastern *Länder* will remain extremely weak for a considerable period of time. This will further accentuate the asymmetry between East and West.

Notes

This chapter was presented as a guest lecture at Princeton University, February 26, 1990; and at a workshop on "Gorbachev and the Germans" held May 10 and 11, 1990, at the Graduate Faculty, New School for Social Research, New York. It has been updated for this book.

1. Since the 1950s the egalitarian features of the educational system of the GDR had become perverted by strong discrimination based on social background and political conformity ("social engagement"). But the fundamental organizational patterns go back to earlier reform movements that were defeated early in West Germany but had strong affinities to the public school system in Scandinavia or in the United States.

2. An open question in this context is, however, whether the unitarizing trend toward uniform solutions that had come to characterize intergovernmental relations in West Germany will not have to be partially reversed because it would otherwise be difficult to accommodate the complex problems arising from German unity. This could also affect the patterns of interstate and federal-state bargaining as they emerged since the late 1960s, when there was a strong preference for equalizing welfare-oriented state intervention through "interlocking politics" (*Politikverflechtung*) and interadministrative bargaining and political logrolling.

The problem has two sides. On the one hand, tolerance of greater heterogeneity in fields such as labor and environmental legislation will be favored by business and by advocates of a supply-side oriented economic policy. Attempts made by the federal government in the first draft of the Economic, Monetary, and Social Union Treaty to suspend some important social guarantees of West German law and thus to transform the GDR into a sort of giant enterprise zone had to be abandoned. But the problem will remain virulent. On the other hand, conservatives might sometimes press for stronger and faster integration, for example to abolish the liberal East German abortion law. In such cultural fields, tolerance for heterogeneity will be necessary if integration shall not fail because of the virulence of cultural conflict. But this requirement may not be easy to reconcile either with the unifying logic of party competition or with established interbureaucratic routines.

Chapter 2

Electoral Politics in the New Germany: Public Opinion and the Bundestag Election of December 2, 1990

Max Kaase

The general election of January 25, 1987, had safely confirmed the status of the conservative and liberal parties and had left Helmut Kohl's position as chancellor of the Federal Republic unchallenged. Yet the election outcome was accepted by winners and losers with little enthusiasm, except for the Free Democratic Party, which had improved its result over the 1983 election mark by 2.1 percentage points. The 0.5 percentage point loss of the ruling Christian Democrats as well as the 1.2 percentage point decrease of the Social Democrats' share of the vote were attributed as much to the low valence of an election whose winner was never in doubt, as to the unattainable goal of SPD candidate Johannes Rau to win an absolute majority of votes (or at least seats) for the SPD. The fact that turnout declined by a substantial 4.7 percentage points fit well with the picture of a low stimulus campaign that had even been interrupted by a lengthy Christmas break.

The January high for the government parties extended through the middle of 1987 and culminated in a victory for the CDU and the FDP in the Hesse state elections on April 5, 1987. From then on, however, the fortunes of the conservative-liberal coalition deteriorated substantially and reached an initial low in the state election in Schleswig-Holstein on September 13—an election that was soon to become known, even beyond the borders of the Federal Republic, as the Barschel election. The magazine *Der Spiegel* revealed that Barschel, who was at that time the state's prime minister, had utilized a variety of illegal means in an attempt to prevent the Social Democratic Party from obtaining a majority. From then on for a period of two years, levels of popular support for the CDU/CSU were consistently lower than for the SPD. The gap between the parties at times grew so large that a public consensus began to emerge that the reigning coalition could hardly expect to win again in the upcoming 1990 election.

Not only the Barschel affair but also dissatisfaction with government policies in the fields of taxes and health services obviously continued to have an impact on public support for the CDU. (A new source tax—the so-called *Quellensteuer*—was to be introduced, taxing capital interest gains at a flat 25 percent rate at the source of income. Moreover, a health care reform proposal was introduced, which aimed at reducing the overall cost of the health care system by limiting expenditures and increasing the share citizens pay for their health services.) As is not unusual in German politics, these deficiencies were attributed mostly to the larger coalition party, the Christian Democrats, and less so to the smaller coalition partner, the FDP. To make things even worse, the sudden electoral surge of the right-wing Republikaner in the West Berlin state election on January 29, 1989 (it received 7.5 percent of the vote), created an additional electoral threat for the CDU/CSU. It now appeared that the CDU could lose not only independent voters in the center of the political spectrum but also conservative voters on the right. Overall, the likelihood that Helmut Kohl would survive the 1990 election seemed pretty slim in the middle of 1989.

However, in the early autumn of 1989 a situation developed that nobody had or could have anticipated. The "unfreezing" of the Communist bloc in Eastern Europe had reached a point where the socialist neighbors of the GDR were no longer willing to play the guardians for those GDR citizens who wanted to leave their country at all costs. On September 11, 1989, Hungary finally opened its borders for GDR citizens to cross into Austria and to continue from there into West Germany. Within three days, 15,000 people took advantage of that opportunity, setting loose the avalanche that, on October 18, swept away Erich Honecker, paved the way for the opening of the wall on November 9, and finally resulted in the disappearance of the GDR as a state in its own right (Glaeßner 1991).

Figure 2.2 shows that the topics of, first, the GDR refugees and then the eventual German unification dominated the political agenda practically up to the eve of election day on December 2, 1990. All other issues fell victim to these dominant themes. With German unification on the political agenda, the campaign plans of the Social Democrats, which had been designed to force the government into a debate on the ecological restructuring of industrial society, evaporated like snow in the sun.

The Road to a New Party System in the GDR

The breathtaking speed with which the seemingly well-entrenched socialist regime fell left a sudden void of acceptable agencies of intermediation to connect citizens and the state in eastern Germany. This was particularly true for the party system, which had seen a hegemonic Communist party (Sozialistische Einheitspartei Deutschlands, or SED) augmented by a set of four basically powerless bloc parties (Christian Democratic Union, or CDU; German Peasants' Party, or DBD; Liberal Democratic Party, or LDPD; and National Democratic Party, or NDPD).

Figure 2.1 The Political Mood of the West German Voting-Age Citizenry, 1987–1990 (vote intention; percentages valid votes)

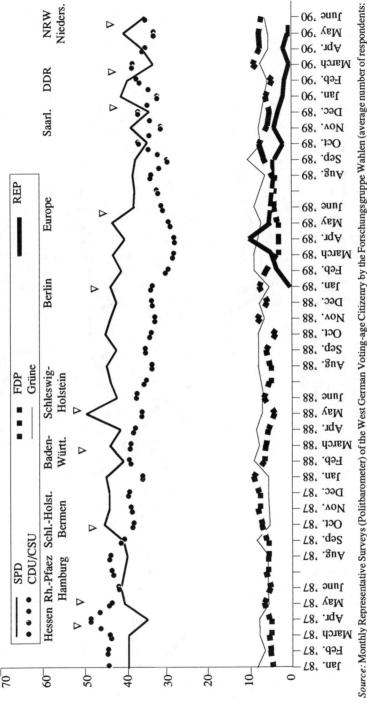

Source: Monthly Representative Surveys (Politbarometer) of the West German Voting-age Citizenry by the Forschungsgruppe Wahlen (average number of respondents: 1,000).

Figure 2.2 Most Important Problems in the "Old" Federal Republic of Germany (percentages based on all respondents)

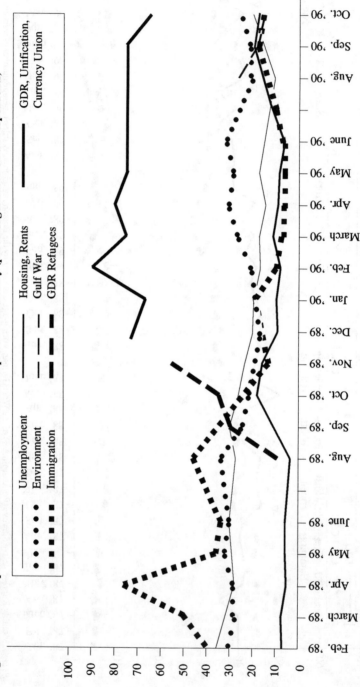

Source: Monthly Representative Surveys (Politbarometer) of the West German Voting-age Citizenry by the Forschungsgruppe Wahlen (average number of respondents: 1,000).

The lack of functioning intermediary structures stimulated various efforts by change-oriented action committees to prevent a situation in which an atomized mass public would permit and encourage status quo elites to grab power once again. In this context the emergence of the round table discussions, which brought together all major political and social forces in the GDR outside the government, was the most influential development (Thaysen 1990). The integration of the round table process into the Modrow government (*Regierung der nationalen Verantwortung,* or "government of national responsibility") in early 1990 marked the final phase of a process during which the citizenry had already written "unification" on its banners while the mix of old and new political elites was still pondering the chances of maintaining the GDR as an independent state that would represent the desired "third way" between socialism and capitalism.

The political and social anomie that threatened to develop after the opening of the Wall forced the GDR government to move the first free election for an East German national parliament from May 6, as had been initially planned, to March 18. This, in turn, compelled parties and other groups to organize as quickly as possible for an effective election campaign. In the limited space of this chapter, it is not possible to describe the crystallization of the twenty-four parties and groupings that finally made it onto the list of official competitors for the Volkskammer election (see Glaeßner 1991, 103–126). However, it is important to note that the first contours of the emerging GDR party system were shaped both by changes in the existing bloc parties and by the recreation of the Social Democratic Party (until January 1990 the Social Democratic Party of the GDR) plus the transformation of a series of sociopolitical movements into quasi-political parties. All former bloc parties participated in the election, either under old or new names, and all of them won seats (SED/PDS: 66 seats; LDPD/LDP: 21 seats jointly with Deutsche Forumspartei [DFP] and FDP; NDPD: 2 seats; DBD: 9 seats; CDU: 163 seats). The Social Democrats obtained 88 seats, the CSU-like German Social Union (DSU) 25 seats, the Bündnis90 12 seats, and the GDR Greens 8 seats. The remaining 6 seats were split among the other 15 competitors.

This election outcome foreshadowed a high symmetry of the East German party system vis-à-vis that of West Germany (with the exception of the PDS). There is little disagreement about the fact that the Volkskammer election, with a 93.4 percent turnout, was basically a plebiscite in favor of German unification (Roth 1990, 383). Additionally, it is widely accepted that it was the ambivalence of the SPD leadership toward unification, especially in the West but also in the East, that turned the tide against the Social Democrats; most polls had forecast an SPD win on election day.

Given the surprise that the election result produced, observers were interested to see whether the local elections on May 6 would confirm or change once again the distribution of party preferences in the GDR.

Although there were some small shifts, the local elections largely corroborated the March 18 election results (Jung 1990, 14–15). The party preferences displayed in these two elections held through the state elections in the five newly constituted *Länder* on October 14 (Gibowski and Kaase 1991, 5).

West Germans and the Politics of Unification

On November 28, 1989, hardly three weeks after the opening of the Wall, Helmut Kohl announced his ten-point plan for German unification in the Bundestag. Many observers believe that this move helped him grab the historical chance offered to him. After that he never lost the political initiative and finally achieved unification on October 3, 1990.

However, in terms of the distribution of party preferences, the period from October 1989 through June 1990 (see Figure 2.1) can be characterized as one of massive public ambivalence and volatility. The state election in the Saarland on January 28, 1990—with Oskar Lafontaine, the potential challenger of Kohl, running for reelection as prime minister—was an outright success for Lafontaine: Not only did his SPD gain 5.2 percentage points compared to the already glamorous 49.2 percent it had received in the 1985 election, but he also managed to keep the Greens (2.7 percent) and the right-wing Republikaner (3.3 percent) out of the *Land* parliament. The date of the election coincided with a public high for the SPD in all of West Germany. A similar situation occurred on May 13, when the SPD maintained its absolute majority of seats in elections to the state legislature of North Rhine–Westphalia and, by getting enough votes to form a coalition government with the Greens, relegated the CDU to the opposition benches in Lower Saxony for the first time since 1976.

Whatever West German voters felt toward the political parties at that time, the goal of unification was never a matter of dissent among the mass public. As Figure 2.3 shows, support for unification among all respondents ranged in the seventies and then continuously stayed at about 80 percent when unification became a realistic alternative. Party preferences affected the level of support (ironically, both Greens and Republikaner voters were most opposed to unification); however, these disparities were in general quite small.

Although support for unification in general was high, the speed at which it should be accomplished was most controversial in both East Germany (see Roth 1990, 383) and West Germany. Lafontaine and the SPD favored a slow process (whatever that meant in concrete terms), whereas the CDU/CSU advocated that unification take place as quickly as feasible. Up until June 1990, a majority of Germans clearly preferred a slow process. According to the Politbarometer polls of the Forschungsgruppe Wahlen, 54

Figure 2.3 West German Voting-Age Citizenry in Favor of Unification

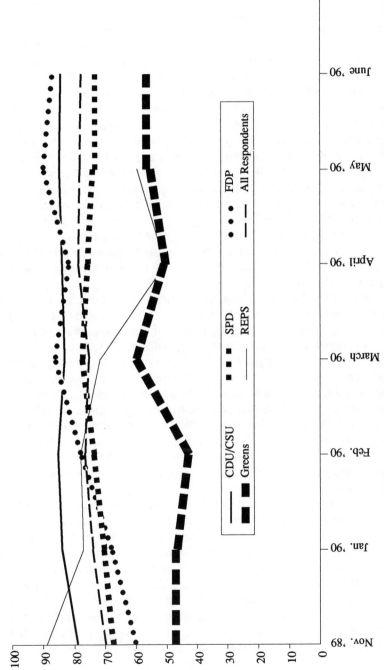

| CDU/CSU | SPD | FDP |
| Greens | REPS | All Respondents |

Source: Monthly Representative Surveys (Politbarometer) of the West German Voting-age Citizenry by the Forschungsgruppe Wahlen (average number of respondents: 1,000).

percent of the 83 percent favoring unification wanted it in 1991 or later, compared to 45 percent who wanted it to take place in 1990. The fact that a majority (60 percent) of CDU/CSU voters wanted unification in 1990, whereas a minority (32 percent) of the SPD voters was in favor of unification in 1990 reflects the nature of a position issue. However, seen from a longitudinal perspective, the June data already marked a shift in public mood toward speedy unification: By June, 35 percent supported Lafontaine's unification policy and 39 percent already supported Kohl's strategy, whereas only 29 percent had supported Kohl's unification policy in May, compared to the 42 percent who had favored Lafontaine's approach then. It is quite likely that the clear-cut unification policy of the federal government, Lafontaine's hesitation to formally declare himself a candidate for the chancellery, and the SPD's split over the first state treaty with the GDR regarding the economic, social, and currency union (which then became effective on July 2), helped swing the public mood in favor of the policy of Helmut Kohl and the reigning CDU/CSU-FDP coalition.

There was, however, more to that swing. As Table 2.1 shows, the government had been successful very early in the game by arguing that, although there might be short-term disadvantages to unification, advantages would by far prevail in the middle to long run.

The data in Table 2.1 are interesting for several reasons. First, although there certainly was a lot of ambivalence with respect to both time frames, a cautious optimism regarding the long-term advantages was clearly the majority opinion. Second, it is surprising to observe how little gross movement occurred in the aggregate distributions of respondents among the response categories over the period of almost half a year. Apparently, once people had made up their minds, the balance of opinion hardly shifted in one direction or another. And third (based on data not shown in Table 2.1), there was little dissent with respect to the long-term consequences—at least among the voters of CDU/CSU and SPD. This, of course, made it very difficult for Oskar Lafontaine to gain credibility with the gloomy picture he continuously painted of the negative consequences, and more specifically the costs, of unification.

When asked what disadvantages they could foresee from unification, respondents mostly mentioned economic ramifications (eventual increases in taxes and unemployment, economic strains, strains on housing). This foreboding also worked against the Social Democrats: Across all voter groups more competence was attributed to the government on economic issues than on any other issue (Kaase and Gibowski 1990a, 752). Thus, in sum, agenda setting and priming worked in favor of the CDU/CSU and the FDP and against the SPD. In addition, this combination of factors also explains the negative electoral outcome of the Bundestag election for the West German Greens, who at no point got into the political and campaigning game. With their resentment toward the unification process, which

Table 2.1 Short-term and Long-term Consequences of Unification as Viewed by the West German Voting-age Citizenry, 1990

Prevailing consequences	Time				
	February n=1006 percent	March n=1020 percent	April n=1023 percent	May n=1008 percent	June n=1028 percent
Short-term					
Advantages	10	12	14	12	12
Both	33	34	36	30	38
Disadvantages	55	52	49	56	48
Don't know	2	2	1	2	2
Total	100	100	100	100	100
Long-term					
Advantages	44	47	46	48	46
Both	43	40	41	39	38
Disadvantages	7	9	8	7	11
Don't know	6	4	5	6	5
Total	100	100	100	100	100

Source: Monthly Representative Surveys (Politbarometer) of the West German Voting-age Citizenry by the Forschungsgruppe Wahlen (average number of respondents: 1,000).

attracted almost all of the public's attention, they were simply overwhelmed by the turn of events.

Getting Ready for the First All-German General Election in the East: The Underlying Structure of Political Orientations

On June 21, 1990, the Economic, Monetary, and Social Union Treaty between the FRG and the GDR was ratified by the Bundestag and the Volkskammer and took effect on July 2. Soon afterward, the two governments began negotiations on the second state treaty, which would define the constitutional and legal framework for unification. This treaty was signed in East Berlin on August 31, 1990, and ratified by the two parliaments on September 20–21. At about the same time (September 12), the Two-Plus-Four Treaty on the Final Settlement with Respect to Germany regulating the external acceptance of unification was signed by the foreign ministers of the four occupying powers and the two German states. In retro-spect, it is still difficult to believe that the tremendous complexities involved in the process of unification were successfully dealt with within a few months' time.

Undoubtedly, one condition that was central to the unbelievably rapid pace of unification was the constitutional background: The GDR decided to surrender its own state identity and join the FRG under Article 23 of the West German Constitution. This decision dismantled the GDR's central-ized structure; through a Volkskammer vote on July 22, the GDR formally reconstituted the five *Länder* of Brandenburg, Mecklenburg-Vorpommern, Saxony, Saxony-Anhalt, and Thuringia (see also Chapter 8). As mentioned above, state parliaments were subsequently elected in these states on October 14 (for the results and an analysis of these elections, see Feist and Hoffmann 1991).

With unification ahead, there was no question that the upcoming gen-eral election in West Germany would be transformed into the first all-German general election since the 1930s. Controversies arose, however, with respect to the electoral laws governing the election (see Chapter 4). A decision by the FRG's constitutional court confirmed that the FRG's elec-toral laws should also be extended to the former territory of the GDR, but that the GDR and FRG would be treated as two separate election areas (*Wahlgebiet West* and *Wahlgebiet Ost*). This regulation was justified by the argument that parties in the much smaller GDR area should have a fair chance to overcome the 5 percent hurdle limiting parliamentary representa-tion. However, the laws permitted the creation of joint lists (*Listenverbindungen*) between Eastern parties or between Eastern and Western parties. The effect of the joint-list decision was that a party or party list surpassing 5 percent in one of the two areas would also be award-ed seats from votes gained in the other area. As will be seen later, this regu-lation turned out to be quite consequential with respect to which parties finally obtained parliamentary representation in the newly elected Bundestag.

Elections in pluralist democracies are *the* instrument of legitimation of political authority. Adopting this instrument equally in West Germany and in East Germany, without further consideration of the different political paths the two Germanies had taken after World War II, would beg the ques-tion of what unification meant in terms of the underlying dimensions of political orientation in the two Germanies, and how a democratic govern-ment will develop in the united Germany. The outcome of the social exper-iment of unification (Giesen and Leggewie 1991; Scheuch 1991) will be, on the one hand, largely determined by how the constitutional and legal framework that has developed in West Germany over the years will be able to cope with the specific problems arising from unification. On the other hand, sociopolitical attitudes and behaviors of the citizens may create a new challenge to that framework; they may even alter it in the long run.

Fortunately, empirical social science research, which was highly politicized and structurally underdeveloped in the GDR (see Thomas 1990), quickly found its way into the GDR after the Wall had been broken down. By mid-1990, the West German commercial institutes of social and market research had established a research infrastructure in the GDR quite on a par with West German standards, thus making survey results available on a regular basis (one example of the latter is the extension of the monthly Politbarometer studies of the Forschungsgruppe Wahlen for the Second German Television Network [ZDF] into East Germany, starting in April 1990). As a consequence, reliable data and analyses became available fairly quickly, providing detailed information on the distribution and structure of political orientations of the East German citizenry, usually in comparison with its West German counterpart (see Bauer 1991a, 1991b; Dalton 1991; Feist 1991; Scheuch 1991; *Der Spiegel* 1991; Weil 1993).

Several core findings of these studies need to be reported. First, in terms of issue priorities, it cannot come as a surprise that there are substantial East-West differences. If the data were interpreted along the lines of value priorities, the East German citizens could be located in an issue space that very much resembles that of the FRG of some twenty years ago (Bauer 1991b, 438–440; Feist 1991, 26). Second, the structure of orientations is less well defined and more diffuse in East Germany compared to the West (Bauer 1991b, 446). Third, many authors observe a surprising and counterintuitively high degree of democratic attitudes in East Germany. This is particularly true with respect to the conflict dimension of democratic attitudes. Various authors attribute this to the specific East German experience of promoting and successfully achieving a peaceful transition from a totalitarian to a democratic political system (Bauer 1991b, 446; Weil 1993, 14–15). Finally, although high support for democratic values and norms does exist in East Germany, Bauer (1991b, 446–451) and Dalton (1991, 11–12) point out that this support is highly contingent on the quality of economic system performance. To put it differently, whereas the long process of democratization in West Germany has finally disentangled general system support from specific outputs of the system and has thereby made it less vulnerable to short-term output fluctuations, this relationship still exists in the East. This, combined with a substantial degree of ambivalence towards other elements of a democratic political culture (Weil 1993, 18–20), makes the integration of the two German citizenries a formidable task.

Conversely, when one compares the political orientations of East and West Germans, one is nevertheless struck by the amount of congruence found across the two populations. The strong personal links continually existing between East and West Germany (Scheuch 1991, 251–261), the penetration of almost all of the GDR territory by West German mass communication media (most notably TV; see Bluck and Kreikenbom 1991, 497), and the general role-model function of West Germany vis-à-vis East Germany (West Germany as a positive reference society) are possible explanations for this phenomenon. One interesting hypothesis put forward in this respect asserts that East Germans had acquired some sort of a "virtual" identification with West German parties long before unification. This could quickly be acknowledged once the Wall was opened and unification was imminent (Bluck and Kreikenbom 1991, 498–501). This approach, incidently, might help to explain why all surveys put the Social Democrats in front before the Volkskammer election. The SPD then quickly lost territory when issue preferences superseded this "virtual" party identification.

The Campaign Agenda of the General Election
in West Germany and in East Germany

I have shown that the political orientations of East and West German citizens in 1990 were partially similar, although there were substantial differences between the two groups. The differences will become more evident as I present theoretical approaches to understanding electoral choices. Over the years, international political sociology has developed a set of theoretical concepts to explain political preferences, which are applied in varying mixes according to the situation of the specific polity in question (for a general description of these concepts see Falter, Schumann, and Winkler 1990). One of these concepts, the cleavage model, refers to the historical conditions necessary for the establishment of long-standing alliances between social groups and political parties. This European perspective was challenged in the United States early on, and later augmented by a model of voting behavior that added political issues and candidates to the picture. West German voting behavior was traditionally characterized and explained by a mix of these two theoretical approaches, suggesting that processes of realignment between social groups and political parties have recently increased the volatility of voters without totally negating the importance of current bonds between voters and their parties (see Dalton and Rohrschneider 1990).

Although the important element of time for learning democracy is lacking in the GDR, there seem to be no a priori reasons why the general explanatory approach developed in electoral sociology should not also be applicable to the GDR. Roth (1990) has argued that the cleavage model is obviously not relevant in the GDR, because the conditions for a pluralist cleavage structure and a multiparty system did not exist (Roth 1990, 370–371). He concludes that voting behavior—at least in the 1990

Volkskammer election—can only be explained by an issue-centered approach. (Schmitt 1992 basically corroborates these findings but, unlike Roth, emphasizes the role of existing party bonds.)

Kaase and Gibowski (1990b, 25–26) have suggested that the lack of currently functioning organizations to mediate sociopolitical interests will reinforce the importance of issue politics and, as a consequence, result in high voter volatility in the former GDR for some time to come. On the other hand, these intermediary structures are also in the process of being established. It is furthermore an open question—and an option for political entrepreneurs—whether and when stable coalitions between corporate intermediary actors and political parties will emerge. (Weßels 1993 has pointed out that the subjective conditions already exist for a system of intermediary organizations quite comparable to those in the FRG.)

What follows from these considerations with respect to the 1990 general election? One conclusion drawn here is that it is important to examine the political agenda of that election. (In order to do so, data will be used that come from an election study jointly conducted by Max Kaase, Hans-Dieter Klingemann, Manfred Kuechler, and Franz Urban Pappi. This study employed not only mass surveys, but also a detailed content analysis of the mass media by Kaase and Schrott 1991.) For the analysis of the political agenda a differentiated coding scheme was developed, which was then applied to the media content analysis and the responses obtained from the open-ended agenda question ("What are presently the most important problems facing Germany?"). This allows a direct comparison of the media agenda and the agenda as it was perceived by individual citizens.

Agenda Priorities of the West Germans

Table 2.2 gives the information for the West German respondents (a maximum of four answers was recorded; on average, each respondent named 2.5 items). Before presenting this information, however, one point of clarification needs to be raised. When coding of the media was already in progress, it became apparent that the unification theme was so overarching that there was hardly any item taken up by the media that did not explicitly or implicitly address the unification theme. As a consequence, an additional code was introduced in order to assess the direct quantitative impact of unification on the agenda. As it turned out, only 17 percent of all media sequences/paragraphs coded had no relation whatsoever to unification (here "the environment" prevailed, with 67 percent without such a connotation), whereas 41 percent contained a direct and 42 percent an indirect reference to unification (Kaase and Schrott 1991, 21). Thus, it must be understood that in 1990 the issues mentioned in almost all instances fall into the context of the unification topic. Varying emphases—if present—among party groups therefore only rarely reflect differences per se but rather what the voters see as the issues most clearly related to the unification theme.

Table 2.2 Issue Priorities in the West German Population and in the West German Media Before the General Election of 1990[a]

	Voting Intentions in the General Election of 1990								West German Media[d]
	CDU/CSU	SPD	FDP	Greens/ Bündnis90	Other Parties	Don't Know/ Not Applicable	All Respondents[b]	All Responses[c]	
Political system	3.2	1.7	6.1	13.0	28.6	2.9	3.9	1.5	24.4
Campaign	1.6	0.8	—	—	—	1.4	1.0	0.4	10.5
Foreign policy	15.7	11.7	6.0	21.6	14.3	13.8	13.6	5.4	13.6
Security policy	4.8	4.2	—	12.9	—	1.4	3.5	1.4	5.3
Unification	29.9	30.6	36.3	39.0	28.6	43.5	35.2	13.9	18.7
Budget/finances	20.5	18.1	21.3	17.3	28.6	12.3	17.3	6.9	4.1
Economy/unemployment	75.6	64.5	81.8	69.5	85.7	52.2	65.4	25.9	8.3
Environment	27.6	26.4	21.2	65.1	14.3	29.0	28.8	11.4	2.7
Social policy	44.9	53.8	48.5	69.5	71.4	41.3	48.0	19.0	5.0
Infrastructure	23.6	33.0	21.2	17.3	—	29.0	27.0	10.7	1.2
Law and order	4.7	9.1	15.2	8.7	14.3	5.1	7.1	2.8	4.6
Education/technology	1.6	3.3	—	6.1	—	0.7	1.9	0.7	1.6
Total N =	127	121	33	23	7	138	449	1,145	4,827
Percent	253.7	257.2	257.6	340.0	285.8	232.6	252.7	100.0	100.0

Source: Developed from Kaase and Schrott 1991.
Notes:
a. Second Panel Wave West of the German Part of the CNEP Study, November 1990.
b. Percentages refer to number of respondents, excluding missing data.
c. Percentages refer to number of responses, excluding missing data.
d. For details see Kaase and Schrott 1991.

However, across all voter groups it is indeed the economic and social implications following from unification that are uniformly of central concern to respondents. Compared to the impact of this dimension, all other aspects—for instance, the effect of unification on the political system and on the foreign policy domain—are of negligible importance. Only the environment, the SPD's initial campaign theme, emerges with some distinction, although, as would be expected, the voters of the Greens accentuate the topic far more than any other group. The relatively small direct emphasis on unification indicates that after the unification on October 3 the item quickly lost its immediate impact (this is in line with the reduced emphasis in the mass media; see Kaase and Schrott 1991, 40–41).

The findings on the public's perception stand in interesting contrast to those on the mass media (although here it has to be kept in mind that the entries in the table collapse media reports for the whole period from July 1 through December 8). Even a differentiation according to week of reporting indicates that the mass media agenda covers a much wider spectrum of themes, including systemic and foreign policy considerations.

Clearly, West Germans were already concentrating on the consequences of unification even before the election had made it complete. While expressing a good deal of concern regarding eventual negative implications (see Table 2.1), the time frame plus the competence assessment in favor of the governing coalition kept these fears from dominating the final voting decision of the West Germans (see also Pappi 1991, 24–25). However, this constellation of factors also serves to show why the coalition did not score the enormous electoral victory that had been predicted by many.

Agenda Priorities of the East Germans

What, then, were the agenda priorities of the East Germans? Table 2.3 contains the equivalent information for this group. With an average of three answers per respondent, the East Germans are even more outspoken on issues than the West Germans. The picture painted above for the West Germans in many ways resembles that for the East Germans, although the contours are much sharper for the latter. There is only one truly overarching theme in the East: the economic and social consequences of unification. Hardly any mention is made of the foreign policy dimensions of unification, and unification itself as an independent theme has almost fully disappeared from the agenda.

Compared to the West, two interesting differences emerge. One is the much larger concern with the political system, reflecting the ongoing process of system transformation. The other is that agenda heterogeneity between the party camps is much greater in the East, although it is difficult to give clear meaning to these differences.

Table 2.3 Issue Priorities in the East German Population and in the East German Media Before the General Election of 1990[a]

	Voting Intentions in the General Election of 1990								
	CDU/CSU	SPD	FDP	Greens/Bündnis90	Other Parties	Don't Know/Not Applicable	All Respondents[b]	All Responses[c]	East German Media[d]
Political system	22.6	14.9	26.2	13.4	16.7	11.7	19.0	6.4	27.0
Campaign	1.8	2.1	7.7	—	—	1.7	2.0	0.7	7.8
Foreign policy	3.7	6.4	—	6.7	16.7	8.3	5.6	1.9	7.5
Security policy	0.9	6.4	—	6.7	8.3	10.0	4.8	1.6	4.1
Unification	2.8	21.3	30.8	—	8.3	20.0	11.9	4.0	10.7
Budget/finances	3.7	6.3	—	—	8.3	1.7	3.6	1.2	4.4
Economy/unemployment	167.0	163.8	123.0	126.7	133.3	151.7	156.6	53.0	17.5
Environment	14.1	10.7	7.7	26.8	8.3	13.3	13.5	4.6	3.0
Social policy	46.2	40.6	69.3	60.0	25.0	56.7	48.6	16.5	4.3
Infrastructure	18.8	12.8	—	20.0	8.3	5.0	13.0	4.4	4.0
Law and order	12.2	29.8	15.4	33.4	16.7	5.0	15.5	5.3	5.9
Education/technology	0.9	2.1	7.7	—	—	—	1.2	0.4	3.7
Total N =	106	47	13	15	12	60	253	746	3,712
Percent	294.7	317.2	307.8	293.7	249.9	285.1	295.3	100.0	100.0

Source: Developed from Kaase and Schrott 1991.
Notes:
a. Second Panel Wave West of the German Part of the CNEP Study, November 1990.
b. Percentages refer to number of respondents, excluding missing data.
c. Percentages refer to number of responses, excluding missing data.
d. For details see Kaase and Schrott 1991.

Again, similar to the West, the media agenda embraces more themes. A reduced emphasis on unification, as well as an increased emphasis on the economy/unemployment themes, is congruent with the views of the public on these matters; causal influences, however, should not be drawn from this coincidence without further investigation.

Reexamining the survey findings, one is struck by the extent to which the East Germans were overwhelmed by uncertainties regarding their economic and social future shortly before the election. These data convey very well the feelings of doom and anxiety that many observers felt were present, and that may have contributed to the almost 20 percent drop in turnout, from the high of 93.4 percent in the Volkskammer election to the low of 74.7 percent in the Bundestag election.

The Bundestag Election of December 2, 1990

A little more than thirty minutes after the polls had closed at 6 PM, the West German television networks broadcast projections that more or less accurately depicted the definite result of the election after every ballot had been counted. Table 2.4 gives the shares of the parties (second ballot only) for all of Germany and separately for the two election areas (area West does not include West Berlin where, because of the four-power occupation, citizens were previously not permitted to vote in general elections).

In political terms, the election yielded a clear-cut result: The CDU/CSU-FDP coalition, which had been in power since 1983, was comfortably reinstated with an overall 1.4 percent increase of its share of votes (second ballot); however, based only on the results from the Wahlgebiet West, the internal balance of power shifted somewhat from the CSU (−0.7 percent) to the FDP (+1.5 percent) and the CDU (+0.5 percent). Given that there had never been the slightest doubt in voters' minds since the summer of 1990 as to who would win the election, and given that Helmut Kohl was unanimously regarded as the one person who had determinedly and skillfully engineered the unification of Germany, one might have expected a better result for the CDU/CSU. However, as has been shown before, the impact of the unification was quickly waning, and the enormity of the problems, especially economic ones, was slowly emerging as an important issue. In a sense, citizens seemed to be happy to get the whole thing over with and return to their normal business after more than one year of permanent overpoliticization.

The SPD, which had fared poorly in the West German polls ever since it was ousted from government in 1982, took yet another loss; with 35.9 percent in the Wahlgebiet West (−1.1 percent) and with an overall result of 33.5 percent, they were pushed back to where they had once been in the late 1950s in terms of electoral success.

Table 2.4 Results of the 1990 General Election (Percentages, Second Ballot)

Turnout and Parties	Germany Percent	Seats	Area West Percent	1990–1987	Area East Percent	1990–VKE[a]
Turnout	77.8		78.5	–5.8	74.7	–18.7
CDU/CSU	43.8	319	44.2	–0.1	41.8	+1.0
SPD	33.5	239	35.9	–1.1	24.3	+2.4
FDP	11.0	79	10.6	+1.5	12.9	+7.6[c]
Greens	3.9	—	4.7	–3.6	0.1	+0.1[d]
Bündnis 90/Greens	1.2	8	—	—	6.0	+1.1
PDS/LL	2.4	17	0.3	+0.3	11.1	–5.3
Republikaner	2.1	—	2.3	+2.3	1.3	+1.3
National Democrats (NPD)	0.3	—	0.3	–0.3	0.3	+0.3
Grey Panthers	0.8	—	0.8	+0.8	0.8	+0.8
Other Parties	1.0	—	0.9	+0.1	1.4	–9.3
Total	100.0	662[b]	100.0		100.0	

Source: Developed from Kaase and Schrott 1991.
Notes:
a. VKE: March 1990 Volkskammer Election.
b. Six Surplus Mandates. There are now 328 constituencies in the Federal Republic (328 direct seats); competitors are elected according to relative majority rule by the first ballot), plus 328 list mandates. The overall distribution of seats is based on the second ballot and follows strict rules of proportional representation, except for the Five Percent clause. For the first time in general elections, the distribution of seats to the parties was no longer based on the second d'Hondt but on the Hare-Niemeyer algorithm.
c. Volkskammer election: BFD.
d. Because the East and West German Greens had decided to remain separate until after the election, the West German Greens could only be elected in East Berlin, where voters found both the East and West Greens on the ballot.

Probably the most surprising result of the election was the disappearance of the West Greens from the Bundestag. Because the Greens had decided not to form a list combination with the East German Bündnis 90/ Greens or unite the parties before the general election, they could not take advantage of the 6 percent the Bündnis 90/Greens were able to garner in the East. In general, three factors caused the downfall of the Western Greens (for details, also from an inside perspective, see Kleinert 1991). First, the internal structure of the party and the tensions between the various party wing elites evoked ideas of conflict and diffuseness of goals. This impression of paralysis was, second, reinforced by the dominant theme of unification, for which the Green party elites were historically and ideologically unprepared. And third, the SPD candidacy of the new left representative Oskar Lafontaine steered a substantial number of voters away from the Greens. In this case the well-known sophistication of the Green voters was, for once, used against them. Voters ultimately punished the Green Party by voting less Green (4.7 percent) with their second than with their first (5.4 percent) ballot (Kleinert 1991, 30–31). As a result, at present the small group of eight East German Bündnis90/Greens deputies is the only parliamentary representation of Green concerns in the Bundestag, although the good results of the West German Greens in the *Länder* elections since January 1991 leave little doubt that the Greens still have a solid voter base that likely will guarantee their reentry into the next Bundestag.

Given the agenda of the election, it did not come as a surprise that the right-wing parties Republikaner and NPD were light-years away from gaining access to the Bundestag. The future of these parties remains open, especially considering the strong showing of the Republikaner in the West Berlin state election in early 1989, in the June 1989 European elections, and in the April 1992 Baden-Württemberg state election, in addition to the performance of the right-wing DVU (Deutsche Volksunion, or German People's Union) in the 1991 Bremen and in the 1992 Schleswig-Holstein state elections. It is even more difficult to anticipate the future electoral results of right-wing parties because there is a distinct lack of theoretical understanding of the conditions under which right-wing parties in Germany do or do not thrive (for some thoughts on the matter, see Kaase and Gibowski 1990a, 758–767).

On the left pole of the party spectrum, the Greens have been replaced, in and outside the parliament, by the SED offspring PDS. Analyses of the Volkskammer election leave little doubt that the 16.3 percent obtained by the PDS came predominantly from the upper elite echelons of the former GDR (Roth 1990, 379; Jung 1990, 9). Kaase and Gibowski (1990b, 24–25) have suggested that the PDS's chances for parliamentary survival are small in the long run; this view is reinforced by its 5.3 percent loss in the 1990 general election, relative to the March 1990 Volkskammer election. Its only chance rests with an eventual function as a left-wing protest party. This assessment, though, is somewhat at odds with Pappi's analysis of the ideologically defined dimensionality of the German party system space. Based on the logic of a rational choice argument, Pappi sees a definite role for the PDS within the German party system (Pappi 1991, 20–23).

The dominant themes of the election and the two candidates for the office of chancellor met an electorate in the West that is still integrated into milieus structurally favoring one of the two large parties. In the aggregate, this can be seen from the way that certain social groups voted in comparison to previous elections (Gibowski and Kaase 1991, 15–17). Lafontaine's policy positions and his controversies with the trade union movement motivated many working-class SPD adherents to vote for the CDU/CSU this time. In the white-collar sector, voter transition was apparently of a more complex nature. Dissatisfied SPD identifiers seem to have moved to the FDP, whereas the SPD was able to compensate for most of these losses with previous Green voters who were attracted by the Lafontaine candidacy. These findings reinforce the notion that a mix of explanatory approaches is still necessary to understand West German voting behavior.

In the East, the lack of well-developed cleavages and structures of political intermediation make a sociostructural approach to understanding regularities in voting behavior less plausible. Let it therefore suffice to say, first, that the *Bundestagswahl* was—as were the three previous GDR elections of 1990—characterized by the extent to which workers supported the CDU. The bleak economic situation in East Germany, which will most likely continue for some years to come, makes it quite unlikely, though, that the 1990 Volkskammer election will serve as a (re-)aligning election in favor of the CDU. Rather, it may well be—and this is supported by 1991/92 survey data—that the "virtual" party identification in the former GDR, which Bluck and Kreikenbom (1991) suggest initially existed predominantly for the SPD, may reemerge (see also Schmitt 1992). This is even more likely after intermediary organizations like the trade unions establish themselves in the former GDR, thereby finally helping to create the kinds of cleavage structures in the East that have slowly evaporated in the West.

One of the most interesting outcomes of the election was the further decrease in turnout in the West and the large drop in the East relative to the March 1990 Volkskammer election. Since 1957, turnout had always been between 87 and 91 percent in the West; 1987 marked the first substantial drop (to 84.4 percent) from those highs.

Concluding Remarks

It took the Federal Republic thirty years to attain at least a certain amount of democratic normality after the interregnum of the Third Reich. Following the initial lead of Konrad Adenauer, a Western orientation has dominated German foreign policy to this very day, and West Germans adopted and identified with political orientations innate to a stable democratic political culture. In this sense elections were normal, but important, interruptions and dramatic high points in the ongoing democratic process.

German unification has changed this idyll—not in principle, but nevertheless in an important fashion—because it merged two states that had developed for more than forty years under political conditions that could not have been further apart. The "natural experiment" of unification is in full swing, and only slowly does the magnitude of the problems—especially economic ones—show. In this sense, the Bundestag election of December 2 was a moment of silence and of reflection, a halt along the way.

Considering that just one year lay between the opening of the Wall and that election, the constitutional and political structure of the new Federal Republic, but also her people, passed the first democratic test quite well. There was no outbreak of nationalistic feelings or a new German *Großmannssucht* (megalomania), but rather a lot of thoughtfulness, a lot of uncertainty regarding the future role of Germany in the world, and, also, a lot of *Kleinmut* (dejection).

The 1992 state elections in Baden-Württemberg and Schleswig-Holstein have signaled to political leaders that voters are presently dissatisfied with the way political actors are coping with the political and social consequences of unification. Politicians have gone almost two years without any state elections. But 1994 will be the year of truth. With state elections coming up in Bavaria, Brandenburg, Berlin, Lower Saxony, Mecklenburg-Vorpommern, Saxony, Saxony-Anhalt, and Thuringia, the European election and a set of community elections, plus the next Bundestag election, political institutions and political culture in the united Germany will be put to the first real test since the Federal Republic was founded in 1949. It is probably little consolation that six more state elections will follow in 1995.

References

Bauer, Petra. 1991a. "Freiheit und Demokratie in der Wahrnehmung der Bürger in der Bundesrepublik und der ehemaligen DDR." In Rudolf Wildenmann (ed.), *Nation und Demokratie: Politisch-strukturelle Gestaltungsprobleme im neuen Deutschland*. Baden-Baden: Nomos Verlagsgesellschaft, 99–124.

Bauer, Petra. 1991b. "Politische Orientierungen im Übergang: Eine Analyse politischer Einstellungen der Bürger in West- und Ostdeutschland." *Kölner Zeitschrift für Soziologie und Sozialpsychologie* 43:433–455.

Bluck, Carsten, and Henry Kreikenbom. 1991. "Die Wähler in der DDR: Nur issueorientiert oder auch parteigebunden?" *Zeitschrift für Parlamentsfragen* 22:495–502.

Dalton, Russell J. 1991. "Communists and Democrats: Attitudes Toward Democracy in the Two Germanies." Paper presented at the Annual Meeting of the American Political Science Association, Washington, D.C.

Dalton, Russell J., and Robert Rohrschneider. 1990. "Wählerwandel und die Abschwächung der Parteineigungen von 1972 bis 1987." In Max Kaase and Hans-Dieter Klingemann (eds.), *Wahlen und Wähler: Analysen aus Anlaß der Bundestagswahl 1987*. Opladen: Westdeutscher Verlag, 297–324.

Falter, Jürgen W., Siegfried Schumann, and Jürgen Winkler. 1990. "Erklärungsmodelle von Wählerverhalten." *Aus Politik und Zeitgeschichte, Beilage zur Wochenzeitung Das Parlament*, B37–38:3–13.

Feist, Ursula. 1991. "Zur politischen Akkulturation der vereinten Deutschen: Eine Analyse aus Anlaß der ersten gemeinsamen Bundestagswahl." *Aus Politik und Zeitgeschichte, Beilage zur Wochenzeitung Das Parlament,* B11–12:21–32.

Feist, Ursula, and Hans-Jürgen Hoffmann. 1991. "Die Landtagswahlen in der ehemaligen DDR am 14 Oktober 1990: Föderalismus im wiedervereinten Deutschland—Tradition und neue Konturen." *Zeitschrift für Parlamentsfragen* 22:5–34.

Forschungsgruppe Wahlen. 1990. Bundestagswahl 1990. Eine Analyse der ersten gesamtdeutschen Bundestagswahl am 2 Dezember 1990, Berichte der Forschungsgruppe Wahlen e.V., No. 61, Mannheim.

Gibowski, Wolfgang G., and Max Kaase. 1991. "Auf dem Weg zum politischen Alltag. Eine Analyse der ersten gesamtdeutschen Bundestagswahl vom 2 Dezember 1990." *Aus Politik und Zeitgeschichte, Beilage zur Wochenzeitung Das Parlament,* B11–12:3–20.

Giesen, Bernd, and Claus Leggewie (eds.). 1991. *Experiment Vereinigung: Ein sozialer Großversuch.* Berlin: Rotbuch Verlag.

Glaeßner, Gert-Joachim. 1991. *Der schwierige Weg zur Demokratie: Vom Ende der DDR zur Deutschen Einheit.* Opladen: Westdeutscher Verlag.

Jung, Matthias. 1990. "Parteiensystem und Wahlen in der DDR. Eine Analyse der Volkskammerwahl vom 18 März 1990 und der Kommunalwahlen vom 6. Mai 1990." *Aus Politik und Zeitgeschichte, Beilage zur Wochenzeitung Das Parlament,* B27:3–15.

Kaase, Max, and Wolfgang G. Gibowski. 1990a. "Die Ausgangslage für die Bundestagswahl am 9. Dezember 1990: Entwicklungen und Meinungsklima seit 1987." In Max Kaase and Hans-Dieter Klingemann (eds.), *Wahlen und Wähler: Analysen aus Anlaß der Bundestagswahl 1987.* Opladen: Westdeutscher Verlag, 735–785.

———. 1990b. "Deutschland im Übergang: Parteien und Wähler vor der Bundestagswahl 1990." *Aus Politik und Zeitgeschichte, Beilage zur Wochenzeitung Das Parlament,* 37:14–26.

Kaase, Max, and Peter R. Schrott. 1991. "Political Information in the 1990 German General Election: Comparing West German and East German Media." Paper presented at the Annual Meeting of the American Political Science Association, Washington, D.C.

Kleinert, Hubert. 1991. "Die Grünen 1990/91: Vom Wahldebakel zum Neuanfang." *Aus Politik und Zeitgeschichte, Beilage zur Wochenzeitschrift Das Parlament,* B44:27–37.

Pappi, Franz Urban. 1991. "Wahrgenommenes Parteiensystem und Wahlentscheidung in Ost- und Westdeutschland: Zur Interpretation der ersten gesamtdeutschen Bundestagswahl." *Aus Politik und Zeitgeschichte, Beilage zur Wochenzeitung Das Parlament,* B44:15–26.

Roth, Dieter. 1990. "Die Wahlen zur Volkskammer in der DDR." *Politische Vierteljahresschrift* 31:369–393.

Scheuch, Erwin K., unter Mitarbeit von Ute Scheuch. 1991. *Wie Deutsch sind die Deutschen? Eine Nation wandelt ihr Gesicht.* Bergisch-Gladbach: Gustav Lübbe Verlag.

Schmitt, Hermann. 1992. So dicht war die Mauer nicht! Über Parteibindungen und cleavages im Osten Deutschlands. Manuscript, Mannheim.

Der Spiegel. 1991. Das Profil der Deutschen. Was sie vereint, was sie trennt. Spiegel Spezial 1, Hamburg: Spiegel Verlag.

Thaysen, Uwe. 1990. *Der Runde Tisch. Oder: Wer War das Volk? Der Weg der DDR in die Demokratie.* Opladen: Westdeutscher Verlag.

Thomas, Rüdiger. 1990. "Zur Geschichte soziologischer Forschung in der DDR." In Heiner Timmermann (ed.), *Lebenslagen: Sozialindikatorenforschung in beiden Teilen Deutschlands, Vol. 64, der Dokumente und Schriften der Europäischen Akademie Otzenhagen.* Saarbrücken: Verlag Rita Dadder, 9–35.

Weil, Frederick D. 1993. "The Development of Democratic Attitudes in Eastern and Western Germany in a Comparative Perspective," in *Democratization in Eastern and Western Europe,* Vol. 1 of *Research on Democracy and Society.* Greenwich: JAI Press (in press).

Weßels, Bernhard. 1993. "Gruppenbindung und rationale Faktoren als Determinanten der Wahlentscheidung in Ost- und Westdeutschland." In Hans-Dieter Klingemann and Max Kaase (eds.), *The First All-German General Election.* Opladen: Westdeutscher Verlag (in press; provisional title).

Chapter 3 _____

Years of Transition: Financing East German Parties in 1989/90

_____ *Peter Lösche*

The German unification process is occasionally described in stereotypes. One such stereotype is the claim that the Federal Republic simply took over the German Democratic Republic in 1989/90, or that the GDR was "colonized" by the FRG, so to speak. Applied to the realm of political parties and the party system, the cliché would indicate that the West German parties simply bought up their East German counterparts and that the East German party system was replaced by the West German system of party competition. It is worth asking whether and to what extent this claim has validity, that is, whether and to what extent the West German parties actually did take over their East German sister organizations. In this chapter, I discuss this question by closely examining the financing of the East German parties before and during the unification year.

The story starts in the mid-1980s with the old regime, when the Stalinist SED dominated other parties such as the CDU, the German Peasants' Party, or the Liberal Democratic Party of Germany (LDPD). Subsequently, this chapter will examine the transitional period of 1989/90 that brought about the merger of some of these parties with their West German sister organizations in 1990. Because four election campaigns had to be organized and financed during the unification year (Volkskammer elections in March, the local elections in May, *Länder* elections in October, and the all-German election in December), the East German parties clearly were badly in need of financial resources during 1990.

What is true generally in the area of party and campaign financing is true specifically in analyzing the finances of East German parties: One has to be a detective. There are many rumors, but almost no precise data; there is much speculation, but the whole story still has to be told; bits of information turn up, but the researcher does not have access to all the sources he needs to put together the mosaic. This is especially true when investigating the claim of absorption of East German parties. Except for one article there are no publications yet by political scientists on the transition of the East German party system or on financing for East German parties.[1] Thus, this chapter explores uncharted territory.

Different Starting Points

In order to understand party and campaign financing in East Germany in 1990 and the transfer of funds and other means of support from West to East Germany, one has to distinguish between the different types of parties that were active at the time of the so-called revolution in the former GDR (which in reality was more the economic collapse and political capitulation of the old Stalinist system than a revolution based on popular uprising). These parties took off from different starting points. Three types of parties can be distinguished: The old parties of the National Front, a reestablished party (the SPD), and newly founded parties and organizations. The following section will give an overview of their sources of funding.

The Old Parties of the National Front

During the existence of the GDR as a separate state before 1990, these bloc parties were put together in a kind of alliance, consisting of the CDU, the German Peasants' Party, two liberal parties, and several mass organizations (for example, the German Federation of Women and the FDGB). This alliance was managed under the leadership and dictatorship of the Stalinist SED. Prior to popular elections, the bloc parties and the mass organizations routinely nominated candidates and agreed on the allocation of parliamentary seats among them. There was no competition whatsoever between the different parties and organizations. Politically and economically the SED controlled everything, including party and campaign financing.

The SED had three sources of income:

1. Direct transfers out of the GDR's state budget. There are good reasons to assume that decisions concerning the respective amounts of money were made in an informal circle of the party's politburo; however, data are not available.
2. Regularly paid dues by more than two million members of the SED (in 1989, these totalled 710 million Ost Marks).
3. Income from enterprises and companies that were formally "people's property" but that were either owned or utilized by the SED (in 1989, this income amounted to 720.3 million Ost Marks).

The SED, using Kommerzielle Koordination (commercial coordination), a department within the SED bureaucracy headed by Alexander Schalck-Golodkowski, may have also invested in foreign companies in capitalist countries. In the GDR Schalck-Golodkowski had established a network of export companies (*Außenhandelsbetriebe,* or AHB), which launched joint ventures with the SED-owned companies abroad. In 1988, AHBs generated profits of 2.137 billion DM (valuta-Mark), of which 1.467 billion were transferred into the coffers of the GDR's finance minister. What happened to the remaining 670 million DM is not known precisely; however, there are indications that these monies were channeled to the SED headquarters.

The other bloc parties also lived on three sources of income: membership dues; subsidies out of the GDR's state budget; and profits from companies managed, but not owned, by the parties. Until 1982 each party received large amounts of money several times a year, brought to it in suitcases (so-called *Koffergeld,* or "suitcase money"). However, on the way from the Ministry of Finance to the different parties some money was lost ("transportation losses"), which meant that some of the cash was stolen for private purposes by the party functionary who was in charge of carrying the money. After 1982, however, subsidies were transferred through the banking system. The total amount of subsidies paid to the bloc parties and the distribution among the respective organizations was decided by a small group of members of the politburo of the SED, including Secretary General Erich Honecker. The minister of finance was not involved in the decision-making process. Between 1984 and 1989 state subsidies were allocated among the bourgeois bloc parties, as shown in Table 3.1.

Table 3.1 State Subsidies for Bloc Parties (in millions of Ost Marks)

	CDU[a]	DBD[b]	LDPD[c]	NDPD[d]	Total
1984	20.4	19.7	4.7	17.4	62.2
1985	39.3	20.3	17.0	24.3	100.9
1986	34.6	21.6	15.4	27.0	98.6
1987	37.0	30.1	15.3	31.4	113.8
1988	32.5	31.1	12.5	26.8	102.4
1989	31.2	30.6	18.1	27.1	107.0

Source: Christoph Lütgert, Norddeutscher Rundfunk, Panorama-Redaktion, letter to the author, 9/13/1990.
Notes:
a. Christian Democratic Union
b. German Peasants' Party
c. Liberal Democratic Party of Germany
d. National Democratic Party of Germany

Furthermore, the LDPD, the National Democratic Party of Germany (NDPD), and the CDU could, much like the SED, draw income from companies that formally were "people's property" but were de facto managed by the parties. These included 30 trading companies, 16 production companies, 9 publishing houses (CDU); 8 companies and 6 publishing houses (NDPD); and 6 publishing houses (LDPD). Profits made by these companies finally ended up in the party coffers. In 1989 party company profits made up 80 percent of the NDPD's income, 40 percent of the LDPD's income, and 12 percent of the CDU's income.

Compared to the parties newly founded in 1989/90, the old bloc parties clearly had a structural advantage with regard to running election campaigns because they could use their organizational infrastructure (including party companies such as publishing houses) to campaign for the East German Volkskammer election, for *Land* elections, and for local elections. However, for the first all-German elections to the Bundestag in December 1990, they were not allowed to make use of this structural advantage. The treasurers of these parties (which meanwhile had merged with West German parties, i.e., the CDU and FDP) had to present affidavits to the speaker of the Bundestag swearing that they would make no use of the organizational infrastructure of the former bloc parties during the campaign.

According to a May 31, 1990, amendment to the East German Law on Political Parties (passed on February 21, 1990), all assets of the bloc parties were put under the care of the Trust Agency for the People's Property (*Treuhandanstalt,* or *Treuhand*), which administered all funds, real estate, enterprises, and other assets. Furthermore, a special investigative commission, set up in 1990, was supposed to report to the Bundestag about the property of all former bloc parties and mass organizations. Although the report was due at the beginning of 1991, it is still pending at the time of this writing. A first draft circulated among commission members in June 1991. There are several reasons for the delay of the report: First, it is extremely difficult to distinguish legally between property owned and used by an organization and property formally owned "by the people" but managed by a party or mass organization. Second, especially in the case of the SED, state and party were almost indistinguishable; especially in the case of the party's very complex network of companies. In early 1990, for example, some of the SED companies were transferred as private property to reliable Communist functionaries. Third, the FDP is trying to gain control of the assets (especially real estate) of the two former bloc parties with which the West German party merged, arguing that this property either had been paid for through membership dues or had been donated to the party.

There is insufficient space to discuss in detail the extremely complex and confusing situation with regard to the former bloc parties' property. In this context, however, party property has to be mentioned as one important source of income for the organizations of the National Front.

The Reestablished Party:
The Social Democratic Party (SPD)

The SPD is the oldest democratic party in Germany. As early as 1946 (i.e., well before the GDR was established), the SPD organization in the Soviet occupation zone was forced to merge with the Communist Party to form the Socialist Unity Party, the SED. In the summer of 1989, several months before the breakdown of the Stalinist system, a group consisting mainly of young Protestant ministers and of engineers reestablished social democracy in the GDR by founding a party they called SDP (for Social Democratic Party). The West German SPD was not involved in setting up and organizing this party. In fact, the Bonn SPD was quite skeptical in the beginning. Thus, initial financing for the newly founded eastern Social Democratic Party depended on small, voluntary contributions. With the breakdown of the Honecker regime, however, the East German SDP became increasingly popular, and looked like the soon-to-be majority party in the upcoming elections. Therefore the West German SPD supported the East German counterpart (now renamed SPD) politically and financially. The two SPDs finally merged before the all-German elections to the Bundestag in December 1990.

In the coerced fusion of 1946, the property that the SPD had owned in the Weimar Republic and that had been confiscated by the Nazis in 1933 was taken over by the SED. Today the SPD is trying to reclaim these old assets, especially real estate (about 70 to 80 plots), publishing houses, and newspapers. According to the secretary-treasurer of the SPD, the party's property in the former GDR has a value of more than one billion DM.

Newly Founded Parties and Political Organizations

This category includes organizations such as Democratic Awakening (Demokratischer Aufbruch), New Forum (Neues Forum), United Left (Vereinigte Linke), Democracy Now (Demokratie Jetzt), and Initiative for Peace and Human Rights (Initiative für Frieden und Menschenrechte). These citizen action groups, which had formed a kind of (potential) political opposition to the Stalinist system in 1988/89 under the umbrella of the Protestant church, cooperated after the breakdown of the Communist regime. Some of them formed a coalition to participate in elections. These organizations were funded by membership dues and small voluntary contributions. Except for two conservative groups, there was no financial support from West German organizations.

According to the Law on Political Parties, each party that participated in the upcoming Volkskammer elections (on March 18, 1990) or that had organized at least 500 members received state subsidies according to certain criteria. These included, among other things, the percentage of votes gained at GDR-wide and local elections, the number of members, other party income, and the amount of money required for staff expenditures. In 1990 the East German parties received direct state support, as shown in Table 3.2.

Table 3.2 State Subsidies to East German Parties, 1990

	First Six Months (Ost Marks) in millions	Second Six Months (Deutsche Marks) in millions
CDU/DA/DSU[a]	48	20
DBA	17	5
PDS[b]	10	N/A
LDPD/NDPD	30	4
SPD	12	14
Bündnis 90[c]	15	1
Grüne/UFV[d]	10	1
Others	16	4

Source: Hans Feldmann, SPD Treasurer's Office, letter to the author, 9/18/1990.
Notes:
a. Christian Democratic Union/Democratic Awakening/German Social Union
b. Party of Democratic Socialism (formerly SED)
c. A coalition of citizen groups
d. Green Party/ecological action groups
N/A: not available

Furthermore, East German parties could draw loans from the GDR's state bank in order to finance their election campaigns. There is no information available at this time indicating if money was taken out.

How Much Financial Support Did East German Parties Get from Their West German Sister Organizations?

While the process of democratization and of party building was taking place in East Germany and when the unification of the country seemed to become a possibility in the near future, West German parties began to look for GDR counterparts with which they could cooperate. In the end, the two

Social Democratic parties came together, and the West German CDU cooperated with two former bloc parties, the East German CDU and the Peasants' Party, and with a political splinter group, Democratic Awakening. The FDP cooperated with the two liberal parties of the former National Front. The Green Party of West Germany favored the coalition of citizen action groups, Bündnis90, but there was no formal cooperation. No West German party, however, would work with the SED, which had changed its name to the Party of Democratic Socialism (PDS).

Of course, cooperation between West and East German parties implied financial aid, and—even more important—in-kind contributions. However, it is almost impossible to obtain precise data or even general information about the kind of support East German parties obtained from Bonn or from regional and local party organizations in the West. In spite of these difficulties, different kinds of financial and in-kind assistance can be distinguished: support from the national party organizations, cooperation between local party organizations, and indirect support from party foundations.

Support from National Parties

Although all kinds of rumors have been and continue to be propagated, my own research as well as investigative reporting in the West German press suggest that the West German parties' executive committees and their offices made no direct transfer payments to their East German counterparts. However, in-kind support was immense.

For example, for most of 1990 about one-third of the 240 employees of the SPD headquarters in Bonn either campaigned in East Germany or helped build an organizational infrastructure for the SPD in the five new states. A special fund of 350,000 DM for traveling allowances was established for party staffers to go to East Germany. Especially in the area of communications and press liaison, the West German SPD provided personnel for its East German sister organization. Furthermore, even before the official merger of the East and West German parties, a party staffer from Bonn was appointed regional secretary-general to each of the five new state-level party organizations, not only to advise East German comrades but also to make sure that the newly established organization worked effectively. However, in retrospect, officials in the SPD's Bonn headquarters regret that the East German Social Democratic Party was treated as an independent sister organization of the Second International as late as mid-1990, thus inhibiting the development of a coherent concept of party building and party organization. It is a reflection of the decentralized structure of the SPD that not only Bonn but also the regional West German party organizations were providing personnel at the same time. Yet, there was no coordination whatsoever between the different organizational levels concerning the effective use of the staffers sent to East Germany. Even today the precise number of staffers sent to East Germany in 1990 from regional party organizations and from the national headquarters is not known. There is only one rough and ready approximation: the closer a regional SPD organization was to the former GDR border, the more extensive and intense was its support for neighboring East German counterparts.

It appears that the Western CDU invested even more money and personnel in restructuring the East German CDU and in election campaigning than did the SPD (two to three times as much, according to speculations in the SPD). At the CDU's party convention on October 1 and 2, 1990, then Secretary-General Volker Rühe indicated that all local party organizations (on the county level) as well as the five CDU regional offices in the new states received new office machinery, office furniture, and stationery from Bonn. On top of that, all kinds of literature were sent to the East German CDU offices. Finally, not only did staffers from the national headquarters as well as from regional CDU offices travel to East Germany; specialized teams to run election campaigns for both Volkskammer and state parliaments were hired from consulting firms.

At first sight the CDU as well as the FDP had a structural advantage over the SPD, because they could fall back on the full-time staffers and voluntary functionaries of the former bloc parties. However, both parties ran into immense problems motivating and mobilizing these people, not only because they had no experience whatsoever in running election campaigns, but also because they were regarded as representatives of the old Stalinist system. Therefore, they came to be a burden on the CDU and the FDP and presented the FDP with all kinds of organizational problems. To shed the negative heritage of the bloc parties, the Bonn FDP headquarters hired consulting firms to run its election campaigns in the GDR, but due to a lack of money and organizational problems, the FDP campaign focused on the local level.

Cooperation Between Local Party Organizations

Close cooperation between local party organizations in West and East Germany proved even more important than the financial and in-kind assistance East German parties received from Western national and regional party organizations. The West German CDU and SPD, both mass parties with memberships of about 700,000 and 900,000 respectively, established formal partnership programs (SPD) and sponsorship programs (CDU) on the local level. Because the West German FDP had less than 70,000 members, they could not organize such a program.

The CDU's program was initiated from the top down; its slogan was "Friends Help Friends." However, within both the CDU and the SPD, the grass roots reacted spontaneously and extremely sympathetically to the destruction of the Wall and the emerging unification process. It is likely that millions of marks' worth of voluntary contributions designed to help their East German counterparts were collected by local West German party organizations, and hundreds of copying machines, typewriters, used and new computers, and other pieces of office equipment were sent eastward. West German party locals printed campaign literature, leaflets, and direct mail for Volkskammer, state, and local elections. Some of the full-time county-level party workers assisted their colleagues in East Germany during the various election campaigns. Probably most important, party volunteers assisted their political friends during election campaigns, handing out leaflets on market squares, distributing direct mail, or placing campaign posters in the villages and towns. Among the party volunteers who spent several weeks in the GDR were former teachers, social workers, and administrators who had recently retired from public service but commanded all the skills necessary for running campaigns.

Indirect Support from Party Foundations

The West German parties represented in the Bundestag (i.e., those that received more than 5 percent of the popular vote in the most recent elections) passed legislation authorizing the formation of so-called party foundations: the SPD's Friedrich-Ebert-Stiftung, the CDU's Konrad-Adenauer-Stiftung, the CSU's Hanns-Seidel-Stiftung, and the FDP's Friedrich-Naumann-Stiftung.[2] Although party foundations formally and legally have to remain separate from their respective parties, they do—indirectly and to some extent directly—perform party functions such as political education and research. These institutions are generously funded through public funds.

After the Wall had come down, party foundations immediately moved into the GDR and became active in the field of political education, and thus supported their respective parties indirectly. Furthermore, party foundations built up an organizational infrastructure that the parties could utilize in some cases. By August 1990, the foundations of the two big parties, the Friedrich-Ebert-Stiftung and the Konrad-Adenauer-Stiftung, had received two million additional DM out of the budget of the Ministry of the Interior for the purpose of political education in the GDR. By September 1990 the Konrad-Adenauer-Stiftung had opened two offices in the GDR, one in Rostock and one in Leipzig, each staffed with four persons. The Friedrich-Ebert-Stiftung had installed an office in Leipzig, and the Hanns-Seidel-Stiftung had set up an office there as well as an office in West Berlin for the purpose of coordinating political education in East Germany. Today, each of the four foundations mentioned above has at least one office in each of the new states. Of course, the kind of political education pursued by the foundations is dominated by the political spirit of their corresponding parties. Thus they serve, at least to some extent, as the parties' propaganda instruments. According to a party staffer in Bonn who manages his party's finances, the party foundations in 1990 got such large amounts of additional funds for use in the GDR "that whenever we would ask for help we would get it." However, he was not willing to explain what kind of help he had been asking for.

The Adoption of the West German Law on Political Parties

More important for the financial situation of East German parties was the fact that the Volkskammer had passed a Law on Political Parties even before democratic elections took place. The law was patterned after the West German Law on Political Parties and provided for the reimbursement of "necessary costs for an appropriate election campaign" out of the national budget. For each registered voter (in East as well as in West Germany there is automatic voter registration), five Deutsche Marks were added to a fund. This fund was then distributed according to the percentage of votes among those parties that had received at least 0.25 percent of the popular vote. For the Volkskammer elections of March 1990, the CDU received 17.6 million Ost Marks (first six months) and 12.9 million Deutsche Marks (second six months); and the SPD received 11.5 million Ost Marks (first six months) and 12.1 million DM (second six months). Following the currency reform of July 2, 1990, the Ost Mark was replaced by the DM, and therefore reimbursement of campaign costs was made in West German currency for the second half of 1990. Public reimbursement of election campaign costs for the state (*Länder*) elections, which were held October 14, 1990, was also regulated by law. However, instead of five Deutsche Marks per registered voter, only two DM were paid into the fund.

Did the West German Parties Take Over
Their East German Sister Organizations?

In preparation for the all-German Bundestag elections, the West and East German parties that had been cooperating before finally merged. Can it be said that the West German parties have now taken over their East German counterparts? (In the context of this chapter, "taking over" is defined in terms of party and election campaign finances.)

Answering this question involves reexamining the types of parties described at the beginning of this chapter and their different origins. East German parties enjoyed two main sources of income, both regulated by the Law on Political Parties: direct subsidies from the GDR's state budget (see Table 3.2) and reimbursement of the necessary costs for an appropriate election campaign. Compared to the situation in West Germany, financial support for East German parties from the (GDR's) national budget took place on a rather large scale. Generous public payments for the reestablished SPD and for the newly founded parties and political organizations enabled them not only to finance the election campaigns but also to hire more full-time staff (in terms of full-time staff in relation to registered voters) than the West German sister organizations. Due to such payments by the state, the East German SPD could hire about 240 full-time employees for its headquarters in Berlin in the summer of 1990, about the same number of staff who worked at the Bonn SPD headquarters. Yet there were dramatic differences in membership of the two parties: The SPD could claim more than 900,000 members in West Germany as opposed to about 20,000 members in East Germany. This led to several warnings from the West German SPD to its East German counterpart not to employ too many staffers in Berlin, because in the long run the party would not be able to pay their salaries. Today, after the merger of the two parties, the number of full-time staffers has been reduced to 126 for the five new states.

For the former bloc parties, the financial situation was not as positive as for the SPD and for the newly founded parties and political organizations. Because each of these parties had employed several thousand staffers under the Stalinist system (the two liberal parties together about 7,000), they had to cut back their personnel immediately and drastically, and pay the remaining salaries out of rather small state contributions, at least compared to the old days under the Communist system. Thus the former bloc parties did depend more on financial assistance from their West German counterparts than the SPD.

Conclusion

West German parties did move into East Germany and support—for political reasons—their counterparts as intensively and extensively as possible. However, neither the CDU nor the FDP nor the SPD took over the respective East German organization financially. East German parties organized and financed their own election campaigns, if not in terms of technical know-how, at least in terms of financial resources.

Since no free and competitive elections had taken place in the GDR for forty years, many believed that the first free elections would at least to some extent determine future patterns of voting behavior and establish a kind of loose party identification. Viewed from the perspective of West German parties, at the time all efforts to support the East German sister organizations seemed worthwhile. During the first six months of 1991, however, the volatility of the East German electorate became obvious. A massive switch in party allegiances seems to be under way: According to public opinion polls, the Social Democrats, who received 24 percent of the East German vote in December 1990 (compared with 42 percent for the CDU) would now get substantially more support than the CDU.

Today there are rising resentments against political parties in the former GDR. Increasing human costs of the unification process, such as high unemployment, disappointment about the free-market economy, and right-wing radicalism, have caused what is called *Parteienverdrossenheit* (party discontentment). The number of party members of the CDU and FDP in East Germany has decreased dramatically, whereas polls suggest that the SPD is benefiting from a modest increase in membership to about 25,000 in all five *Länder*. To stem the tide of antiparty resentment the CDU, FDP, and SPD have focused on building their organizational infrastructure in the former GDR. In terms of party finance, the state party organizations in East Germany increasingly depend on subsidies from their Bonn headquarters. Today there are no more direct public subsidies for organizational purposes (as there were in the GDR in 1990). Because the organizational structures of the CDU and FDP are deteriorating and the SPD still has to set up a coherent structure, the collection of membership dues does not work very well. According to SPD estimates, the party needs 40 million DM for the next four years in order to establish its organization, hold party conferences, pay for intraparty communication, and run election campaigns in the five new states. Therefore the national party convention in September 1990 passed a resolution requiring all party members to pay an additional 10 percent in party dues for the special purpose of helping their friends in East Germany.

Notes

1. See Ute Schmidt, "Die Parteienlandschaft in Deutschland nach der Vereinigung," *Gegenwartskunde* 4/1991:515–544. All data and information in this paper are either taken from current press sources or from interviews/correspondence with party staffers and journalists. For comparative campaign and party financing, see Herbert E. Alexander (ed.), 1989, *Comparative Political Finance in the 1980s* (Cambridge: Cambridge University Press); and Arthur B. Gunlicks (ed.), *Comparative Campaign and Party Finance in North America and Western Europe* (Boulder: Westview Press, 1992).

2. The Green Party has also established a foundation, but only very recently, with somewhat different priorities, and on a much smaller scale.

Chapter 4

Political Elites and Electoral Rules: The Composition of the Bundestag, 1949–1990

Christopher Anderson

When the Berlin Wall fell on November 9, 1989, few people would have predicted that, little more than a year later, a unified Germany would elect its first all-German parliament. Yet it soon became apparent that the 1990 West German federal elections, which had initially been planned as the regular Bundestag elections for the old Federal Republic, would be the first free elections in both parts of Germany since 1932.[1] When the GDR decided to accede to the old Federal Republic and adopt its institutional framework, the new federal states also had to be integrated into the electoral structure of the new Germany. As a result, electoral laws and all the rules governing electoral politics turned into hotly contested issues shortly before the 1990 German election campaign, when the political parties began jockeying for the best starting position into the new German electoral politics.

It is widely believed that the laws that govern electoral systems have politically nonneutral consequences. The most famous consequences are those that affect the number of parties in a system (Duverger 1954; Rae 1967; Riker 1976; Lijphart 1990). Electoral rules, however, do not simply impose such nonneutral consequences on the participants in the governing process; they also provide them with strategic opportunities. Moreover, and maybe more important, the electoral rules are not dictated by some magic force, but structured by the participants in the governing process themselves.

Electoral rules can be said to have two kinds of consequences: First, they determine the chances of political parties to be represented in the parliament. Second, they influence the likelihood that different types of candidates (e.g., women, minorities, experts) are represented (Lijphart 1991; Rule 1987). Electoral laws thus structure both the political and demographic composition of legislatures.

This chapter serves two tasks: First, it will describe the issues surrounding proposed changes in German electoral laws prior to the December

1990 election. Second, it will also examine the composition of the new Bundestag, and thus characterize some of the aggregate consequences of German electoral law.

The Politics of German Electoral Law

The German electoral system provides for two paths to the national parliament: (a) single-member, simple-majority districts and (b) proportional representation (PR).[2] Half of its members are nominated and elected directly in districts (*Wahlkreise*) by simple majority vote. The other half of the Bundestag members are nominated by the political parties at the *Land* (state) level and elected via party lists. A voter has two votes on election day: A first vote for the district candidate and a second vote for the political party. The voter can split these votes whichever way he or she wants. The total number of parliamentary seats that a party is entitled to is determined by the overall percentage the party receives nationwide on the second vote, that is, through the PR element of the electoral system. However, a party must gain at least 5 percent of the popular vote (or win three districts directly) in order to be represented in the Bundestag. The winners of the district races are automatically members of the Bundestag, whereas the remaining seats that the party is entitled to are filled with the candidates from the rank-ordered party lists that exist separately in each state. If a party wins more districts than it would be entitled to, given its success on the second vote, the party keeps those extra seats. These extra seats are also called surplus mandates (*Überhang-mandate*). Once in the Bundestag, the legislators (*Abgeordnete*) have equal status as representatives irrespective of the mechanism by which they were elected.[3]

Political parties use the party lists to secure the election of preferred candidates by placing them high on the rank-ordered lists. It is crucial to note that these candidates typically include parliamentary leaders as well as candidates that would only have a marginal chance of winning a district seat (Kaack 1969). Most of the district candidates are also safely placed on the party lists so that their election to the Bundestag is secured even if they lose their district races. It is widely believed that political parties try to balance the composition of their parliamentary groups in the Bundestag by including candidates with particular characteristics, such as religious denomination, interest group membership, regional affiliation (Kitzinger 1960; Loewenberg 1967; Loewenberg and Patterson 1979; Nohlen 1978), or, more recently, expertise in new technologies (Kaack 1988).

The electoral rules thus condition the composition of the German Bundestag in two ways: First, they limit the number of political parties with the help of the 5 percent threshold and thus ensure the relative cohesiveness of the party system; second, they provide the political parties with opportunities to structure the composition of their parliamentary groups to include lawmakers with certain desirable characteristics.

An agreement concerning the electoral law reached between the two German states during the negotiations leading to the Unification Treaty simply stated that the 5 percent threshold would continue to apply in federal elections. In addition, the creation of combined lists between parties in the East and the West would be allowed. This meant that the GDR would simply adopt the West German electoral laws upon accession to the FRG. The agreement pleased, albeit for different reasons, both the incumbent (West German) CDU/CSU-FDP coalition as well as its main opposition, the SPD. If the 5 percent threshold was applied in all of Germany, marginal parties such as the Republikaner on the right of the political spectrum and the PDS on the left would stand almost no chance of being represented in the new Bundestag. This would help the CDU/CSU with conservative voters because it would prevent an electoral success by the Republikaner, which consistently scored below 5 percent in public opinion polls in the West and had virtually no organizational structure in the East. It would also spare the SPD the potential embarrassment of sharing the opposition benches with former Communists (PDS), and quite possibly turn prospective PDS/LL (Party of Democratic Socialism/Left List, formerly Socialist Unity Party) voters into Social Democratic supporters. Even though the PDS had polled 16.4 percent in the East German elections of March 1990, it virtually did not exist as a political party in the West and would have been very unlikely to score above 5 percent in all of Germany. The electoral chances of the various small citizens' initiatives that had helped bring about the ouster of the Communist regime were ironically even worse than those of the former Communists. On the other hand, the law would allow the CSU to carry its little East German sister-party, the DSU, into the new Bundestag by virtue of combined party lists.

The smaller political parties vehemently opposed this agreement between the two German governments. As a consequence, the Greens, the PDS, and the Republikaner filed a complaint (*Organklage*) with the Federal Constitutional Court, claiming that small parties were at a disadvantage under these rules. The exceptions were those parties that were acceptable as partners to bigger West German parties. In a ruling handed down on September 29, 1990, little more than two months before the election, the Federal Constitutional Court declared the agreement on the electoral law unconstitutional. In particular, the court held that the possibility of creating combined lists was insufficient to counterbalance the disadvantages of the 5 percent threshold (von Beyme 1991, 174). The application of the 5 percent threshold in all of Germany would de facto establish a 6 percent clause in the West and a 23.7 percent threshold in the East, given that the eastern parties were not organized in the West (this applied in particular to the smaller parties). The ruling also revoked the opportunity for cooperation of parties that did not compete regionally. This essentially voided the CSU's strategy of lifting the DSU into the new Bundestag. The court found that only a few eastern parties (i.e., the DSU) had a fair chance of finding a sufficiently strong western ally, and stated that "this was considered a violation of the principle of equal opportunity for all comparable groups" (von Beyme 1991, 174). Even though the 5 percent threshold was in principle upheld, the court mandated that it would be applied separately in the two Germanies for this particular election.

Despite the fact that the agreement between the two German states would have simply extended the territory to which the electoral rules applied, it is clear why the de facto consequences were considered desirable by the major political parties. Given the organizational difficulties for the smaller parties in the former GDR, one can justifiably speak of attempted strategic manipulations of the electoral rules by the major western political parties. Had the proposed electoral laws been implemented, the new Bundestag would probably look very different than it does today. It is not likely that the PDS/LL or the Greens/Bündnis90[4] would have been represented in the 1990 Bundestag had the 5 percent threshold been applied to the entire nation without any East/West distinction.

The electoral laws governing election to the first all-German Bundestag basically resembled those that had been used in West Germany since the founding of the Federal Republic, with the crucial exception of the separate 5 percent hurdle. Another important but strategically less significant modification concerned the number of deputies in the Bundestag. As the size of the country increased by virtue of unification, the Bundestag expanded as well. Instead of redrawing electoral districts for the entire nation, new districts were created in the East, while the old Western districts were left intact. As a result, 80 new districts were created in the former GDR and Berlin and added to the old 248 districts that had existed in the West. Because the principle of electing half of the members from the districts and the other half from the party lists was to be maintained, the new Bundestag was now to include 328 directly elected members and 328 deputies elected from party lists. Consequently the new Bundestag consisted of a sizable majority of experienced and professional politicians from the West (most of whom had considerable seniority) and a minority of inexperienced (in western politics), unpolished new members from the East, most of whom had been catapulted into political office within the past year.

The Composition of the New Bundestag

When the election results were in, it turned out that the new Bundestag would have more members than initially planned (662 instead of 656) as a result of six surplus mandates. The governing CDU/CSU-FDP coalition had won a decisive victory, while the outcome was a considerable debacle for the SPD, and even more so for the Greens. The West German Greens failed to gain representation in the Bundestag, missing the 5 percent threshold by only 0.3 percent. Its small pendant in the East, an alliance of citizens' groups and the new East German Greens, managed to jump the East German hurdle with 5.9 percent of the popular vote. The PDS/LL managed to poll 9.9 percent of the vote in the former GDR but only 0.3 percent in the West. To many observers, the FDP was the big winner of the December elections, gaining 10.6 percent in the West and 13.4 percent in the East; this constituted one of the party's best election results ever. At the beginning of the Bundestag's twelfth session, the distribution of seats was therefore as follows: CDU/CSU 319,[5] SPD 239, FDP 79, PDS/LL 17, and Greens/Bündnis90 8.

Given that candidate recruitment in Germany is largely recruitment by political parties, what should the new Bundestag look like? Which criteria of qualifications and characteristics were to be applied in the selection of candidates? Keeping in mind that self-selection naturally played some part as well, it is important to consider the problems involved in recruiting candidates for elective office from a society that had just thrown off the burden of an authoritarian regime and where individual involvement with the Communist state (as a party member, a member of a mass organization, or a collaborator with the secret service) was widespread. Under these conditions, what kinds of individuals would one have expected to represent the former GDR in the Bundestag? Moreover, how would they compare to those representing the old Federal Republic?

It is by no means obvious what the consequences of the East German transition to democracy should be with regard to political elites and electoral competition. Given the radical changes in East Germany during the course of the unification process, the lack of democratic political experience, the lack of Western-style political infrastructure, and the lack of professional democratic politicians, one might expect significant differences in the social and political composition of the representatives elected from the GDR and the old Federal Republic. Many of the "old" elites were swept from power during the unification year, and a number of political parties were created from scratch.

Some researchers have argued, however, that the West German party system and its competitive logic were transferred to the East during the unification year (Kaase and Gibowski 1990; Lehmbruch 1990). Given that forty years of Communist rule left no room for the socialization and experience of partisan attachments as they are usually developed in Western nations (Roth 1990), these scholars view the East German partisan landscape as having been invaded by the strategically highly skilled West German party machines[6] (see Chapters 2 and 3). Such an invasion should have created considerable continuity in the compositional patterns of the new Bundestag.

However, significant differences might also exist in the East. It is not clear to what extent the argument of a party transfer can be extended to the area of candidate recruitment and organization. The CDU, the FDP, and the PDS/LL could rely to some extent on an established organizational infrastructure they had inherited from the old bloc parties (CDU and LDPD) and the SED, whereas the newly created eastern SPD and the Greens/Bündnis90 were at an obvious disadvantage in that regard. The CDU, FDP, and the PDS/LL had access to a pool of party members who had not necessarily been tainted by the old regime, even though many of them may have been associated with it in some fashion for quite some time (*Mitläufer,* or "fellow traveler"); the Protestant church and citizen groups provided a much smaller pool of potential candidates for the SPD and the Greens/Bündnis 90.

The combination of party transfer in voters' minds and organizational continuity would lead us to expect relatively few significant differences between the representatives from the East and the West for CDU and FDP, although there might be differences in the composition of the members elected from the SPD and Greens/Bündnis 90. It is curious that the East German break with the past may have affected the newly established democratic forces to a greater extent than those that could utilize old structures to compete in the new electoral environment.

Overall, then, the composition of the new Bundestag was likely to be influenced by several competing factors: The break with the Communist past, the western logic of party competition, the existence of a partisan infrastructure that provided access to a pool of acceptable candidates, and the logic of German electoral law. As indicated above, the two main consequences of electoral rules are examined in this essay: The sociodemographic and the political composition of legislatures. The following section will examine some of the standard demographic characteristics of legislators, such as age, gender, and education, while the latter part of this chapter explores the parties' strategic position in the new electoral arena.

Age and Education

As Figure 4.1 shows, the average age of Bundestag members has oscillated between 50.0 (1949) and 46.6 (1972) years over the course of the Federal Republic's existence. The new Bundestag's mean age of 48.7 years fits in well with that of its predecessors.

However, politically interesting differences emerge from comparing the members who were elected in the former GDR with those elected in the old Federal Republic. First, Easterners are younger than Westerners. While the average age of deputies representing the West hovers around 50 years

Figure 4.1 Average Age of Bundestag Members, 1949–1990

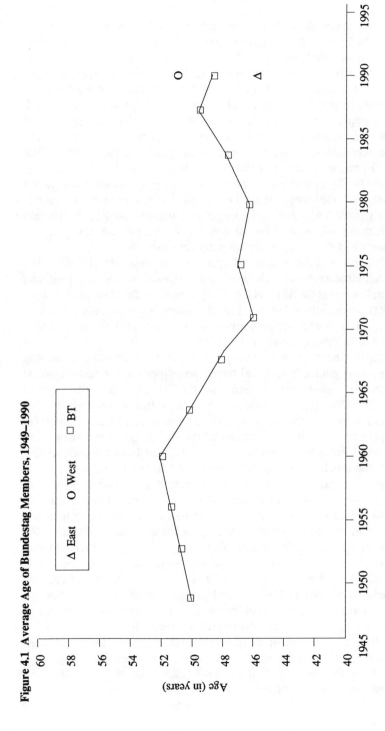

Sources: Schindler, Peter. 1984. *Datenhandbuch zur Geschichte des Deutschen Bundestages 1949 bis 1982.* Baden-Baden: Nomos Verlagsgesellschaft; Schindler, Peter. 1988. *Datenhandbuch zur Geschichte des Deutschen Bundestages 1980 bis 1987.* Baden-Baden: Nomos Verlagsgesellschaft; *Kürschner's Volkshandbuch Deutscher Bundestag.* 1990. Rheinbreitbach: NDV Neue DarmstUadter Verlagsanstalt.

for the three major parties,[7] deputies elected from the East are substantially younger (44.5 versus 49.9 years). Second, in contrast to their western counterparts, among whom the age differences between males and females are relatively small, the CDU women elected in the East are much younger than their male colleagues (38.0 versus 46.0 years) and thus more similar in age to those from the Greens/Bündnis90 and the PDS/LL (average age 36.0 and 35.3 years, respectively). The youngest male deputies elected in East Germany come from the SPD (43.5 years), whereas the oldest male deputies represent the former Communist party, that is, the PDS/LL (49.8 years). Given the novelty of the SPD relative to the old Communist party, this result hardly comes as a surprise. Clearly, the age difference between East and West indicates that the novelty of democratic electoral politics meant a greater involvement of younger activists and candidates, whereas the differences within the group of representatives from the East points to the influence of other factors such as party organization.

As the party of the middle and upper-middle class, the CDU/CSU has traditionally had comparatively weak ties to unions and industrial workers in general, whereas the SPD, as the classical party of the trade union movement, has historically relied on labor and unions; more recently it has also been aligned with white-collar workers and technocrats. This has also been reflected in the composition of the legislature.

Since the inception of the Federal Republic, the CDU/CSU Bundestag members have generally included higher proportions of the self-employed and university graduates compared to the SPD (Kaack 1988; Mueller 1983). CDU/CSU delegates have also been more likely to have held a job of higher occupational status before their election to the Bundestag (Mueller 1983). The profile of deputies from the FDP, a party with a history of representing business interests, independent business owners, and farmers, has usually been similar to that of the CDU/CSU members.

When one examines the distribution of formal education, which can also be taken as an indicator of social status, one finds patterns that resemble those for the distribution of age. In the past forty-some years there has been a trend toward the *Akademisierung* (academization; Schindler 1984, 197) of the Bundestag. In essence this means that the proportion of members with college-level educations has increased dramatically since 1949 (see Figure 4.2).[8] The daily business of a highly developed and differentiated legislature appears to have required ever higher levels of expertise and skill. Naturally, the proportion of individuals in the general population who acquired college degrees has risen significantly as well.

In 1980 82.5 percent of all Bundestag members had attended college, compared to only 44 percent in 1953. The new Bundestag (77.9 percent) falls between the levels of 1980 and 1987 (71.5 percent). Until 1983 there had been quite distinct differences between the political parties with regard to their Bundestag members' levels of formal education. The FDP and

Figure 4.2 Bundestag Members with College Education (in percent), 1949–1990

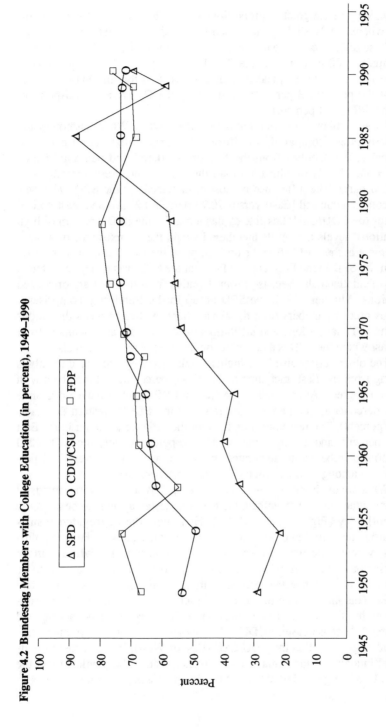

Sources: Schindler, Peter. 1984. *Datenhandbuch zur Geschichte des Deutschen Bundestages 1949 bis 1982.* Baden-Baden: Nomos Verlagsgesellschaft; Schindler, Peter. 1988. *Datenhandbuch zur Geschichte des Deutschen Bundestages 1980 bis 1987.* Baden-Baden: Nomos Verlagsgesellschaft; *Kürschner's Volkshandbuch Deutscher Bundestag.* 1990. Rheinbreitbach: NDV Neue DarmstUadter Verlagsanstalt.

CDU/CSU had the greatest proportions of members who had gone to college, whereas only slightly more than half of the SPD members had done so. These differences appear to have been narrowed by 1990. The Greens/Bündnis90 (100 percent) and the PDS/LL (88.2 percent) have the greatest proportions of college-educated members. We find that the FDP leads the rest of the pack (82.3 percent), followed by the CDU/CSU (77.5 percent) and the SPD (74.1 percent).

These numbers, however, tell only half the story. When Easterners and Westerners are compared, a uniform and curious distinction emerges: Ironically, the deputies from the former "workers' and peasants' state" have *higher* levels of education than those from the West, regardless of political party. The difference is most pronounced for the SPD (94.1 percent college-educated [East] versus 70.73 percent [West]) and least noticeable for the CDU/CSU. Possible explanations for the SPD's pattern of high educational levels among its members include the nonexistence of a labor movement in the East before the unification of the two Germanies, the novelty of the SPD in the East, and the fact that the SPD was to a great extent a party of intellectuals. Because fewer deputies from the East are organized in unions (Mueller 1992), the SPD group in the Bundestag comprises a curious mix of members from the West where the ties between the unions and the SPD have a long and institutionalized tradition, and members from the East where the SPD is a new creation led mainly by intellectuals.

The other parties also have higher levels of college-educated members coming from the East, including a significant percentage of members with doctoral degrees. Almost half of the eastern FDP deputies have a doctorate (47.1 percent) as compared to a quarter of the FDP's western delegates (25.8 percent). The respective numbers for the SPD are a quarter in the East (28.4 percent) and a fifth in the West (19.0 percent). Only the CDU/CSU has more members with doctorates among the western deputies (30.3 percent) than among their eastern colleagues (26.6 percent).

What are the implications of these findings? When the overall trends of age and education are examined, the new Bundestag appears to be a picture of continuity (Figures 4.1 and 4.2). However, the aggregated results obscure potentially important and noteworthy consequences. Female politicians, who in the past had to prove their electability (which can be expressed as a function of age equaling experience) and thus tended to be older than male Bundestag members, are now younger across all political parties. This may be due to a change in attitudes about candidate recruitment within the parties. The unification of Germany may have accelerated this trend, because eastern CDU delegates are, for example, younger than any other group within the CDU/CSU (East or West). Whether these trends will ultimately produce greater issue diversity cannot be predicted, but the example of Angela Merkel (now Minister for Family Affairs and deputy chairperson of the CDU and a protégé of Chancellor Kohl) might indicate greater recognition for women or eastern deputies who appear to be more progressive with regard to social issues.

What seems to be more important, however, is the fact that the eastern politicians are a good deal younger than their western counterparts. This indicates that the transition toward a democratic form of government in the East has brought younger candidates and activists to the fore. To what extent that has political consequences cannot be answered conclusively here. Youth coupled with no seniority appears to be an indicator for reduced influence in the Bundestag at least in the short run, especially since the deputies from the East constitute only roughly one-fourth of the Bundestag. In addition, although the overall numbers suggest that the new Bundestag is not more nor any less educated than its predecessors, the differences between the eastern and the western deputies show that a greater proportion of Easterners has gone to college. The eastern part of Germany is thus represented in the new Bundestag by individuals with extraordinarily high levels of formal education. While they may be younger than representatives from the West, they may find it relatively easy to adapt to their new political environment.

Women in the Bundestag

Even though women constitute the majority of eligible voters in the German electorate, they have traditionally been greatly underrepresented in the Bundestag (see Figure 4.3). Between 1949 and 1980 the number of female Bundestag members fluctuated between 8.8 percent (1953) and 5.8 percent (1972). With the beginning of the 1980s and the electoral success of the Greens, however, the big parties have been under increasing pressures to involve a greater number of women in party politics and eventually to nominate more women for election to the Bundestag. Aside from the pressure for change based on ideological factors, the proposals to include more women at all political levels were also seen by party strategists as a means to make parties more attractive for women voters.

Beginning in 1983, the number of female Bundestag members increased markedly: from almost 10 percent of the delegates to 15.4 percent in 1987. The 1990 election brought another increase in the number of female deputies elected to the Bundestag. More than one-fifth of the Bundestag members are now women (20.5 percent). Even though the reasons for this development are likely to be complex, some preliminary explanations can be given. The increase is almost certainly *not* a result of the unification because the percentage of women members from the East is almost identical to that from the West (21.6 versus 20.3 percent). Given the minimal political activity and influence of the Volkskammer until 1990,[9] it may be assumed that the old levels of female representation there were of less political consequence than current ones. Rather, the increase should be

Figure 4.3 Proportion of Women in the Bundestag (in percent), 1949–1990

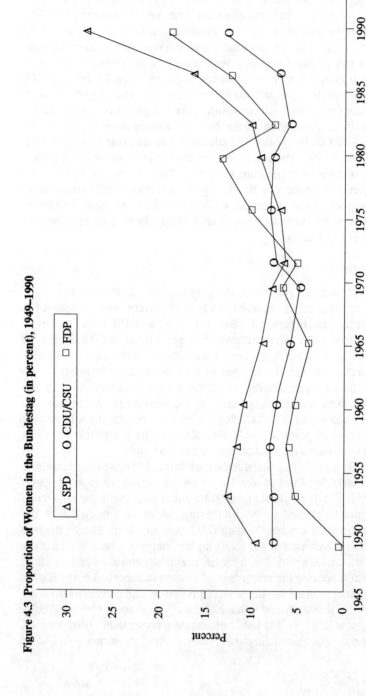

Sources: Schindler, Peter. 1984. *Datenhandbuch zur Geschichte des Deutschen Bundestages 1949 bis 1982.* Baden-Baden: Nomos Verlagsgesellschaft; Schindler, Peter. 1988. *Datenhandbuch zur Geschichte des Deutschen Bundestages 1980 bis 1987.* Baden-Baden: Nomos Verlagsgesellschaft; *Kürschner's Volkshandbuch Deutscher Bundestag.* 1990. Rheinbreitbach: NDV Neue DarmstUadter Verlagsanstalt.

seen as real and, especially in the case of the Greens and the SPD, artificially induced with affirmative action–like quota programs that require a certain number of party functionaries to be female. In the case of the SPD 40 percent of all party offices are supposed to be held by women.

There have been distinct patterns of female representation. First, the push for more female representation did not show results until the 1980s. Second, aside from the Greens who had 35.7 percent (1983) and 56.8 percent (1987) women among their Bundestag deputies, the commitment to include more women delegates seems to have been strongest in the SPD and weakest in the CDU/CSU. Political and social worldview coupled with institutional barriers may explain some of these differences. What is finally noteworthy is that despite the official SED rhetoric before the fall of the GDR, the proportion of women involved in the political process at the elite level (here expressed as the number of women elected from all mainstream political parties) was *not* significantly different in the East than in the West. However, given that the CDU/CSU, SPD, and FDP have more than doubled the proportion of women serving in the Bundestag, it appears evident that the greater involvement of women in party politics and as representatives in the Bundestag will alter the political landscape considerably.

The trends considered in this section give a first quick look at the composition of the new Bundestag. In the aggregate, the new Bundestag does not differ radically from the old one, yet interesting and noteworthy subtle distinctions exist.[10] Some of the most noteworthy differences are found between the SPD on the one hand and the descendants of the old bloc parties on the other hand. Whether the relative similarity of East and West German Bundestag members results from planned recruitment on the part of the western political parties or local idiosyncracies or self-selection is difficult to assess with the data at hand. It is also difficult to speculate about the political implications of demographic trends without considering the institutional arrangements and structures that constrain German electoral politics. Thus, the next section will examine the composition of the Bundestag with regard to the strategic positions of the political parties.

The Strategic Position of German Parties

As mentioned above, the German electoral system provides for two paths to the Bundestag. It is well known that the political parties are not equally successful in single-member districts. Consequently, they have different strategic opportunities to get desirable candidates elected to the Bundestag. Figure 4.4 shows the *Wahlkreise* won by the CDU/CSU, which almost exactly mirror the success of the SPD in the *Wahlkreise,* given that these are usually the only parties winning direct mandates. These data provide one possible preliminary test of the hypothesis that the West German party system was transferred to the East; it is possible to partially trace the connection between the parties' strategic position and the composition of the Bundestag. Should the party that wins the majority of district seats in the West also win a majority of districts in the East?

Figures 4.4 and 4.5 give the proportion of districts won directly by the CDU/CSU since 1949 (Figure 4.4) and the proportions of safe seats as a percentage of all seats won by the CDU/CSU and the SPD (Figure 4.5).[11] As a general rule the CDU/CSU wins more districts than the SPD (except for the SPD's heydays in 1969 and 1972). This trend was not broken in 1990. Indeed, the CDU/CSU won more than 70 percent of the district seats (71.3 percent). However, the CDU/CSU was considerably more successful in the East with regard to direct seats won (84.5 percent) than in the West (67.7 percent). As a result, the SPD had one of its most dismal showings since the 1950s, winning only 27.7 percent of the district races overall. It did much better in the West (31.9 percent) than in the East, where it captured only 12.7 percent of the direct mandates. Thus, the CDU/CSU enjoyed its advantage in the election of district deputies in both the East and the West. However, success in district races cannot be treated completely separately from the success of the party lists, given that the voter has two votes in the polling booth. Indeed, there is a quite considerable correlation between the success in district races and the second vote (Pearson's r=0.78).

On the surface, it appears that the West German pattern was replicated in the East. However, the figures do not show the depth of the parties' successes. The proportion of safe seats may be used as an indicator for depth of success. Keeping in mind that the CDU/CSU has always had a higher proportion of safe seats (as a proportion of district races won), both parties were less successful in the districts than before. In fact, there has been a continuous decline in the proportion of safe seats won by both parties since 1972. In 1990, the CDU/CSU had the lowest proportion of safe seats since 1949 and the SPD had its worst result since 1965. With regard to East/West differences, both parties won fewer seats with 55 percent of the vote or more in the East than in the West. Indeed, the CDU only won 10 percent of its districts with 55 percent or more in the East, and the SPD had no direct candidate winning 55 percent of the vote in this part of the country.

In general, successful district candidates performed better in the West than in the East, regardless of party; the mean vote for *Wahlkreis* candidates in the West was almost 50 percent (49.5 percent), whereas the successful Easterners won with an average of 44.2 percent. Although this is certainly a function of the split among three or more parties in many races in the East (with the FDP and PDS/LL often running relatively strongly), these results may also be an indicator for potential volatility in East German electoral politics. Overall, however, the results of the 1990 election are well in line with the parties' results in the 1980s.

Figure 4.4 Proportion of *Wahlkreise* Won by the CDU/CSU (in percent), 1949–1990

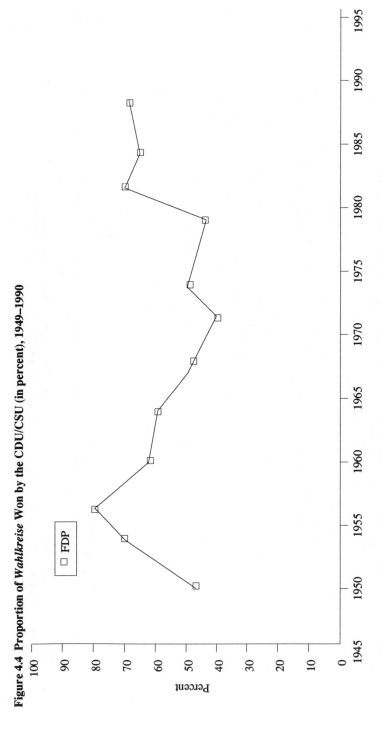

Sources: Schindler, Peter. 1984. *Datenhandbuch zur Geschichte des Deutschen Bundestages 1949 bis 1982.* Baden-Baden: Nomos Verlagsgesellschaft; Schindler, Peter. 1988. *Datenhandbuch zur Geschichte des Deutschen Bundestages 1980 bis 1987.* Baden-Baden: Nomos Verlagsgesellschaft; *Kürschner's Volkshandbuch Deutscher Bundestag.* 1990. Rheinbreitbach: NDV Neue DarmstUadter Verlagsanstalt.

Figure 4.5 Safe Seats Among *Wahlkreis* Seats Won by CDU/CSU and SPD (in percent), 1949–1990

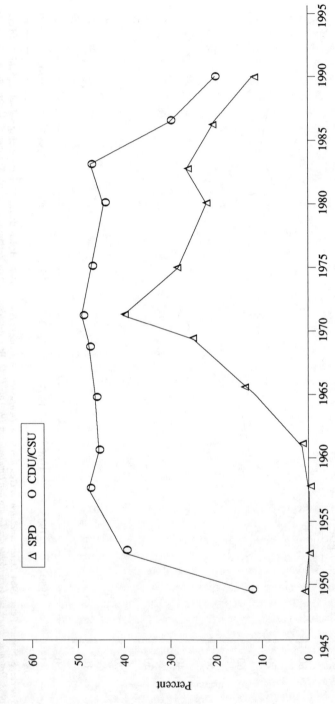

Sources: Schindler, Peter. 1984. *Datenhandbuch zur Geschichte des Deutschen Bundestages 1949 bis 1982.* Baden-Baden: Nomos Verlagsgesellschaft; Schindler, Peter. 1988. *Datenhandbuch zur Geschichte des Deutschen Bundestages 1980 bis 1987.* Baden-Baden: Nomos Verlagsgesellschaft; *Kürschner's Volkshandbuch Deutscher Bundestag.* 1990. Rheinbreitbach: NDV Neue DarmstUadter Verlagsanstalt.

Given the novelty of the electoral system for eastern voters, one might have expected a greater number of local idiosyncrasies that could feasibly have led to a greater success of individual, locally known, candidates. Yet the CDU/CSU won districts in the East in a very similar proportion to the West. The notable exceptions are the success of the PDS/LL's party chief Gregor Gysi in East Berlin and the FDP's Uwe Lühr in Hans-Dietrich Genscher's old home town of Halle. These two were the only non-SPD and non-CDU candidates to win districts in the East. However, such idiosyncrasies are rare. The eastern pattern appears to be driven mainly by political party, not candidate personality, and in a way that resembles the western pattern to a remarkable degree.

The analyses of the Bundestag's sociodemographic composition and of the parties' strategic positions can be related by examining the success of women candidates elected via different electoral mechanisms. Earlier work has demonstrated that PR systems, in contrast to first-past-the-post systems, favor the representation of minorities in general (see Lijphart 1991), and women in particular (Rule 1987). Germany, with its mixture of PR and single-member districts, is no exception to that rule: Women have traditionally constituted a small minority of Bundestag members, and women have traditionally been elected to the Bundestag via the party lists. Since women have historically had the status of a minority in elective office, it is plausible that party lists are their more natural route to the Bundestag, while the districts are the more natural locus for the election of candidates broadly representative of the parties. Figure 4.6 shows the proportions of female *Wahlkreis* delegates for the two major political parties since 1949.

Upon closer inspection, several features stand out: There was very little change in the number of female district deputies between 1949 and 1983. However, the latter half of the 1980s brought a substantial increase in the number of female district delegates in the 1987 and 1990 elections. It appears that political parties have found women to be electable district candidates only in the past decade (even though the percentage is still substantially smaller than that of women elected overall; see Figure 4.3). This is true in particular for the SPD, even though the SPD has always had a higher proportion of female district delegates than the CDU/CSU. However, both parties have increased their female contingent considerably during the 1980s, and the proportion of women in the new Bundestag seems to follow the trend begun in the 1980s. This may be due to a combination of factors such as external pressure, change of recruitment mechanisms, change in social structure, and self-selection on the part of potential female candidates. Most interesting in this context is the fact that there is virtually no difference between the proportions of women elected in *Wahlkreise* in the East and the West. If one leaves out the SPD (only one woman won a district seat for the SPD in the East), one finds that the

Figure 4.6 Proportion of *Wahlkreise* Won by Women (in percent), 1949–1990

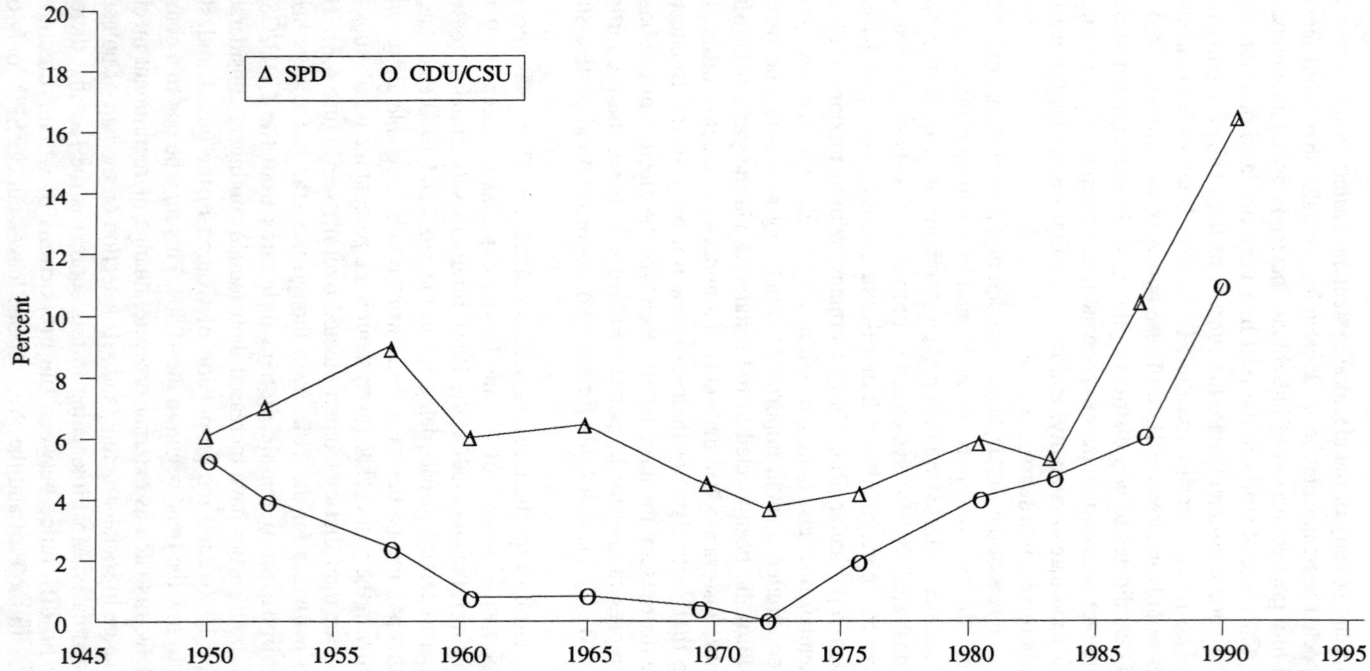

△ SPD   ○ CDU/CSU

Sources: Schindler, Peter. 1984. *Datenhandbuch zur Geschichte des Deutschen Bundestages 1949 bis 1982.* Baden-Baden: Nomos Verlagsgesellschaft; Schindler, Peter. 1988. *Datenhandbuch zur Geschichte des Deutschen Bundestages 1980 bis 1987.* Baden-Baden: Nomos Verlagsgesellschaft; *Kürschner's Volkshandbuch Deutscher Bundestag.* 1990. Rheinbreitbach: NDV Neue DarmstUadter Verlagsanstalt.

proportion of CDU/CSU women elected in *Wahlkreise* is virtually identical in the East and the West.

Overall, the strategic positions of the two major parties have changed little in 1990, and the differences between East and West are slight. The CDU/CSU all but dominated the eastern district races; this comes as no surprise considering that the majority of voters in the East appeared somewhat allergic to socialist politics after forty years of SED dictatorship. Combined with Lafontaine's unattractive message, this attitude probably hurt the SPD more than any other party. Given these special circumstances, the similarities between the East and the West with regard to the success of female district candidates are even more striking. The pattern appears to be one of continuity, not change.

Conclusion

The electoral rules that governed the 1990 Bundestag elections served as a temporary modus vivendi for a unique electoral situation that had developed as part of the unification process of the two German states. Because the electoral laws allowed for a separate 5 percent threshold in the two Germanies, the PDS (the successor party to the East German Communist party), as well as an alliance of East German citizens' groups (Bündnis90), achieved representation in the first post-Communist, all-German parliament. However, it is highly unlikely that the former Communists will be able to survive electorally after the 1994 election when the 5 percent threshold will apply to the entire nation, whereas the Bündnis90 stands a reasonable chance of being represented again by way of cooperation with the West German Greens.

The composition of the Bundestag has changed considerably between the founding of the Federal Republic in 1949 and its enlargement in 1990. Representatives are better educated today than they were forty years ago, a greater number of delegates are women, and district races have become more competitive over time. At the aggregate level the new Bundestag does not seem to be radically different from its eleven predecessors. Yet the pattern is one of apparent continuity with certain hidden distinctions. Whether the differences that were found are indeed relatively small or substantively significant cannot be determined conclusively and are subject to debate. Given the radical changes that took place in East Germany in 1989 and 1990 and eastern citizens' lack of experience in democratic electoral politics, it would not have been implausible to expect more significant differences in the composition of the new Bundestag. Yet extreme demographic differences are, by and large, absent. Instead, homogeneity prevails within the parties' parliamentary groups among members elected from the eastern and the western parts of the Federal Republic. The most significant and interesting differences are the younger age of eastern deputies (especially among CDU women), and their higher level of education (particularly among the SPD and FDP deputies). Radical differences with regard to the strategic positions of the parties are also difficult to detect. Finally, although the CDU/CSU was particularly successful in the East, it is not clear whether these successes are sustainable in the future (Koelble 1991).

Even though extreme dissimilarities do not exist, we do find support for the thesis that the East is different from the West, albeit to a lesser degree than anticipated. To equate this finding and the other relative differences described in this chapter with support for the party-transfer thesis may be premature for several reasons: First, there may have been a party transfer in voters' minds that was supplemented by continuity in party organization and infrastructure for some parties (CDU, FDP, PDS). Those parties that could rely on an established party apparatus and organizational structures in the eastern half of Germany (CDU, FDP, and PDS) gained the most support in the East and show the least variation with regard to their composition, and in particular with regard to their strategic position. This could help explain some of the differences in votes won by the CDU and the FDP on the one hand and the SPD and the Greens/Bündnis90 on the other hand. Second, the success of the CDU in the East may not run as deep as it appears at first glance. The antipathy toward socialist (or social-democratic) ideas after forty years of Communist rule, coupled with fact that many of the districts split ideologically and cannot be considered safe for the CDU, may indicate a more tenuous support for the CDU than meets the eye. To some extent the electoral situation in the former GDR can be compared to that of the Federal Republic after 1949. The system is in flux. It is unlikely that any party has developed a permanently superior or inferior position in the East that would already have institutionalized gains or made it impossible to reduce losses. It may thus be true that the West German party system was indeed exported to the East and made functional through the existing infrastructure that facilitated the recruitment of appropriate candidates. Whether the export of the West German party system has already established the future electoral pattern will to a considerable degree depend on the performance of incumbent politicians and organizational efforts in the East.

Notes

I would like to thank John Sprague, Karl Kaltenthaler, and Arend Lijphart for helpful suggestions and comments on various ideas and earlier drafts of this chapter.

1. This characterization is not exactly correct because the 1932 election was also held in parts of Germany that were later made parts of Poland and Belgium.

2. The German system, once unique, is now being imitated in Central and Eastern Europe. The first free elections to the Hungarian and Bulgarian parliaments

in 1990 operated under electoral rules not exactly identical but very similar to the German system.

3. For a quick overview of the electoral system, see Max Kaase (1984), "Personalized Proportional Representation: The 'Model' of the West German Electoral System," in Arend Lijphart and Bernard Grofman (eds.), *Choosing an Electoral System*. (New York: Praeger), 155–164.

4. The Greens/Bündnis90 is the electoral alliance of the East German Greens and a number of citizen initiatives that had helped bring about the ouster of the Communist regime. Bündnis90 stands for Alliance 1990. PDS/LL stands for Party of Democratic Socialism/Left List.

5. This number is 318 today because one of the Bavarian CSU members, a twelve-year Bundestag veteran named Ortwin Lowack, left the CSU in April 1990 and has not joined a new party or parliamentary group.

6. These scholars do not suggest, however, that the transfer of the German party system should extend to candidate recruitment and organizational patterns. For a view that suggests some level of party identification on the part of voters in eastern Germany, see Bluck and Kreikenbom 1991.

7. There is only one member elected in the West who is not a member of the CDU/CSU, SPD, or FDP: Ulla Jelpke (PDS/LL), who was elected via the party list from North Rhine–Westphalia.

8. For 1990 I followed the classification scheme used by Schindler's *Datenhandbuch zur Geschichte des Deutschen Bundestages* and Kürschner's *Volkshandbuch Deutscher Bundestag*. This scheme classifies all members who attended and/or graduated from college (Universitäten, Pädagogische Hochschulen [PH], Fachhochschulen [FH], college-level Akademien). It should be mentioned that the coding of college-level education is not without problems, especially with regard to the comparability of the different types of colleges that existed in the former GDR and the FRG.

9. In the last East German parliament (Volkskammer) 32.2 percent of the deputies had been female (*Journal für Sozialforschung* 1, 1991: 91).

10. This is, of course, partially a function of the smaller number of East German representatives.

11. Percentages, instead of the actual number of seats, are given since the total number of Bundestag deputies has changed over time. Between 1949 and 1953 there were 242 directly elected members. With the accession of the Saarland the number was increased in 1957 to 247. From 1965 until 1987 the number was constantly at 248 directly elected members, and, as mentioned above, in 1990 the number was increased to 328. In 1990 the PDS/LL and the FDP each won one district in the East and in 1949 there were a number of small parties that also won a small number of direct seats. These are not included here. In general, however, the CDU and the SPD have won the district races. Since the numbers of districts won by these two parties mirror each other almost exactly, only the percentage of districts won by the CDU is shown here. A safe seat is defined as a seat for which the member receives 55 percent or more of the vote, following the standard usually employed by political scientists and used in the *Datenhandbuch zur Geschichte des Deutschen Bundestages*.

References

von Beyme, Klaus. 1991. "Electoral Unification: The First German Elections in December 1990." *Government and Opposition* 26, 1:167–184.

Bluck, Carsten, and Henry Kreikenbom. 1991. "Die Wähler in der DDR: Nur issue-orientiert oder auch parteigebunden?" *Zeitschrift für Parlamentsfragen* 22:495–502.

Deutscher Bundestag: *Amtliches Handbuch des Deutschen Bundestages*. Rheinbreitbach: Neue Darmstädter Verlagsanstalt, 1987.

Duverger, Maurice. 1954. *Political Parties*. New York: Wiley and Sons.

Journal für Sozialforschung. 31 (1991):1.

Kaack, Heino. 1967. *Zwischen Verhältniswahl und Mehrheitswahl*. Opladen: Leske Verlag.

———. 1969. *Wahlkreisgeographie und Kandidatenauslese*. Opladen: Westdeutscher Verlag.

———. 1971. *Geschichte und Struktur des deutschen Parteiensystems*. Opladen: Westdeutscher Verlag.

———. 1988. "Die Soziale Zusammensetzung des Deutschen Bundestages." In Uwe Thaysen, Roger Davidson, and Robert G. Livingston (eds.), *US-Kongress und Deutscher Bundestag*. Opladen: Westdeutscher Verlag.

Kaase, Max. 1984. "Personalized Proportional Representation: The 'Model' of the West German Electoral System." In Arend Lijphart and Bernard Grofman (eds.), *Choosing an Electoral System*. New York: Praeger, 155–164.

Kaase, Max, and Wolfgang Gibowski. 1990. "Deutschland im Übergang: Parteien und Wähler vor der Bundestagswahl 1990." *Aus Politik und Zeitgeschichte* 27:14–26.

Kitzinger, Uwe. 1960. *German Electoral Politics: A Study of the 1957 Campaign*. Oxford: Clarendon Press.

Koelble, Thomas. 1991. "After the Deluge: Unification and the Political Parties in Germany." *German Politics and Society* 22:45–59.

Lehmbruch, Gerhard. 1990. "The Process of Regime Change in East Germany." Paper presented at the workshop "Gorbachev and the Germans." New School for Social Research, New York, May 10–11, 1990.

Lijphart, Arend. 1990. "The Political Consequences of Electoral Laws, 1945-85." *American Political Science Review* 84, 9:481–496.

———. 1991. "Constitutional Choices for New Democracies." *Journal of Democracy* 2, 1:72–84.

Loewenberg, Gerhard. 1967. *Parliament in the German Political System*. Ithaca, NY: Cornell University Press.

Loewenberg, Gerhard, and Samual C. Patterson. 1979. *Comparing Legislatures*. Boston/Toronto: Little, Brown.

Mueller, Emil Peter. 1983. *Soziale Strukturen im X Deutschen Bundestag*. Cologne: Deutscher Instituts-Verlag.

———. 1992. "Wirtschaftliche und soziale Interessen im XII. Bundestag." *Zeitschrift für Parlamentsfragen* 23, 1 5–16.

Nohlen, Dieter. 1978. *Wahlsysteme der Welt: Daten und Analysen*. Munich: Piper.

Rae, Douglas W. 1967. *The Political Consequences of Electoral Laws*. New Haven: Yale University Press.

Riker, William H. 1976. "The Number of Political Parties: A Re-examination of Duverger's Law." *Comparative Politics* 9:93–106.

Roth, Dieter. 1990. "Die Volkskammerwahl in der DDR am 18.3.1990." In Wolfgang Merkel and Ulrike Liebert (eds.), *Die Politik der Deutschen Einheit*. Opladen: Leske und Budrich.

Rule, Wilma. 1987. "Electoral Systems, Contextual Factors and Women's Opportunity for Election to Parliament in Twenty-Three Democracies." *Western Political Quarterly* 40:477–498.

Schindler, Peter. 1984. *Datenhandbuch zur Geschichte des Deutschen Bundestages 1949 bis 1982*. Baden-Baden: Nomos Verlagsgesellschaft.

————. 1988. *Datenhandbuch zur Geschichte des Deutschen Bundestages 1980 bis 1987*. Baden-Baden: Nomos Verlagsgesellschaft.

Chapter 5

The Rise of Right-Wing Extremism in the New Germany

Gerard Braunthal

Right-wing extremism is on the rise in many parts of the world. In Eastern Europe and the Commonwealth of Independent States, ultraconservative, nationalist parties have gained numerous adherents. In Western Europe, right-wing parties have done well in local, state, national, and European Parliament elections in recent years. Building on the fears of voters about a wave of immigrants competing for scarce jobs and housing, political parties—such as the Nationalist Front parties in Britain and France and the Freedom Party in Austria—have pitched their electoral campaigns to racist and xenophobic views held by many citizens.

This chapter focuses on one West European country—Germany— where the political right has become the center of national and international attention as a result of a wave of assaults by right-wing youths against immigrants and leftists. Among older generations, their well-publicized actions, especially since the unification of West and East Germany in 1990, have rekindled memories of Nazi assaults on Jews and political dissidents during the Hitler era. To gain an understanding of the developments since 1990, it is first of all important to define what I mean by right-wing extremism; second, to trace right-wing developments in the Federal Republic; and, third, to assess right-wing activity in eastern Germany prior to, and since, unification. In such a survey, it is important to ask what the root causes for the rise of right-wing extremism are: Will it grow to such proportions that, in a worst-case scenario, the democratic system collapses and a neo-Fascist system triumphs? To prevent such a catastrophe, what means should be used to counteract the present extremist movement?

Right-wing extremism in Germany encompasses political parties and action groups whose members hold authoritarian, antiliberal, nationalistic, Volk, and racist views. They worry about their own future in a rapidly changing society; are intolerant of minorities, including foreigners and homosexuals; and reject a pluralist society that values democracy and human rights. They emphasize the need for law and order in a patriarchical, harmonious society free of conflict. They are intolerant of differing opinions, unable to make compromises with others, convinced of their mission, ready to accuse their enemies of conspiring against them, and, in some cases, willing to go underground and/or use violence to accomplish their ends. Many, but not all, right-wing extremists are neo-Fascists or neo-Nazis, who still make use of the symbols of the past, glorify the leaders of, and structure their organizations on the Nazi model.

Right-Wing Parties in the FRG

The collapse of Nazism in Germany in 1945 never resulted in a widespread reexamination of the questions of responsibility and guilt for the Nazi government's evil deeds. Many people repressed their feelings and could not confront their own past. This contributed to a perception that fascism could not be all that bad. Since the founding of the FRG, recruits to the right-wing movement have joined for a variety of reasons. They have been buffeted by the ill effects of a capitalist system that produced economic crises and unemployment, a technological modernization process that widened the schism between the haves and have-nots, changes in the social class system (including the breakup of many nuclear families) leading to downward mobility, and the rise of intergenerational tensions. Many who felt confronted by changes over which they have had little control and intractable political, economic, and social problems joined right-wing groups and parties, seeking a sense of worth and camaraderie (Butterwegge 1990).

Most of these right-wingers, primarily young males, have not been unemployed, according to a 1992 five-year study of youth in Bielefeld, a medium-sized city in western Germany. Rather, as apprentices or on jobs that were not too fulfilling, they felt estranged from the established political parties.[1] This study does not typify the profile of East German rightists who are primarily unemployed.

From 1949 on, rightist leaders in West Germany capitalized on the latent neo-Nazi and ultraright views of a small segment of the population. They formed dozens of small groups, usually numbering less than 100 members, harboring old and new Nazis, neo-Nazis, bored youth who knew little about the Nazi period, and those who favored violence or terrorism. Some, such as the Nationalist Front, founded in 1985 and led until his death by Michael Kühnen, or the German Alternative, founded in Bremen in 1989, see themselves as revolutionary cadre organizations and have maintained contact with Fascist groups in other countries.[2]

Rightist leaders also formed several political parties to give dissatisfied voters a vehicle to express their disagreement with government policies. During the first two years of the FRG, the neo-Nazi German Reich Party

(Deutsche Reichsspartei, or DRP) and the Socialist Reich Party flourished, but in 1952 the constitutional court declared the latter unconstitutional.

In a second cycle of right-wing political activity, the extreme-right German National Democratic Party (NPD) was founded in 1964. Five years later, it claimed 28,000 members. Between 1966 and 1969 it received more than the necessary minimum of 5 percent of the votes in seven out of eleven *Länder* elections to qualify for seats in the *Land* legislatures, but it never obtained 5 percent of the vote in any Bundestag election. The NPD's days of glory coincided with the death of the German economic miracle, rising unemployment, and ailing coal and steel industries. Since the 1960s, with few exceptions, such as the 1989 municipal election in Frankfurt, it has not fared well in local, state, and national elections. The party has lost attractiveness as a result of a national economic recovery, internal feuds, and the rise of rival parties.

In the current third cycle, to be assessed fully, the Republikaner (more popularly known as the REPS) have been active since the early 1980s. The party was founded in 1982 by Franz Schönhuber and some dissidents from the CSU, the conservative Bavarian affiliate of the CDU. The dissidents assailed the lack of intraparty democracy in the CSU and criticized the one billion DM loan that Bavaria's minister-president, Franz Josef Strauss, had extended to the GDR.

Schönhuber had been a sergeant in the Waffen-SS during World War II; in the postwar period he became a newspaper editor in Munich. From 1975 to 1982 he was the host of a popular political talk show on Bavarian television. One author characterized him as a "kind of Phil Donahue with the politics of 1960s George Wallace" (Ely 1989, 2). In 1982 he was fired from his post because of the publication of his autobiography, in which he boasted of his SS background. In 1985, he became party chairman.

Like the French rightist National Front leader, Jean-Marie le Pen, Schönhuber is a skillful and demagogic speaker. He has survived much infighting and many power struggles within the party, always careful to keep right-wing extremist planks out of the party program. Thus, the Office for the Protection of the Constitution, the domestic government intelligence agency, does not include the REPS in its yearly listing of left- and right-wing extremist parties, even though the party stands close to the threshold of extremism.

To maintain this aura of respectability, the REPS are ostensibly committed to the preservation of the state and the democratic order. They support the introduction of the initiative and referendum at the national level, the direct election of the president, more citizen participation, and the establishment of the post of ombudsperson. Furthermore, they prohibit members from wearing paramilitary uniforms.

However, these populist and anti-elitist positions are offset by nationalist, xenophobic, and traditionalist ones. Party statements, for example, deny that Germany was solely responsible for World War II and praise the "community of German patriots." The program, prior to 1990, called for German unification, with an implicit neutral status in relation to the then existing two-power blocs. In 1992, it opposed the strengthening of the European Community at the expense of weakened German sovereignty. In domestic policies, the program underlines the need for law and order. It warns about a flood of immigrants pouring into Germany, thereby undermining the social net and making the country a "welfare office for the whole world." Party programs demand the protection of the environment as a means of saving the "soil" and call on women to nurture a family and children in the home. Moreover, the party shows no sympathy for the feminist movement, abortion rights, homosexuals, and AIDS patients.[3]

In the electoral arena, the REPS participated first in Bavarian and Baden-Württemberg elections—conservative south German areas in which they continue to have strength. By 1989, they had built up a nationwide organization, with a membership of over 20,000. That year they scored their greatest success when, most unexpectedly, over 90,000 West Berlin voters cast their votes for the party in the January *Land* election. This vote, 7.5 percent of the total, gave the party eleven seats in the Berlin legislature and two nonvoting seats in the Bundestag. (At the time, all Berlin deputies could participate in parliamentary debates but could not vote.) In June, the REPS received two million votes, or 7.1 percent of the West German national vote, in the supranational European Parliament election, gaining six seats, including one taken by Schönhuber. In the election, the REPS scored highest in Bavaria, especially in the foothill region of the Alps, where about 750,000 voters, or nearly 15 percent, supported them. They also did well in conservative areas of Baden-Württemberg.

This unexpected electoral backing of a then relatively unknown right-radical party caused consternation and alarm in West Germany and abroad. Polling institutes, journalists, and authors sought to identify the party's members and voters and the causes for their support (Klär et al. 1989; Leggewie 1989; Stiller 1989). In the 1989 elections, the REPS received the greatest support from eighteen-to-twenty-four-year-old men, who cast twice as many votes for the party as women. According to one specialist, men show a higher interest in new political movements than women. In addition, most of the young and better educated women were repelled by a party that was patriarchical, aggressive, and ready to use force, and that furthermore lauded the place of women in the home (Roth 1990).

In the West Berlin election, the party did well in working-class districts, especially in areas containing numerous low-cost housing projects and few social and cultural amenities. Many persons with low incomes and minimal education, who have been shown to be more prone to accept right-wing propaganda than others, live in such areas in social isolation. The party also received support from other social classes, especially from lower- and middle-class employed persons, including salaried employees and civil servants who fear their own social decline as the technical intelligentsia and other "yuppified" groups make their climb up the social ladder.

In addition, numerous small shopkeepers and farmers voted for the REPS, the latter because the party promised to restrict food imports from abroad that competed with the farmers' own products. Many policemen cast their votes for a party that stood above all for law and order. They considered themselves scapegoats for the government's controversial policies, such as the building of nuclear energy plants, that had sparked massive protest demonstrations and clashes with the police. Moreover, many of these policemen were originally from conservative rural areas but served in large cities with multiethnic groups. In West Berlin, these groups included alternative culture youth and Turks, neither of whom were overly fond of the police (Ely 1989, 6).

In the West Berlin election, most REPS voters had voted for the CDU in the previous election, but a sizable number had also switched allegiance from the SPD. Thus, it would be erroneous to see many REPS voters as fanatic neo-Nazis; rather, they are persons protesting the government's policies, such as allowing many foreigners to come into Germany, failing to build enough low-cost housing units, or tolerating high unemployment. REPS voters are characterized by one writer as the "nice, quiet neighbors next door," who make foreigners, rather than Jews, the new scapegoats (Castner and Castner 1989, 33).[4] Their reaction to a threatening economic, social, and cultural environment stems from an ultraconservative mindset. They seek new forms of community as the traditional social milieu of family, neighborhood, and clubs dissolves. As a consequence, they support the REPS or other right-wing groups.

In the early 1990s the REPS still represent a threat to the established system, despite a momentary loss of support. Their leaders' anti-Semitism, for instance, though mildly expressed, constitutes a challenge to the boundaries of free expression. Schönhuber has stated that the Jews themselves were responsible for anti-Semitism in Germany because they had the temerity to constantly meddle in national affairs that did not concern them. He characterized the German Central Council of Jews as the "fifth occupying power" on German soil. In 1989, he said that history books needed to be rewritten: "We do not allow that our history be permanently reduced to Auschwitz" (Roth 1990, 45–46).

Such statements also emanate from right-wing academic circles in their attempt to revise history, and they lend support to the views expressed by many Germans in public opinion polls over the years. In a January 1992 poll (released on the fiftieth anniversary of the Wannsee conference at which top Nazi leaders decided to eliminate the Jews), 27 percent of the respondents in the united Germany stated that Hitler would have been a great statesman if he had not persecuted Jews or plunged Germany into war. Nearly half (42 percent) said that the Nazi government had positive as well as negative aspects. Sixty percent believed that "a certain amount" of anti-Semitism would always be present in Germany. Slightly more concurred with the statement that forty-six years after the war "we should not talk so much anymore about the persecution of Jews." Nearly two-thirds said that Germans "don't trust themselves to express their true opinion about Jews."[5] On the basis of a wide range of questions, the pollsters concluded that 13 percent were convinced anti-Semites, 39 percent held some anti-Semitic views, and that 48 percent were free of anti-Semitism.[6]

The REPS have mirrored the views of many Germans not only on the Jews but also on the issue of reopening the eastern border question. After German reunification in October 1990, Chancellor Kohl delayed a pledge to recognize the permanence and inviolability of the German-Polish border, as had been demanded by Poland. He feared alienating those ultraconservative voters who—prior to 1945—had lived in areas that are now parts of Poland, Russia, the Czech Republic, and Slovakia. These voters, it was feared, might defect from the CDU/CSU and vote for the REPS, whose leaders stated that Silesia, East Prussia, and the Sudetenland should be incorporated into a united Germany. Kohl's delaying tactic on the border question in turn produced concern in Poland and other East European states about the power of a resurgent Germany.

Kohl need not have worried about the REPS's electoral chances in 1990. He was the one who stole their thunder by demanding a speedy unification of both Germanies. The nationalist slogans heard on the streets of GDR cities after the breakdown of the Wall in November 1989 came from citizens ready to endorse the Christian Democrats and not the REPS. As nationalism became more legitimate and respectable, the REPS lost much of their appeal. In campaign speeches in the former GDR, Schönhuber stated that eastern Germany must not become a "Coca-Cola republic." He assailed American influence in the Federal Republic, which was supposedly undermining traditional German values. He also called for the speedy return home of the remaining Soviet units stationed in eastern Germany.[7]

These statements did not have the desired effect of gaining new support for the party, especially in eastern Germany, where the REPS had been prohibited from campaigning for a few months prior to reunification because authorities deemed them to be unconstitutional. On appeal to a court, the ban was lifted. Serious infighting among REPS leaders further blemished the party's image. As a result of these problems and Kohl's effective campaign of capitalizing on the nationalist issue, the REPS could not repeat their earlier electoral successes. In the first national election held in the newly united Germany on December 2, 1990, they received less than one million votes, or 2.1 percent of the total. Nearly half came from dissatisfied voters who had previously supported one of the major parties (330,000 CDU and 110,000 SPD voters). Once again, the REPS did best in

Bavaria, garnering 5 percent. In Berlin, their support had slipped from 7.5 to 3.1 percent. Yet, as a result of the explosive issue of foreigners in Germany, they gained nearly 11 percent of the vote (fifteen seats in the legislature) in the Baden-Württemberg election of April 1992, thereby becoming the third strongest party in that *Land*. (In 1988, they had mustered only 1 percent of the vote.)

Other Right-Wing Parties

There are other parties on the right currently competing with the REPS and the NPD for votes. The most important one is the German People's Union (Deutsche Volksunion, or DVU), which was founded as an association in 1971 by the Munich-based right-wing publisher Gerhard Frey. His publications include the *Deutsche National-Zeitung* and *Deutsche Wochen-Zeitung* (combined circulation 100,000). After Frey transformed the association into a party in 1987, the Office for the Protection of the Constitution placed it in its "right-wing extremist" category. The DVU program is xenophobic and nationalist. It talks of the need to "Germanize" the Germans, warns about the invasion of foreigners (in 1992, an estimated 500,000 asylum-seekers and 150,000 ethnic Germans from Eastern Europe arrived in Germany), defames democratic institutions, makes light of Nazi crimes, and denies German responsibility for World War II. It has opened branches in the former GDR, intending to recruit new members there.

While the REPS have been making the headlines since 1989, the DVU received renewed attention in September 1991 when it scored well in the Bremen *Land* assembly election. It received more than 6 percent of the vote, giving it six seats in the legislative assembly. As a result, the SPD lost its twenty-year-old absolute majority and had to form a coalition cabinet. During the campaign, the political asylum question became the most controversial issue. According to Article 16 of the Federal Republic's constitution, persons persecuted on political grounds shall enjoy the right of asylum. Only a small percentage of asylum-seekers qualify for permanent residence on that basis. The others come primarily to work and improve their standard of living.

DVU leaders accused Bremen authorities of being more generous to applicants for asylum than leaders in other *Länder*. Such applicants were given individual housing and social security payments in cash rather than canteen meals, while waiting for a long time for courts to decide whether they could stay as genuine political refugees or be subject to deportation. (Most of those who are to be deported manage to stay in Germany illegally.)

DVU leaders emphasized that only those foreigners escaping political persecution in their home countries should receive political asylum. One of the party's campaign posters read: "The boat is full—Stop the flood of asylum-seekers." Election leaflets warned that allowing more foreigners to come to Germany would lead to "the destruction of European culture."[8]

As a result of such charges, some of which were also raised by other groups, the SPD-controlled Bremen assembly decided reluctantly that no more than 300 applicants a month were to be allowed to stay in the city while their cases were being considered. Poles and Romanians were barred because the exodus of people from these two countries was too great. This legislative fiat did little to reduce the xenophobia toward foreigners, including the many guest workers and their family members who had lived in Bremen and elsewhere for decades (in 1991, there were 4.8 million foreigners in Germany). About 10 percent of the Bremen residents come from countries such as Portugal, Italy, Spain, the former Yugoslavia, and Turkey. They have been working in fish-processing plants and at other jobs that most Germans shun. In recent years, their numbers have been augmented by ethnic Germans from the former Soviet Union and Eastern Europe, who have a constitutional right of resettlement in Germany.

The controversy over foreigners in Germany is part of a worldwide problem of interstate migration that needs to be addressed at national and international levels. In the meantime, it provides a ready-made issue that the DVU and conservative German parties, aware of popular discontent, have exploited for electoral gains. This was made evident once more in a 1992 election in Schleswig-Holstein, where the DVU gained 6.3 percent of the total vote and six seats in the legislature after not even having entered the electoral campaign four years earlier.

This survey of right-wing groups and parties in western Germany, with an emphasis on the most recent period, indicates that political activities of the right have occurred on a cyclical basis. In periods of economic downturn and social dislocations the groups became more active and gained new members, and the parties achieved some major successes. But the organizations did not fare as well during periods of economic upswing and social stability.

Right-Wing Media

Any political organization needs to mold public opinion in order to have an influence on public policies, recruit members, and gain votes in elections. Rightist parties receive support from ultraright publishing houses, which publish newspapers and journals with a combined yearly circulation of millions. Journals, some short-lived and some long-lived, feature articles assailing liberal public policies. In one instance, an author wrote that the Germans were dying out because women were not fertile enough.[9] Other authors, including revisionist historians, argue that the Nazi crimes were no different than those committed by Stalin in the Soviet Union. Some of these writings are pure apologia for the deeds of Nazi leaders, and the authors do not shun the themes of racism and biological determinism. Conservative television and radio commentators also influence the climate of opinion, even though most of them distance themselves from extremist positions that go beyond the constitutional threshold.

After the 1990 national election, right-wing journals, such as *Nation und Europa* and *Nation,* attempted to dispel the gloom among rightist leaders about the poor election results. The journals debated ways of improving membership recruitment. One editor urged the formation of cadre organizations on the model that Michael Kühnen, the deceased leader of the National Front, had advocated for years.[10] Another journal reprinted a position paper by the NPD youth organization, which endorsed the ideology of the new right. This ideology glorifies the nation as the key political unit, but rejects National Socialism. It calls for the protection of nature and a limit to immigration because the population pressure on the country would otherwise be too great. In 1991, the CSU Bavarian minister of the environment, at a CSU rally, made a similar argument about immigration.[11]

The effect of the right-wing media on public opinion is hard to gauge. Undoubtedly, rightist publicists found an audience not only among members of the extremist organizations but also among conservative CDU/CSU adherents. Thus their extremist views gained a degree of respectability that they might not have enjoyed otherwise. Whenever these views were persuasive to a broad audience, as in the case of immigration, the major parties had to adopt more conservative policies.

The Emergence of the Right in the GDR

Totalitarian or authoritarian states by their very nature allow no groups or political parties to organize that would threaten the political elite's hold on governmental power. The citizens, whose civil liberties are greatly limited, are expected to be loyal to the regime and quash any dissident ideas. In the GDR, the Communist regime that ruled the country from 1949 to 1989 was never fully able to hold down the population. Opposition groups, clustered in churches, sought to open the closed system to ideas of democratic pluralism. The Western media wrote about these groups, whose members often favored a democratic socialist alternative, but paid little attention in the 1980s to emerging underground right-wing groups. As a result, little was known about them.

The GDR regime suppressed the news about their rise in the early 1980s as much as possible. Such news would have given lie to official propaganda that the GDR state was anti-Fascist (and that the FRG was the sole successor to the Nazi state). The reality was that it could not stamp out dissident ideas, although it tried to stamp out dissident groups. The regime had to expect that there would be supporters of the far right in any society, especially because the bulk of the population had supported the Nazi government during the Hitler era. After World War II, the Communist authorities did not allow public discussion of how people could confront their own past and their complicity or guilt in what had happened (Frindte 1990).

By the 1980s, only a few of the old fanatic Nazis, who had formed the backbone of the movement when Hitler assumed office in 1933, were still alive. Instead, young men were in the vanguard of the rightist movement. They were influenced by West German neo-Fascist groups and television and radio programs from West Germany, including West Berlin. They rejected the Communist system less for its oppressive nature than for not maintaining traditional German petty bourgeois and nationalist values. Freya Klier, a left dissident who was expelled from the GDR in 1987, writes: "The German values of discipline and strong forms of authority and so forth were also the values of the SED. . . . These kids were educated with a militaristic old Prussian value system and, not surprisingly, their protest against the system is in fact a protest against the system's failure to live up to its own values."[12]

The right-wing youth had a penchant not only for order and nationalism but also for anticommunism, anti-Semitism, and xenophobia. Thus, some of them desecrated Jewish cemeteries and painted anti-Semitic graffiti on buildings. Many turned against foreign workers from Third World countries, viewing them as interlopers who attacked German women, imported AIDS, received preferential treatment from the state, and lived better than the average GDR citizen (Brück 1991, 191–200).

These exaggerated views did not correspond to the facts. The 170,000 foreign workers from Mozambique, Angola, Cuba, Poland, Vietnam, and other Communist countries took jobs that Germans shunned. They lived in overcrowded shelters built especially for them in outlying city suburbs that lacked social amenities. Often they were treated as third-class citizens, were harassed while shopping, and were denied service in bars. The government failed to integrate them into German society (Hockenos 1990, 107).

These facts, however, did not deter the right-radical youth, especially skinheads, from committing violent acts against such a weak subgroup. Only a minority of skinheads—dressed in steel-toed boots, rolled-up jeans, bomber jackets, and sporting razor-thin haircuts—were on the political right, but their violence often has been more aggressive and brutal than that committed by their West German counterparts.

Prior to the crumbling of the regime in 1989, rightist skinheads were involved in the worst outbreak of violence in East Berlin. On October 17, 1987, thirty of them, carrying bicycle chains and bats, stormed into the headquarters of the human rights movement located in the Prenzlauerberg

Zion Church, where a punk concert was in progress. They injured dozens in the audience while shouting "Sieg Heil," "Jewish swine," and "rabble out of the German church." The police arrested four skinheads, who subsequently received sentences of one to four years for "hooliganism." The SED-controlled press covered up this act of violence for one month (Hockenos 1990, 108).

Around 1987, the fascos (or faschos) organized for conspiratorial work. Older and more educated than the skinheads, they were strongly committed to a Fascist program. They wanted to reestablish the German Reich, abolish socialism, and get rid of American and Soviet soldiers on German soil. Glorifying violence, they made contacts with Western neo-Nazi organizations, including those in the United States and Canada (Hockenos 1990, 109).

After the peaceful revolution of November 1989, skinheads marched in packs, with arms outstretched in the Nazi salute, in the huge weekly demonstrations held to protest the GDR regime. They demanded unification, shouted nationalist slogans, and favored a greater Germany. When the media featured their participation, they had achieved their purpose of drawing attention to themselves and to their demands. They were not the only ones to insist on swift unification, but their demands, running counter to those of the leaders of the citizens groups, who favored a democratic socialist East German state, shifted the political dialogue to the right.

Eastern Germany After 1989

Since the downfall of the GDR regime and the subsequent unification of the two states in 1990, right-wing groups in eastern Germany have escalated their physical violence against foreigners and left-wingers. The end of the Communist government and its ubiquitous secret police (Stasi) meant that these groups could organize in a free society and operate with fewer restraints than before. In 1991, the police estimated that there were 2,000 hard-core neo-Nazis who engaged in violence, supported by about 15,000 sympathizers and 50,000 others who supported their ideology but not their tactics. In 1992, the number of hard-core neo-Nazis had risen to an estimated 3,300, with an additional 1,700 in western Germany.

The root causes for youth being predisposed to neo-Nazism or ultranationalist ideology and then joining right-wing groups have already been noted. In the post-GDR era, other causes include much anomie, fueled by high unemployment and uncertainty about future job prospects during the transformation of a command economy into a free-market economy. This was accentuated by a new rootlessness, lack of orientation, and social dislocation among the population. These sociopolitical factors left a mark on desperate, frustrated, less-educated young men, who often came from bro-

ken homes. Many angry youth, who had grown up in the repressive
Communist era, viewed themselves in the post-1990 period as second-class
citizens in relation to the *Wessis* (West Germans). As compensation, they
attempted to make life miserable for the defenseless foreigners (Heitmeyer
1990).

The reports about racial violence in eastern Germany as well as in
western Germany are disquieting. From January to November 1992, the
number of right-wing attacks against foreign workers and Romanian gypsies in eastern Germany reached a peak of 661 (another 975 in western
Germany), not matched since the racial violence of the early Nazi years.[13]
Football rowdies and hooligans, some of whom study law and medicine or
work as clerks during the week, were also involved in violence against foreigners on weekends. Right-radical attacks led to frequent, bloody con-
frontations with left-wingers and Turkish or other foreign youth. The
understaffed and insufficiently armed East German police were not able to
quell the attacks and counterattacks.

In Dresden, one of the key centers of neo-Nazism, an immigrant from
Mozambique was killed when skinheads beat him up in a streetcar and then
hurled him to the street. A few of the ringleaders received jail sentences of
up to four years. In a Dresden suburb, five skinheads drove up to a cultural
center in which left-wing punks and other leftists were having a dance. The
skinheads accosted a Mozambican worker in front of the center and held a
knife to his throat. A group of punks rushed out of the center to assist the
victim. A brawl ensued and the skinheads fled. By the time the police
came, all was quiet.

Neo-Nazis have firebombed several hostels for foreigners, terrorizing
the inhabitants. Hoyerswerda, in northern Saxony, was the scene of repeated violence. The town of 70,000 had 240 asylum-seekers and 70
Mozambican and Vietnamese workers. In September 1991 a group of neo-
Nazis attacked Vietnamese men selling goods on the market square. The
police dispersed the neo-Nazis. Soon thereafter 120 skinheads tried to
storm one of the two hostels for foreigners. Some German neighbors
cheered on the attackers, yelling "Niggers and Fidschies [Asian foreigners]
go home." During the following days, the skinheads, armed with trun-
cheons, stones, steel balls, bottles, and Molotov cocktails, caused further
violence on the streets. Another seventeen people were injured, a few seriously.

As a result, members of the Human Rights League and about 100
members of the *Autonomen* (tough left-wing youth) provided protection to
the foreign workers in their hostels. This time, a large police contingent,
reinforced by Dresden police and border guards, attempted to keep both
sides apart. The police had to use dogs, tear gas, and water cannons to
maintain order; they arrested thirty people.

In August 1992, hundreds of skinheads, bored and frustrated by their lack of job opportunities, rioted for nearly a week in Rostock, a port on the Baltic Sea racked by high unemployment (40 percent) and poverty. During that time they firebombed a ten-story hostel housing Romanian gypsies, forcing the evacuation of its residents to another area. These attacks, which the police could hardly contain, precipitated more violence against foreigners in both parts of Germany in the following months, as well as the torching of buildings in the former Sachsenhausen and Ravensbrück concentration camps. In November 1992, in western Germany, the attacks were capped by the firebombing of a home in a small town in Schleswig-Holstein, in which three Turkish women burned to death. Much of the population in Germany and elsewhere was horrified and fearful of developments that had parallels to the last years of the Weimar era.

Government officials are stumped on how to provide better protection for foreigners in the long run. Proposals range from removing asylum-seekers to more hospitable towns to fencing in their hostels. None of the proposals has proven satisfactory. When foreign workers leave eastern Germany upon the expiration of their work contracts, as many already have, and fewer political asylum-seekers are admitted into the country, violence may shrink unless a new group of victims is found.

Skinhead attacks on foreigners reflect a bias that is not restricted to a small minority. A 1990 survey of 2,700 youth in Saxony indicates that 15 to 20 percent of them were intolerant, nationalist, anti-Semitic, and authoritarian. Five percent were attracted to rightist parties for ideological or social reasons. These youth were primarily high school students and apprentices, including skinheads and members of the REPS, but not university students and those employed.[14]

In late 1990, a Cologne social research institute carried out another study in eastern Germany for the Bonn government. The respondents—adult Germans, foreigners, and experts—confirmed the xenophobic attitudes prevalent in the former GDR. More than 70 percent of the foreigners polled said that Germans had insulted or reviled them; 20 percent reported physical abuse. Many said that they were afraid to leave their apartments in the evenings. Paradoxically, Turks were at the top of the list of foreigners who were least liked among German respondents, even though few, if any, had any personal contact with Turks.[15]

Conclusion

This survey of right-wing extremism in the two former German states and the newly united FRG indicates the presence of a dual right-wing movement that operates at the levels of political and direct action. Observers have worried about the tactics of members of direct action groups, who have engaged in incessant violence, especially against foreigners. Such violence endangers the democratic system that has such tender shoots in eastern Germany.

There is also cause for concern that the political culture is moving to the right. Most parties have become more nationalist and conservative on the political asylum issue. In addition, there is the at present unlikely possibility that the CDU/CSU might some day enter into a coalition with a far-right party in order to maintain or regain political power. Even "friendly fascism" could sneak in through an escalation of violence and calls for a strong leader to cope with it, police excesses, an increased surveillance of citizens and foreigners, and restrictions on their civil liberties.[16]

Yet the likelihood of fascism triumphing is remote. Although a number of parallels can be drawn between the late Weimar period on the one hand, when Nazi and Communist forces battled one another on the streets in a period of high unemployment and social dislocation, and the present period on the other hand, there are also significant differences. First, democracy seems solidly established in western Germany, despite the excesses committed by extremist groups and their occasional victories in shaping the political agenda, such as on the political asylum question. Second, even though the NPD and the REPS did well in *Land* elections, they were not able to maintain their electoral momentum in the 1990 national election. Right-wing party organizations have been fragmented and have not yet produced a charismatic leader who could mobilize a greater share of the electorate. Third, violence in eastern Germany is bound to subside eventually as economic conditions improve and youth gain employment and a sense of self-worth.

Such optimism about the future needs to be tempered by the unpredictability of events. The likelihood of fascism emerging again would be reduced if immediate steps were taken to deal with the root causes of the xenophobia and violence that have made the headlines in recent years.

In eastern Germany, the population will need to cope with what it sees as a "massive destruction" of its identity and a "downgrading of East German consciousness" since unification.[17] On the question of individual and collective guilt, the older people will also need to cope with their past behavior and attitudes during the Nazi era, once the younger generation begins to ask questions. But such a dialogue may not take place because attention is currently focused on how people can come to terms with their behavior during the GDR era.

At the same time, government leaders, teachers, and others in positions of authority should make more forceful appeals for the citizenry to be tolerant of minorities and to stop all violence. One psychoanalyst stated: "We need a revolution for humanity in our country."[18] A similar sentiment must have motivated organizers in all parts of Germany in late 1991 and 1992, who scheduled numerous public demonstrations, rallies, and rock concerts to indicate that many Germans felt sympathy for foreigners. One rock concert in Berlin was held under the motto, "I am a foreigner." In Cologne, demonstrators carried placards that read, "Dear foreigners, please don't leave us alone with these Germans."[19] In November 1992, at a mass rally of 350,000 persons in Berlin, marred by leftist protests against government policies, President Richard von Weizsäcker said: "We should never forget what caused the failure of the first republic in Germany. Not because there were too many Nazis too soon, but because for too long there were too few democrats."[20]

The president's warning was an implicit plea for tolerance toward foreigners in Germany. Polls taken in 1991 indicate that 60 percent of German respondents show support for foreigners living in Germany. The 40 percent opposed resent the increased outlays for refugees and the perceived large-scale abuse of the right to political asylum.[21]

The government will have to tackle the question of immigration of foreigners from Eastern Europe and Third World countries with sensitivity and fairness. Germany (and other West European countries) contends that it can admit only a limited number of people. But legally admitted immigrants should be integrated and assimilated and gain full rights, including the vote in local elections and eventual citizenship. German government efforts, limited so far, to help shore up the economies of East European countries so that people may build up an existence at home rather than emigrate to Germany and elsewhere, is a step in the right direction.

In sum, if current economic and social problems in Germany are eased, participatory democracy is encouraged, and more deep-seated causes for the perpetuation of right-wing extremism are addressed, and if the perpetrators of violence are severely punished, then there is hope that the democratic system of the new Germany will be strengthened rather than weakened.

Notes

1. The "Bielefelder Rechtsextremismus-Studie" by Wilhelm Heitmeyer, cited in *Die Zeit*, May 29, 1992.

2. For a yearly list of rightist (and leftist) groups and parties, see the annual reports, entitled *Verfassungsschutzbericht*, of the Federal Office for the Protection of the Constitution (Bundesverfassungsschutz).

3. See Die Republikaner: *Parteiprogramm 1990*. Bonn, 1990. Also personal interview with Bavarian REPS official, Munich, December 10, 1990.

4. Bartholomäus Grill in *Die Zeit*, February 17, 1989; quoted in Castner and Castner, 1989: 33.

5. EMNID poll of West Germans, East Germans, and Israelis commissioned by *Der Spiegel*, January 13, 1992.

6. *Der Spiegel*, January 20, 1992, p. 44. West Germans were more anti-Semitic, pro-rightist, and hostile to foreigners than East Germans.

7. *New York Times*, November 30, 1990.

8. On immigration, see Federal Ministry of the Interior (BMI), *Innenpolitik*

No. 4, 1991; BMI, "Survey of the Policy and Law Regarding Aliens in the FRG," V II 1–937 020/15 (January 1991, mimeo); *Christian Science Monitor*, November 19, 1991.

    9. Cited by *Die Zeit*, May 11, 1990.

    10. Karl Richter, editor of *Deutsche Rundschau*, writing in *Nation und Europa*, November 1990, cited in *Die Tageszeitung*, November 4, 1991.

    11. *Die Tageszeitung*, November 4, 1991.

    12. Freya Klier, *Fatherland of Lies: Growing Up in the GDR*, n.p., cited in Paul Hockenos, "Fascism in the Antifascist State," *Z*. Boston, March 1990, p. 107.

    13. *New York Times*, October 28, 1992.

    14. Most of the polled youth reject right-wing extremism. Yet only 20 to 30 percent were willing to participate in counterdemonstrations, hand out leaflets, and work in anti-Fascist groups (Wilfried Schubarth and Walter Friedrich, "Einstellungen ostdeutscher Jugendlicher zu Rechts- und Linksextremismus" [Freudenberg Stiftung, May 1991, hectographed]).

    15. *The Week in Germany*. New York, March 1, 1991.

    16. The expression "friendly fascism" is the title of a book by Bertram Gross, *Friendly Fascism: The New Face of Power in America* (New York: M. Evans), 1980.

    17. Personal letter from Ulrich Heublein, Central Institute for Youth Research, Leipzig, to author, December 16, 1991.

    18. *Stuttgarter Zeitung*, November 2, 1991.

    19. *Christian Science Monitor*, November 18, 1991.

    20. *New York Times*, November 9, 1992.

    21. German Information Center, "Foreigners in Germany: Guest Workers, Asylum-Seekers, Refugees, and Ethnic Germans—Facts and Reflections." New York, November 1991.

References

Brück, Wolfgang. 1991. "Jugend als soziales Problem." In Walter Friedrich and Hartmut Griese (eds.), *Jugend und Jugendforschung in der DDR: Gesellschaftspolitische Situationen, Sozialisation und Mentalitätsentwicklung in den achtziger Jahren*. Opladen: Leske und Budrich, 191–200.

Butterwegge, Christoph. 1990. "Gesellschaftliche Ursachen, Erscheinungsformen und Entwicklungstendenzen des Rechtsradikalismus." In C. Butterwegge and Horst Isola (eds.), *Rechtsextremismus im vereinten Deutschland: Randerscheinung oder Gefahr für die Demokratie?* Berlin: Links, 14–18.

Castner, Hartmut, and Thilo Castner. 1989. "Rechtsextremismus und Jugend." *Aus Politik und Zeitgeschichte*, 41–42/89 (October 6, 1989): 33.

Ely, John. 1989. "Republicans: Neo-Nazis or the Black-Brown Hazelnut? Recent Successes of the Radical Right in West Germany." *German Politics and Society* 19, Fall 1989: 2.

Federal Ministry of the Interior (BMI). 1991. *Innenpolitik* No. 4, 1991; BMI, "Survey of the Policy and Law Regarding Aliens in the FRG." V II 1–937 020/15 (January 1991, mimeo).

Forschungsgruppe Wahlen, Mannheim. 1991. "Wahl in Bremen: Eine Analyse der Bürgerschaftswahl vom 29 September 1991." *Bericht* 66: October 4, 1991 (mimeo).

Frindte, Wolfgang. 1990. "Sozialpsychologische Anmerkungen zur Entwicklung rechtsradikaler Tendenzen in der DDR." In C. Butterwegge and Horst Isola (eds.), *Rechtsextremismus im vereinten Deutschland: Randerscheinung oder Gefahr für die Demokratie?* Berlin, Links: 90–91.

Gross, Bertram. 1980. *Friendly Fascism: The New Face of Power in America.* New York: M. Evans.

Heitmeyer, Wilhelm. 1990. "Einig Vaterland—Einig Rechtsextremismus?" In C. Butterwegge and Horst Isola (eds.), *Rechtsextremismus im vereinten Deutschland: Randerscheinung oder Gefahr für die Demokratie?* Berlin: Links, 116–132.

Hockenos, Paul. 1990. "Fascism in the Antifascist State," *Z.* Boston, March 1990: 107.

Klär, Karl-Heinz et al. (eds.). 1989. *Die Wähler der extremen Rechten II.* 3 vols. Bonn: Demokratische Gemeinde–Vorwärts.

Leggewie, Claus. 1989. *Die Republikaner: Phantombild der neuen Rechten.* Berlin: Rotbuch.

Roth, Dieter. 1990. "Die Republikaner." Aus Politik und Zeitgeschichte (supplement to Das Parlament), B 37-38/90, September 14, 1990.

Schubarth, Wilfried, and Walter Friedrich. 1991. "Einstellungen ostdeutscher Jugendlicher zu Rechts- und Linksextremismus" (Freudenberg Stiftung, May 1991, hectographed).

Stiller, Michael. 1989. *Die Republikaner: Franz Schönhuber und seine rechtsradikale Partei.* Munich: Wilhelm Heyne.

Part 2
Political Institutions and
Policy Choices:
New Challenges

Chapter 6

Necessary Illusions: The Transformation of Governance Structures in the New Germany
Wolfgang Seibel

The unified Germany is not simply an extended version of West Germany before November 9, 1989, but a new Germany. The forces that have made this entity different from the West German model are revealing themselves in the emerging structure of governance. In this chapter I attempt a preliminary account of this evolving structure of governance. I address three questions: first, how the process of unification is being managed politically; second, what crucial problems and dilemmas are likely to emerge and how the German political system will deal with these issues; and third, how the process of unification will affect general structural change in the German polity.

The Political Management of Unification

The German Democratic Republic was a cornerstone of the Soviet imperium. Nonetheless, when the revolution came to East Germany, it occurred with a swiftness and thoroughness unmatched in Eastern Europe. The Communist state was rapidly and entirely dismantled, and East Germany was absorbed into a healthy national economy and into a democratic system with a stable institutional framework.

The unification of East and West Germany less than eleven months after the Berlin Wall crumbled in November 1989 is a story of remarkable political success. The structural inertia that mainstream political scientists had seen at the heart of the West German political system vanished—at least for a time—under the challenges of the year 1990. The incrementalism of the corporatist approach to political coordination was nowhere in

This chapter is adapted with permission of *Le Revue Tocqueville* Volume 23 Number 1, 1992: 177–197.

evidence, and vigorous decisionmaking replaced more cautious methods of problem solving. No courts intervened to slow the pace of change, and, most surprising for many, the chancellor himself displayed leadership.

It would be a mistake, however, to attribute full credit for reunification to purposeful political management. Certainly, the Germans were lucky to have pragmatic and skillful leaders during the most challenging and exciting days of their postwar history. But international conditions also furthered the process of reunification. And there is good sense in acknowledging that unification was shaped by the autodynamics of core elements of the German polity, especially the political parties, the government bureaucracy, and the legal system.

Because 1990 was an election year in both parts of the still-divided country, the political parties took an active part in the process. The prospect of unification, which began to seem credible during the first months of 1990, almost immediately stimulated partisan debate among the parties (Lehmbruch 1990; see also Chapter 1). The governing Christian Democrats quite quickly assumed a dominant position. The representatives of the small, fragile civil rights movement in East Germany that had initiated the revolution of 1989, as well as the representatives of the West German Social Democrats, were entangled in intellectual debates about the process of unification. The Christian Democrats, on the other hand, did not burden themselves with such niceties. Their message was simple: unification as soon as possible. This outlook was dramatically upheld by the voters in the first free elections in East Germany on March 18, 1990, when the Christian Democrats won more than 40 percent of the vote. This was a bitter surprise for the Social Democrats, because what is now East Germany had been a stronghold of the democratic left before Hitler came to power in 1933.

After March 18, 1990, the urgency implicit in the Christian Democrats' platform as well as the need to sustain the collapsing East German economy became forces that drove the unification process. The Social Democrats lost their ability to influence this process because they continued to misjudge the political psychology of unification, which was seen throughout Germany as a long-awaited event of historic proportions. Failing to grasp the political advantage of a positive message, they felt obliged to emphasize the complicated side of unification. Accordingly, the party was soundly defeated in the first all-German elections, which were held on December 2, 1990.

Another force that propelled the process of unification was bureaucratic professionalism. During spring and summer 1990, task forces within the federal bureaucracy drafted the legal framework for unification. Officially, this process took the form of negotiations between representatives of two independent states. However, West German bureaucrats soon dominated this process when the lack of professional expertise on the East German side became clear.

One may well admire the handiwork of the West German bureaucrats, who quite smoothly bound a formerly totalitarian state into the complex West German state structure and the country's free but highly regulated economy. This process was accomplished through two state treaties, the Economic, Monetary, and Social Union Treaty, which entered into force on July 2, 1990, and the Unification Treaty itself, which became effective on October 3, the day of German unity. On that day in 1990, the German Democratic Republic became part of the Federal Republic of Germany. The two state treaties provided the framework under which the political and economic institutions of West Germany were to be extended to East Germany (Lehmbruch 1991).

As a matter of fact, there was no alternative to speedy unification in 1990. The dynamics of this process were controlled by structural elements in the West German polity, although it can legitimately be seen as a success of political leadership: Certainly, Chancellor Helmut Kohl well deserved his victory in the December elections. Nonetheless, the speed of unification—and the political and administrative techniques that were used to accomplish it—inevitably caused or aggravated the dilemmas characteristic of large-scale transformation, not only in East Germany but in the entire country.

The Unanticipated Consequences of Unification: Crucial Dilemmas

One can hardly imagine a more unbalanced phenomenon than the economic and political integration of East and West Germany. East Germany has sixteen million inhabitants, West Germany sixty-two million. East Germany struggles to achieve 10 percent of West German GNP, and a difficult struggle it is. Labor productivity in East Germany is only 30 percent that of West Germany. Manufacturing technology is outmoded, and the infrastructure—especially transportation and telecommunications—is run-down or nonexistent.

The currency union of July 2, 1990, exposed the East German economy to the world market, deprived it of its traditional markets in Eastern Europe, and weakened East German industry. East German consumers prefer to buy West German goods with their new Deutsche Marks; as a result, East German industrial output in summer 1991 was only 60 percent of its level in the fall of 1990. Official unemployment approached 16 percent in the winter of 1992. When the short-term laborers, many of whom have no real employment at all, and other beneficiaries of related public subsidies are counted, unemployment figures reach 32.6 percent (Deutsche Bundesbank 12–1991, 36; Sachverständigenrat 1991, 109). In addition, there are substantial regional and structural imbalances within the East German economy. The northern part of East Germany is the least industrialized in the country, whereas the southern part is largely dominated by chemical and textile industries. What is more, East Germany is the most intensely polluted area in Europe. Measured by West German environmental protection standards, roughly ten million of East Germany's sixteen million people are living in health-threatening conditions (Sauberzweig 1992).

Under these circumstances, the government is in an especially delicate position. First, the East Germans' strong expectation of prosperity, reinforced by optimistic pronouncements during 1990 and 1991, has created tremendous political pressure for the government to take a more active role in the economic system and to guarantee individual welfare. Second, as education, transportation, telecommunications, and other elements of the economic infrastructure have heretofore been the almost exclusive purview of the state, there are few private entities capable of participating in the task of reconstruction, and there are none capable of taking responsibility for it. Finally, the state is the owner of the single biggest company in the world. A special state-owned holding company, the *Treuhandanstalt,* still owns several thousand companies, hotels, restaurants, pharmacies, libraries, and other enterprises, which together employ 1.6 million people. The German government is under a great deal of stress. The question is how the German governance structure will respond to this pressure.

Coping mechanisms are an established field of psychological research. What we know from the work of Leon Festinger (1957) or Irving Janis (1972) is that individuals under stress fall back on routines, instead of exploring alternatives, and that action is subject to justifying ideologies, especially when people experience Festinger's famous cognitive dissonance. The ongoing process of societal and political integration in Germany is very likely to cause such dissonance, and one can expect the government to turn to the structural routines manifest in political traditions and constitutional constraints in its response.

The success of the West German model, which meshes a market economy with democratic statehood, has been due to the remarkable flexibility of institutional routines. The institutional setting of federalism and the tight but elastic net of paragovernmental coordination and decisionmaking are responsible for this institutional flexibility. How the German political system makes use of this kind of elasticity in coping with the stress of unification remains an open question.

As I have already mentioned, at its outset the competition between political parties led politicians to simplify unification, to describe the process in broad, rather euphoric terms. This simplification was, in effect, a mechanism through which individuals and the body politic tried to avoid the costs of acknowledging complexity. This approach, however, left Germans vulnerable to being surprised by the unanticipated consequences of reality.

This is one way to describe what has happened to the German government since the fall of 1990, especially with regard to the financial and organizational consequences of reunification. One, if not the basic, simplification of unification was the assumption that the integration of the former GDR into the market economy and into the constitutional state would be a self-financing process. Another illusion, fostered perhaps by the legalistic tendency of German state culture and widespread admiration for the traditions of German public administration, was that the Unification Treaty, commonly viewed as a legal masterpiece, was a self-implementing mechanism. Both illusions were to be destroyed soon after October 3, 1990.

The Illusion of a Self-Financing Unification

Government officials expected that upon unification an influx of private capital would flow into the state-controlled East German economy. They regarded the *Treuhandanstalt* as a transitional entity, destined to sell off its holdings. They also expected the *Treuhandanstalt* to refinance government expenditures for modernizing infrastructure (Milbradt 1992). Under these circumstances, the cost of unification would be borne by East Germany alone.

This assumption may have encouraged the governing Christian and Free Democrats to reject firmly any tax increases for unification in the all-German election in the fall of 1990. Above all, the assumption of a self-financing transformation of East Germany made it easy to tolerate the provisional and paraconstitutional fiscal arrangements described in the Unification Treaty of August 1990. In it, the West German federative fiscal system was imposed on East Germany with some remarkable exceptions.

As in the United States, most local administrative tasks in Germany are assumed by the states—the *Länder*. One difference is that the German fiscal system redistributes tax revenues raised by the individual states so that the states and the municipalities in West Germany have comparable fiscal strength. If they extended this system to the East German *Länder,* the West German states would have faced sharp cutbacks in their revenues. Accordingly, the Unification Treaty excluded their East German counterparts from this redistribution mechanism. In its place, the federal government and the *Länder* created a special fund—the Fund for German Unity (*Fonds Deutsche Einheit*)—to raise additional revenue for the East German states. This fund is financed primarily through borrowing. Everyone assumed that the fund was a temporary measure, and that the East German *Länder,* by virtue of privatization and steady economic growth, would soon be able to stand on their own, ready to participate in the established fiscal mechanisms used to allocate state revenues. Accordingly, the Fund for German Unity was limited to four years, and its yield to the East German *Länder* was initially calculated to decrease in sharp steps each year until 1994.

As it turned out, however, a host of obstacles to the privatization of the state-owned enterprises in East Germany emerged almost immediately. The Communist government had formed giant conglomerates, the so-called *Kombinate,* which have proven difficult to dismantle into viable economic units that would be attractive to investors. Furthermore, the Communist regime had not only expropriated private business, it had neglected to maintain files and documents on any kind of property. As a result, one of the main obstacles to private investment has become the "property question"—the time-consuming process of verifying the status of almost all real estate and the land it stands on. Yet another obstacle to private investment is the potential risk from polluted soil and water. These risks can be borne by the *Treuhandanstalt,* but they are ultimately transferred to the taxpayer. In addition, East Germany is not a preferred location for industry because transportation and telecommunications networks are inadequate. Finally, although the East German educational system had provided a trained work force, West German managers have been reluctant to move to East Germany and to send their children to East German schools and universities. Without the infusion of modern management, promising private enterprise in East Germany will wither.

Although reliable figures are difficult to obtain, roughly 8,000 businesses employing 3,550,500 workers had been privatized by the end of 1992. This represents 77 percent of the *Treuhandanstalt*'s holdings. These enterprises were privatized because they had the potential of being profitable, and the *Treuhandanstalt* has become more inefficient on balance than before. The *Treuhandanstalt,* with its approximately 2,900 relatively inefficient enterprises, has become a black hole in the federal budget. In 1992, the *Treuhand* deficit has reached 250 billion Deutsche Marks, the equivalent of $150 billion. What is more, the *Treuhandanstalt*'s efforts to streamline its operations by closing hundreds of plants has not helped the government. The government has had to pay relatively generous unemployment benefits to hundreds of thousands of people.

Difficulties with privatization shattered the simplistic belief in a self-financing transformation of the East German economy. It became clear that unification required gigantic public transfers from West to East Germany. These transfers put the fiscal system under additional stress. Soon after the elections of December 2, 1990, the reelected government had to break its promise of not increasing taxes. Needless to say, the opposition did not hesitate to stigmatize this as the "tax-lie" and accused the government of fraudulently winning the election. Even with additional tax revenues, the federal government has been forced to expand the budget deficit dramatically. Although the current budget deficit of 5 percent of GNP appears relatively modest compared to other Western industrialized countries, one has to bear in mind that as recently as 1989 the West German deficit came only to 0.5 percent of GNP (*Sachverständigenrat* 1991, 131, 134). Accordingly, the International Monetary Fund felt obligated to urge the German government on October 9, 1991, to reach a sober account on the costs of unification and its effect on budget policy and deficit spending.

One-third of the federal budget is now spent in the former East Germany, although it has only one-fifth of the country's population. This disproportion means that there is a net transfer of public money from West to East Germany of 9,500 Deutsche Marks per capita per year. For an appropriate comparison, we can turn to the Marshall Plan fund, which transferred 800 Deutsche Marks per capita per year after 1947. In fact, the transfers to East Germany are so great that they represent 70 percent of East German GNP in 1991 (Institut der deutschen Wirschaft [after this IdW] 1991). But most of these federal transfers are not intended for productive investment. Sixty-two percent are spent subsidizing social benefits such as unemployment compensation and housing subsidies.

Whatever the result of this gigantic transfer of funds, it cannot compensate for the flawed financial basis of unification. Difficulties with privatization and the precarious East German economy have revealed the provisional fiscal arrangement described by the Unification Treaty to be totally inadequate. There remains a pressing need for public investment. And despite the billions of Deutsche Marks spent for transfer pay, the East German *Länder* and their municipalities are still discriminated against in terms of tax distribution. In 1991, the East German *Länder* and municipalities received only 85 percent of the per capita tax revenues that their West German counterparts received (Milbradt 1992).

Any attempt to revise what was meant as a temporary arrangement will produce a characteristic dilemma. Either the federal government must continue to finance *Länder* budgets through direct subsidies, an activity that lies outside the range of its constitutional authority, or the East German *Länder* can insist on a constitutional solution that would provide them access to the pool of revenue raised by the West German states. In the first instance, the federal budget deficit would be increased and an unconstitutional relationship institutionalized indefinitely. In the second scenario, conflict between East and West German *Länder* can be expected to increase sharply.

The problems that were ignored during unification are resurfacing in ways that threaten to weaken the federative relationships that lie at the heart of the German polity (Benz 1992). Ironically, the strength of the federal system has produced the fiscal problems that undermine its influence. The West German *Länder* used their veto power to prevent the East German *Länder* from sharing in the redistribution of state revenues, thus showing the Achilles heel of German federalism, namely its inertia when it comes to redistributing income (Scharpf 1976). In times when redistribution becomes a pressing issue, this sort of peripheral inflexibility is bypassed by central decisionmaking.

The Illusion of a Self-Implementing Unification

As established by the federative character of the constitution, the German *Länder* are responsible for the bulk of public administration, for instance, education at all levels, the judicial system, and the police. In addition, most federal legislation is carried out by the *Länder* as well. Much of this administrative burden is borne by the municipalities under the auspices of the respective *Länder* government. The problem that Germany faced in 1990 was that there were no *Länder* in East German territory. To solve this deficiency, five new *Länder* were created in spring 1990: Saxony, Thuringia, Brandenburg, Saxony-Anhalt, and Mecklenburg–West Pomerania. With the exception of Saxony and Thuringia, these *Länder* had originally been created arbitrarily by Communist planners in 1947, and they disappeared in 1952 when the Communist government replaced them with fourteen administrative districts. The *Länder* that were reconstituted in 1990 are at best a throwback to a brief era in the history of the GDR, without historical or economic justification.

There had been a short, intense debate on the territorial reorganization of the East German *Länder* when they were first reestablished in spring 1990, which focused on optimal size and economic structure (Blaschke 1990). But these discussions were brushed aside in the euphoria that marked the year. As they stand, the East German *Länder* do not balance the regional and structural disparities of the East German economy. Furthermore, the new *Länder,* with the exception of Saxony, have roughly half the inhabitants of their West German counterparts, creating imbalances between East and West.

Although hastily reconstructed, East German *Länder* play such a crucial role in the dialectic of unification that it is unlikely that they will be redrawn along more rational lines. The newly created *Länder,* along with the shift toward municipal self-administration, symbolize the new democracy for East Germans. No matter how artificial their boundaries, they give East Germans the same sort of regional identity that their West German counterparts possess. From the point of view of the federal government, the new *Länder*'s weaknesses in population and economic strength were an advantage. These weaknesses would enable it to absorb more effectively the still existing GDR, which interfered with the growth of a federal identity in the East. The West German *Länder* adjusted to the formation of the new states by pushing through an adjustment in the representation ratio in the chamber of states, the Bundesrat, and one which is relatively detrimental to the East Germans.

The imbalances between East and West German *Länder* are particularly evident at the level of counties and municipalities. East German counties and villages have, on average, only one-half the territory and one-third the population of their West German counterparts. This leads to disparities in the allocation of resources for modernizing infrastructure. There is general agreement that territorial reform on the local level must be achieved, although there is little consensus about the process of this reform.

The problem is that any reform at the local level would destabilize newly developed governments and reinforce the existing tendency to defer decisionmaking to central authorities. Furthermore, the newly emerging class of local dignitaries—the mayors, the county commissioners (*Landräte*), and the like—not surprisingly oppose any territorial reform that might diminish their own power, legitimacy, or standing.

The problems at the local level are compounded by the structural legacies of the GDR. At first glance, local administration is the only element of organizational continuity in the East German public sector. In fact, local administration in the GDR differed substantially from the West German norm. Many activities that are considered core competencies by West German administrators were relegated to the central government. This is especially true for social services, transportation, energy, and sewage disposal. In the GDR, all these services had been owned and run by the state-owned enterprises, the already-mentioned *Kombinate*, or VEB (*Volkseigene Betriebe*, or "people-owned enterprises"). After unification, local administrators in East Germany had to reassemble this network of services under municipal control. Pressures to modernize these services provided strong incentives to turn the more profitable activities, such as power supply and sewage disposal, over to private firms with the capacity to make the requisite investment. The problem with this approach is that, in the long run, it undermines the basis of healthy municipal finance. Municipalities are left with only those programs that run at a loss. This in turn tends to undermine the political and administrative credibility of local administration as a whole.

Thus, the desire to simplify the problems of unification colored the perception of public administration in East Germany. The Unification Treaty itself did not even enumerate the organizational prerequisites for its own implementation. Although the Communist regime in East Germany had long been accused of totalitarianism, there was no perception of what totalitarianism implies for the functions of public administration. In fact, the old regime's bureaucracy was hardly a true bureaucracy. It lacked almost all of the attributes that Max Weber described, such as a commitment to abstract rules instead of personal decisionmaking, a professional staff, or clear-cut patterns of horizontal and vertical organization. In the GDR, the rule of law as a principle of administrative decisionmaking was unknown. There was only a single textbook on administrative law. There was no standard career pattern for civil servants, except through party affiliation and ideological training (Derlien 1992). With some important exceptions, primarily in the foreign service and police, the dominant pattern of bureaucratic behavior apparently was what Colin Campbell (1987, 483) calls "politicized incompetence." Administrative life was dominated by the arbitrariness of party rule and the preferential treatment meted out for political loyalty rather than professional standards.

Accordingly, one of the most destructive legacies of the old regime in East Germany is the poorly trained corps of civil servants. As Derlien has pointed out (1992), this is a new development in the history of German public administration, a history that spans many changes of regimes and the subsequent transformation of public service. The professional bureaucracy endured and provided consistency when governments changed in 1918 and 1933. This pattern was followed in the West after 1945, but the bureaucracy was dissolved as a professional institution in East Germany, especially after the GDR was founded in 1949. This has created an unprecedented problem for East Germany. Whereas new German governments faced the challenge of securing the loyalty of the bureaucratic elites when they took power, the new democratic regime in East Germany faces the much greater challenge of securing the professional competence of the entire state apparatus. To make matters worse, some core areas of the modern state, such as fiscal administration, were simply not practiced in the GDR. At the same time, bureaucrats in East Germany are charged with putting into practice thousands of West German laws and regulations overnight.

Although legions of West German civil servants helped establish modest offices in the East, public administration in East Germany still functions only in the most rudimentary ways. Most of the complex regulations of the German welfare state are not being carried out properly. The absence of reliable and efficient decisionmaking among public authorities in East Germany is a serious obstacle to private investment and economic growth. The shortage of trained personnel in its tax collecting agencies is so severe that unpunished tax evasion is currently one of the few incentives to private entrepreneurship that the practice of public administration provides (*Bundesrechnungshof* 1991).

Although political loyalty is no longer a criterion for placement or advancement in the East German civil service, many of the experienced bureaucrats who can be found in East Germany rose through the party system under the Communist regime. The few exceptions who were not Communist Party members usually belonged to the so-called bloc parties. These were non-Communist parties established to create the illusion that the GDR was a multiparty system. (Christian Democrats and Liberal Democrats were set up as counterparts to parties in West Germany. When the country was unified in 1990, the East German Christian Democrats and Liberal Democrats merged with their West German counterparts; in fact, the East German Free Democrats [formerly Liberal Democrats] now have twice the membership of the original West German party.) Consequently, East Germans have few alternatives but to chose former Communist and bloc party members to fill executive positions. Although the loyalty of these technocrats is not questioned by the elected officials who appoint them to senior positions, many are known to the electorate as loyal functionaries of the Communist regime, and they are not credible representatives of the newly democratized state.

Their usefulness is further compromised by the association with the infamous Stasi (from Ministerium für Staatssicherheit). Almost anyone belonging to the functional elites of the GDR had some contact with the Stasi, and the disclosure of secret service collaboration is an obsession with German journalists. During the summer of 1991, a first wave of revelations from Stasi files shook the governments of the East German *Länder*. In winter 1992 the Stasi-revelations became almost a hysteria and, in a way, this appeared to be some kind of psychological compensation for the political incompetence to deal appropriately with the material consequences of unification.

The organizational weakness combined with the shortage of trained personnel also impedes enforcement of the rule of law—or what Germans refer to as *Rechtsstaat*. The education of lawyers was a highly ideological process in the GDR, and East German lawyers gained a reputation as ideological hard-liners. The Unification Treaty stipulated that East German judges be screened for evidence of their commitment to due process. This task is assigned to committees composed of East German legislators and West German lawyers. It is estimated that after this review only one-third of the judges will remain in office (*Frankfurter Allgemeine Zeitung*, October 4, 1991).

In West Germany, the upper echelons of the civil service are staffed by lawyers, who are cognizant of the oversight that the courts maintain over the executive branch. In East Germany after fifty-six years of totalitarianism, this relationship has been obscured. According to experts, few decisions by East German authorities conform to West German standards of court control (Namgalies 1992).

The Transformation of Governance Structures:
The Prussian Model?

Despite all of these problems, it would be a mistake to assume that the Germans failed to plan for unification. Certainly, some of the problems I have mentioned would have been easier to manage had they been anticipated, but rational planning is not the usual way that political systems solve their problems, and it may even be counterproductive under certain circumstances. In Germany, without some of the crude simplifications that marked unification, the will and energy necessary to carry out the process would have been lacking. This is an example of what Noam Chomsky (1989) calls the "necessity of illusions." Certainly, the attempt to engage in comprehensive planning for unification would have bogged down the process before it started. Nonetheless, now that unification is underway, I will take the occasion to evaluate where it is going.

The process of unification, it is thus far clear, is more than the simple transfer of economic and political institutions from West Germany to East Germany. In West Germany, these institutions are embedded in the social structure. In East Germany, without this social structure, these institutions exist as a set of parameters that constrain social and political action. There is no reason to assume that the sum of these actions will produce institutions that are identical or even similar to what we have known in West Germany; there is also no reason to presume that they will not transform the institutions that characterize the Federal Republic of Germany as a whole.

This situation is one reason for scholarly attention to both the short-term and long-term structural changes in the German polity. As I pointed out, the process of political and administrative change most often reflects a series of compromises and stopgap measures rather than the decisive clarity of a comprehensive plan. On the other hand, this series of short-term responses has long-term significance. In fact, the less explicitly controlled this process is, the more likely that it is shaped by implicit assumptions. These assumptions reflect legitimate issues in everyday decisionmaking and are shaped by political tradition and culture. In this respect, the challenge for scholars is to inquire into the structure of these short-term changes with the goal of seeing their long-term trend.

It is helpful to see unification in light of German history. Optimists hope that the unified Germany will resume the economic and political success that the West German model has enjoyed since the 1950s. This is clearly the goal of the present generation of political leaders. It is important to bear in mind, however, that the West German model is the consequence of a unique historical situation. There is no model for the reunited Germany, at least no successful one.

After 1945, Germany was dismantled, and the parts reconstituted as the West German Federal Republic were the most Western state in German history. Four hundred years ago, the Latin and Western orientation of the German identity was removed by Martin Luther's reformation. When modern statehood emerged in Germany two centuries later, it was dominated by the Electorate of Brandenburg and the Kingdom of Prussia. The Prussian state itself was a compromise between a modern, centrally controlled government and a premodern caste system that placed political power in the hands of the provincial aristocrats, the *Junker*. Only in the western parts of Germany did modern societal structures such as an awakening bourgeoisie, capitalist entrepreneurship, and free associations emerge to produce a more modern political process.

In Prussia, as in other areas of Eastern Europe (Schöpflin 1990), the state itself was the central agent of modernization. The power of the state grew in several stages, most rapidly after Napoléon decisively defeated Prussia in 1806. The scholarly debate on the *Sonderweg,* Germany's separate path in modern history, has revealed that the process of modernization has been deviant in the sense that the gap between economic, administrative, and political modernization widened during the nineteenth century. There was no liberal revolution in Germany, as there was in Britain and France, and neither the German bourgeoisie nor the working class ever achieved the political power necessary to transform the German state into a democracy. The bourgeoisie, although integrated ideologically under the Second Empire after 1871, never wielded political power, and there was no place in the state administration for representatives of the working class. As a consequence, the state remained removed from the vast majority of society. Until 1914, the higher ranks of the German government were dominated by the *Junker.* The distance between state and society facilitated the emergence of political irrationality and authoritarianism. It was the combination of these premodern forces with a modern, efficient bureaucracy that allowed Hitler to carry out his horrifying agenda.

The Weimar Republic of 1918 and 1919 made a first attempt to escape from the *Sonderweg,* with well-known consequences. The Federal Republic of Germany, however, represents a successful attempt to deviate from the *Sonderweg.* First of all, it did so geographically. West Germany was successful, in large part, because of its Western orientation. There was no force attracting it from the East. Prussia was not only dissolved as a state, its political tradition was uprooted geographically. The world of the *Junker* east of the river Elbe was destroyed forever. The traditions that had emerged in West Germany—the tradition of civil self-consciousness and an entrepreneurial bourgeoisie—exerted their attractions without competition. Chancellor Konrad Adenauer, the mayor of Cologne until 1933, became the symbol of the Westernness of the new Federal Republic. Against strong opposition even within his own Christian Democratic Party, he soberly abandoned the option of a hasty unification of the divided Germany in favor of solidly allying the Federal Republic with Western institutions of capitalism and democracy. The tiny western city of Bonn became the geographical symbol of the new Germany. The governance structure that evolved succeeded to an exceptional degree in promoting its economic and political stability because it possessed two key qualities: federalism and corporatism.

These qualities emerged for several reasons. After World War II, the geographic axis of the country spun round from East-West to North-South. The North-South axis had never before figured prominently in German history, and it gave the country greater stability because it was, to begin with, economically more homogeneous than the East-West axis that prevailed during preceding regimes. These governments were forced to address the sharp contrast between an industrialized West and an agricultural Northeast. The homogeneity that characterized West Germany facilitated the distribution of political and economic power in a way that was geographically balanced and that reinforced existing stability. For the first time in German history, federalism was well grounded in economic as well as in constitutional terms. Although central planning and coordination has been plagued by political inertia, West Germany displayed a high degree of decentralized flexibility, especially in terms of regional planning, provision of infrastructure, and economic development (Benz 1985).

Moreover, for the first time in history, the German state was thoroughly embedded in its social context. The aristocratic agrarian elite had disappeared as a political class in and of itself. It was replaced by a party system that incorporated all social strata under the auspices of democratic processes. More important, however, the party system acted as an interlocutor between the state and the organized interests of society. There were no pressure groups—whether economically or ideologically motivated—that lacked political representation in the party system and a corresponding degree of political integration. The loose alliances that emerged under this system were a precondition for the establishment of paragovernmental coordination among the interest groups to influence regulation, for instance in industrial relations and social security. Although this paragovernmental style of policymaking, known as neocorporatism, bypasses the constitutional order and, especially, weakens the power of parliament, it relieves government from the political burden of coordination costs and establishing legitimacy. Since the mid-1970s, corporatism has provided the political elasticity needed to support the welfare measures during economic crises (Scharpf 1987, 212–251).

West Germany did not entirely escape the legacy of the *Sonderweg,* however. There remained a latent distance between democracy and statehood. One of the reasons for the evolution of corporatism was that during the period of state modernization in the eighteenth and nineteenth centuries, neither of the new social classes, the bourgeoisie nor the working class, had any exposure to the self-consciously democratic state. The state did not present itself as a vehicle for democratic processes. Furthermore, democracy had not shown itself to be equal to the economic challenges that Germany faced in the twentieth century. As a result, the German body politic has placed its trust in social welfare measures. Accordingly, the West German constitutional identity is based on economic growth and social welfare (on *soziale Marktwirtschaft,* or "the social market economy") rather than on the vigor of democratic institutions. Especially for the left, "social welfare" has become synonymous with "democracy" (Noelle-Neumann 1992). In contrast to the citizens of other Western democracies, Germans tend to perceive democracy as a policy rather than a formal order of politics (Fraenkel 1963). Because West Germans have no deep-seated faith in the stability of democratic institutions, their domestic policy becomes slightly hysterical in times of crisis, as it did, for instance, during the first wave of terrorism in the 1970s. Significantly enough, the *soziale Marktwirtschaft* was elevated to a quasi-constitutional principle in the Economic, Monetary, and Social Union Treaty in 1990.

The assets of the West German system of government—federalism and corporatism—unfortunately do not transfer to the political management of unification. They are not transferable because the state structure and the social makeup of East Germany do not provide the context in which they might flourish. The dominant style of governance in East Germany possesses many of the structural properties of the old regime and, accordingly, does not have much in common with the West German model. State centralism continues to be the prevailing pattern of decisionmaking, as the new *Länder* will remain, at least for the next decade, entirely dependent on the federal government for funds and organizational support. Party rule as a structural characteristic of governance will continue to predominate, not because of the continued influence of the Communist Party, of course, but because the West German party machines are indispensable for the transfer of knowledge and expertise. In West Germany, however, the party system has been balanced by the vertical fragmentation of the state into three levels (the federal, state, and local governments) and by a civil-service system that serves as a counterweight to party patronage (Mayntz and Derlien 1989). There are currently no such counterweights in East Germany.

In East Germany, the power of the central state is reinforced by its economic role. Despite unification, the *Treuhandanstalt* will continue to be the largest enterprise in the world because privatization and the unemployment that accompanies privatization will meet both economic and political obstacles. The state-owned *Treuhandanstalt* will continue to function as a vehicle for employment and will exert a tremendous influence on economic policy. Even in decentralized form, the *Treuhand* will continue to limit the discretion of individual *Länder* and municipalities.

Another reason for the dominance of the central government in East Germany is that it does not grow out of a social context. Fifty-six years of totalitarianism have eliminated the intermediary organizations that prevail in West Germany and that still exist, to some degree, in other East European societies. Civil society has been almost completely destroyed in East Germany (see Bendix 1991). Although voluntary associations have mushroomed since the fall of 1989 (see Seibel 1991b), they do not provide the established and extensive base required for the corporatist style of political decisionmaking. Attempts to practice corporatism, in the process of restoring health care and in social policy, have been staged by West German actors. Although the number of small- and medium-sized businesses is growing, there is no culture of cooperation between business and government. The municipalities do not have appropriate mechanisms to respond to issues raised by businesses. This situation makes urban and regional development more government-centered and technocratic than it ever was in West Germany.

Thus, the prevailing pattern of governance emerging in the new Germany is another instance of the partial modernization that characterized Germany in the past. Here again, the accelerated modernization of the economy and state structure has not been accompanied by an equivalent modernization of civil and political culture. This discontinuity is one of the important causes of social tensions and political conflicts that have surfaced in Germany, conflicts that are exacerbated by the realization that East Germany is not going to enjoy, at least not immediately, the economic prosperity that unification had been expected to bring.

The legacy of totalitarianism, as expressed in attitudes and social behavior, makes East Germans reluctant to accept the advantages of democracy. Whereas eight out of ten West Germans consider democracy to be the best type of government, only three out of ten East Germans do so (*Frankfurter Allgemeine Zeitung,* September 30, 1991, 13). In addition, 82 percent of the East Germans consider themselves "second-class Germans" (EMNID 1991). This sort of frustration is expressed in hostility and physical aggression against minorities. In the East German city of Hoyerswerda, a group of violent young people laid siege to a shelter for immigrants to the applause of bystanders. Violence has also increased in West Germany. In September 1991 alone, more than 100 shelters for immigrants were attacked violently in Germany (*Die Zeit,* October 11, 1991, 20).

The stubbornly backward social and political culture also affects the modernization of the state. Because East Germany lacks a tradition of private enterprise, the central government must assume a dominant role in economic modernization. And it must do so without the corporatism that guides policymaking in West Germany. Like Prussia in the eighteenth and nineteenth centuries, the state is the main promoter of economic modernization, and, as in the days of the Prussian aristocrats Karl Freiherr vom und zum Stein and Prince Karl August von Hardenberg, the state is preoccupied with modernizing its own apparatus. Given its separation from social structures, there may be a tendency for the state to become rigid rather than elastic in its practices.

The hope that East Germany will be reconstructed according to the West German model will not be fulfilled. This hope, although a necessary illusion in Chomsky's sense, is an expression of the aspiration for unification rather than a hardheaded assessment. Germany is having, in the words of Fritz Stern, a second chance. Although it is difficult to predict exactly how it will use that second chance, one may describe the obvious consequences of German reunification for governance structures and one may at least speculate about the appropriateness of the new structure to bear the huge challenge of unification.

Notes

This chapter is a revised version of a lecture at the Woodrow Wilson School of Public and International Affairs under the auspices of the Council on Regional Studies, Princeton University, October 17, 1991. I am indebted to Ezra Suleiman, Director of the Council, for kindly hosting the lecture and to James McAdams, Gerhard Lehmbruch, Heinrich Mäding, Charles Maier, Susan Rose-Ackerman, Manfred G. Schmidt, and Kathleen Thelen for helpful comments. The usual caveat applies.

References

Bendix, Reinhard. 1991. "Staat, Legitimierung und 'Zivilgesellschaft'." *Berliner Journal für Soziologie* 1:3–11.

Benz, Arthur. 1985. *Föderalismus als dynamisches System. Zentralisierung und Dezentralisierung im Föderativen Bundesstaat.* Opladen: Westdeutscher Verlag.

———. 1992. "Reformbedarf und Reformchancen des Kooperativen Föderalismus in Gesamtdeutschland." In Wolfgang Seibel, Arthur Benz, and Heinrich Mäding (eds.), *Verwaltungsreform und Verwaltungspolitik im Prozess der Deutschen Einigung.* Baden-Baden: Nomos.

Blaschke, Karlheinz. 1990. "Alte Länder—Neue Länder. Zur der Territorialen Neugliederung der DDR." *Aus Politik und Zeitgeschichte,* June 29, 1990.

Bundesrechnungshof. 1991. *Bericht über Aufbau der Steuerverwaltung in den neuen Bundesländern und Berlin (Ost).* Frankfurt am Main. VIII 1/2/3. 20 80 07 (91).

Campbell, Colin. 1987. "Administration and Politics. The State Apparatus and Political Responsiveness." *Comparative Politics* 19:481–499.

Chomsky, Noam. 1989. *Necessary Illusions: Thought Control in Democratic Societies.* London: Pluto Press.

Derlien, Hans-Ulrich. 1992. "Professionalisierung und Säuberung." In Wolfgang Seibel, Arthur Benz, and Heinrich Mäding (eds.), *Verwaltungsreform und Verwaltungspolitik im Prozess der Deutschen Einigung.* Baden-Baden: Nomos.

Deutsche Bundesbank. 1991. *Monatsberichte der Deutschen Bundesbank.* Frankfurt/Main: 12–1991.

EMNID. 1991. Umfrage Ost-Deutschland 23 Oktober–11 November. Bielefeld, mimeo.

Festinger, Leon. 1957. *A Theory of Cognitive Dissonance.* Evanston: Row, Peterson and Company.

Fraenkel, Ernst. 1963. *Deutschland und die westlichen Demokratien.* Stuttgart: Kohlhammer.

Institut der deutschen Wirtschaft. 1991. Dokumentation: Transferzahlungen an die neuen Bundesländer. Köln, mimeo.

Janis, Irving. 1972. *Victims of Groupthink: A Psychological Study of Foreign Policy Decisions and Fiascoes.* Boston: Houghton Mifflin.

Lehmbruch, Gerhard. 1990. "Die improvisierte Vereinigung: Die Dritte Deutsche Republik." *Leviathan* 8:462–486.

———. 1991. "Die Deutsche Vereinigung: Strukturen und Strategien." *Politische Vierteljahresschrift* 32:585–604.

Mayntz, Renate, and Hans-Ulrich Derlien. 1989. "Party Patronage and Politicization of the West German Administrative Elite 1970–1987—Toward Hybridization?" *Governance* 2:384–404.

Milbradt, Georg. 1992. "Die Finanzausstattung der Neuen Bundesländer." In Wolfgang Seibel, Arthur Benz, and Heinrich Mäding (eds.), *Verwaltungsreform und Verwaltungspolitik im Prozess der Deutschen Einigung*. Baden-Baden: Nomos.

Namgalies, Johannes. 1992. "Institutionelle und personelle Gesichtspuntke des Aufbaus der Verwaltungsgerichtsbarkeit in Mecklenburg-Vorpommern." In Wolfgang Seibel, Arthur Benz, and Heinrich Mäding (eds.), *Verwaltungsreform und Verwaltungspolitik im Prozess der Deutschen Einigung*. Baden-Baden: Nomos.

Noelle-Neumann, Elisabeth. 1992. "Der Zeitgeist ist das Kapital der Sozialdemokratie. Die Deutschen und ihr Sozialstaat." *Frankfurter Allgemeine Zeitung*, February 19:5.

Sachverständigenrat zur Begutachtung der Gesamtwirtschaftlichen Entwicklung. 1991. Die Wirtschaftliche Integration in Deutschland: Perspektiven—Wege—Risiken. *Jahresgutachten* 1991–92. Stuttgart: Metzler-Poeschel.

Sauberzweig, Dieter. 1992. "Handlungsbedarf und Handlungszwänge des Kommunalen Umweltschutzes in den neuen Bundesländern." In Wolfgang Seibel, Arthur Benz, and Heinrich Mäding (eds.), *Verwaltungsreform und Verwaltungspolitik im Prozess der Deutschen Einigung*. Baden-Baden: Nomos.

Scharpf, Fritz W. 1976. "Theorie der Politikverflechtung." In Fritz W. Scharpf, Bernd Reissert, and Fritz Schnabel (eds.), *Politikverflechtung*. Kronberg: Athenäum, 13–76.

———. 1987. *Sozialdemokratische Krisenpolitik in Europa*. Frankfurt/New York: Campus.

Schöpflin, George. 1990. "The Political Traditions of Eastern Europe." *Daedalus* 119:55–90.

Seibel, Wolfgang. 1991a. "Verwaltungsreform in den ostdeutschen Bundesländern." *Die öffentliche Verwaltung* 46:198–204.

———. 1991b. Nonprofit Organizations in East Germany. A newspaper survey compiled for the Johns Hopkins International Nonprofit Sector Project. Konstanz, mimeo.

Chapter 7 _____

The Basic Law Under Strain: Constitutional Dilemmas and Challenges

_____ *Donald P. Kommers*

When and under what circumstances should a people give to itself a new constitution? This question assumed considerable importance in Germany at the beginning of the movement toward reunification. Constitutions usually come into being when a people wants to make a fresh start, either because it has thrown off the yoke of some colonial or imperial power, or because it wants to secure rights that have been or are being threatened, or simply because it feels the time has come to codify in a single document preconstitutional rules, traditions, and values it cherishes and would wish to perpetuate. None of these conditions applied to Germany in 1990, the year of German unity.

Yet conditions were ripe for a new constitutional settlement. After all, the creation of a single unified state would alter the fabric of German society, making it more Protestant, more Eastern oriented, and more culturally and regionally diverse. Still another measure of significant change would be the sudden presence of sixteen million people—a full quarter of the population—with little or no experience with democracy. In West Germany too, even before unity, stirrings of constitutional reform could be heard against the backdrop of widespread discontent rooted in economic woes, environmental blight, and accelerated social change, not to mention problems of governance spawned by a fragmented and ossified party system. Surely, many observers argued, these changes and conditions would trigger the start of a new era of constitutional government in Germany.[1]

The Constitution and German Unity

Some Germans hoped that national unity would produce a fresh constitution right at the outset. The Basic Law itself provided an authoritative basis for just such a change; as the Preamble indicates, it was framed originally as a transitional document pending Germany's reunification.[2] Articles 23 and 146 also emphasized the document's impermanence: Article 23 applied the Basic Law "for the time being" to the existing states of the Federal Republic of Germany as well as to "other parts of Germany" upon "their accession" (*Beitritt*), whereas Article 146 provided for the Basic Law's own expiration "on the day on which a constitution adopted by a free decision of the German people comes into force." Each of these articles loomed large in the debate over how Germany should be brought together again. In short, they specified alternative procedures by which unity could take place: Either by a simple act of accession, which would mean the immediate extinction of the German Democratic Republic and its absorption into the political system of the FRG (Article 23), or by establishing a new constitution drafted and approved by all the German people (Article 146).[3]

One can see why many Germans might have found the preferred route to unity in Article 146. This route would have allowed the entire German people to reconstitute itself as a nation. It would have done so by adopting a constitution drafted by a popularly elected constituent assembly and approved in a popular referendum, infusing the new document with the kind of democratic legitimacy that the Basic Law arguably lacked.[4] A constitutional convention with a substantial eastern representation would also have had the opportunity to produce a document fusing the liberalism of the Basic Law with the values of human solidarity espoused by reform-minded democrats in East Germany. Writing and ratifying a new constitution, however, would have been a long and arduous affair at a time when the unification train moved forward with unbelievable speed. Accession under Article 23 would keep the train moving at full tilt, whereas the use of Article 146 would slow it down.

The problem of which procedure to use was bound up in part with the question of Germany's legal status after World War II. FRG leaders had always maintained that Germany continued to exist as an independent state even after its destruction and occupation in 1945. According to this theory, the FRG represented not a successor state but rather a rebuilding of the "German Reich" created between 1867 and 1871, a view the Federal Constitutional Court has repeatedly affirmed.[5] Although the Basic Law did not extend to the whole of Germany, it affirmed the unity of the German people, mandated reunification as a paramount constitutional goal, and proclaimed the fundamental illegitimacy of the East German regime. Unity by accession, therefore, would simply enlarge the territory of the Federal Republic and allow the state to retain its existing legal personality. Armed with this theory—one supported by continued Four Power control over Germany as a whole—legal scholars could plausibly argue that Article 23 provided the most salutary and expeditious means of unifying Germany.[6]

In addition, some international lawyers argued that the GDR's accession under Article 23 would raise fewer doubts about the continuing validity of West Germany's international treaties. Here too the debate revolved around the problem of state succession versus continuity. If the use of Article 146 were to result in the creation of a Germany different from the Federal Republic, it was argued, "all international treaties concluded by the former Federal Republic would have to be renegotiated, including the NATO Treaty and the Treaty of Rome on the EC."[7] Mindful of this problem, the European Community went so far as to advise the Germans to employ Article 23 as the most appropriate vehicle for the nation's passage to unity.[8]

Needless to say, the GDR would have to consent to its own dissolution under Article 23. After all, the East German regime was recognized as a separate entity in international law, one consequence of its admission (along with the FRG) to the United Nations under the terms of the Intra-German Basic Treaty of 1972. In addition, the Constitutional Court pointed out in the 1972 Basic Treaty case that the GDR could only "accede" to the FRG by a free decision of its people;[9] that is, only a democratically elected East German parliament could lawfully accede to the Federal Republic. With incredible rapidity, that is what happened. On March 18, 1990, in the GDR's first free general election, East Germans voted heavily in favor of instant reunification, whereupon the new parliament proceeded forthwith to reestablish the five *Länder* (states) of Brandenburg, Saxony, Mecklenburg–West Pomerania, Saxony-Anhalt, and Thuringia.[10] Shortly thereafter, in accordance with Article 23, the parliament resolved to accede to the Federal Republic on October 3, 1990. When that day arrived, the German Democratic Republic ceased to exist.

Treaty-Mandated Changes in the Basic Law

On two previous occasions in this century—1918 and 1949—Germans were required to remake or adjust their constitutions within the context of unique international settings. It happened again in 1990 with the signing of the Unification Treaty between the GDR and the FRG (August 31, 1990) and the "Two-Plus-Four" Treaty on the Final Settlement with Respect to Germany (September 12, 1990).[11] Under the Two-Plus-Four Treaty, pursuant to which the Allied powers finally relinquished their rights over Berlin and Germany as a whole (thus restoring the German nation to full sovereignty), the GDR and FRG governments promised to ensure that an all-German constitution would conform to all treaty provisions, particularly those dealing with Germany's borders.[12] The Unification Treaty incorporated these assurances. In the two-plus-four talks, the two German governments agreed to confine the borders of a united Germany to the territory over which they currently ruled. Accordingly, the treaty provided for the repeal of Article 23,[13] effectively freezing Germany's existing borders, for there are no "other parts of Germany" left to accede to the FRG. The treaty further amended the Basic Law to delete references to the goal of reunification contained in the Basic Law's Preamble and Article 146. As revised, the Preamble declares that "the German people . . . have achieved the unity and freedom of Germany in free self-determination" and "[this] Basic Law is thus valid for the entire German people,"[14] whereas Article 146, while dropping the reference to reunification, retains language allowing the German people to adopt a new constitution. Whether the changed wording of Article 146, however, establishes the Basic Law in perpetuity is a disputed issue to be taken up later in this essay.

Although the swift path to German unity left no room for major constitutional surgery, the Unification Treaty amended other provisions of the Basic Law to reflect the reality of national unity and also to accommodate certain vital interests of the GDR's population. First, the treaty altered Article 51 (2) to mirror the new balance of power in the Bundesrat, the national parliamentary body in which the *Länder* are corporately represented. Previously, each *Land* had between three to five votes in this body, depending on its population. Under the treaty, each *Land* was to have, as before, at least three votes, but *Länder* in excess of seven million inhabitants—presently Baden-Württemberg, Bavaria, Lower Saxony, and North Rhine–Westphalia—would now have six instead of five. *Länder* with more than two and six million inhabitants would now have four and five votes respectively.

The addition of five medium-sized eastern states under the old system would have added significantly to the voting strength of these states generally, which would have come at the expense of the more populous and wealthier states. And so, at the Bundesrat's own initiative, the count was changed to create a better balance of power among the states. In addition, with a sixth vote, the most populous states would cast a total of twenty-four votes, enough to give them a veto over most legislative measures, including amendments to the Basic Law, which required a two-thirds vote.[15]

Second, and most important, the Unification Treaty inserted a new Article 143 into the Basic Law, a transitional provision that allowed the new *Länder* to deviate from existing constitutional requirements for a period of two years (until December 31, 1992) in policy areas in which years of separate practices in the old GDR would not permit the Basic Law's immediate application. The new provision was one way of getting around the sensitive issue of abortion, concerning which East and West Germany had radically different policies. It was also thought that the settlement of disputes about expropriated property in East Germany, involving tens of thousands of claims, would have to be shielded against attack under constitutional provisions dealing with the right to property.[16]

In short, the eastern *Länder* were given a grace period of two years to bring their policies into conformity with the Basic Law's standards. With respect to abortion, the two parts of Germany would be allowed to follow their respective practices and procedures pending the passage, by the end of 1992, of a new law applicable to all of Germany. What made abortion and property rights, two issues taken up in greater detail below, so important in the aftermath of unity is that they touch core constitutional values that are unamendable under the Basic Law.

Third, and less controversial, Article 143 allows the eastern *Länder* to deviate from certain sections of the Basic Law on federal-state relations for a period of five years (up to December 31, 1995). These sections deal with revenue sharing, financial equalization payments, apportionment of tax revenue, and judicial administration.[17] Clearly, the new *Länder* would be unable to meet the terms of these provisions or to execute the powers granted by them in light of their depressed and outdated economies and the time that it would take to reform the old system of judicial and public administration. Indeed, five years would hardly be enough time to equalize the standards of East and West, but the time frame was deemed sufficient to amend the federal provisions of the Basic Law to reflect a more realistic division of power between the *Länder* and the national government.

Finally, the Unification Treaty holds out the promise of major constitutional reform in the near future, for it advises the contracting parties (GDR and FRG) to request "the legislative bodies of united Germany" (i.e., Bundestag and Bundesrat) to consider other constitutional amendments that may be warranted as a consequence of national unity.[18] In particular, the treaty mentions the constitutional relationship between the *Länder* and the federation, the possible incorporation of Berlin into the *Land* of Brandenburg, the prospect of introducing state objectives into the Basic Law, and the employment of Article 146 for the purpose of reconsidering more fundamental reforms and holding a popular referendum to approve the document as a whole. As noted earlier, Article 146, as amended, repeats the language that envisions the termination of the Basic Law "on the day on which a constitution adopted by a free decision of the German people comes into force."[19]

Reunification in Court

Four treaties prepared the groundwork for reunification: the Economic, Monetary, and Social Union Treaty (May 18, 1990), the East-West Election Treaty (August 20, 1990), the Unification Treaty (August 31, 1990), and the Two-Plus-Four Treaty on the Final Settlement with Respect to Germany (September 12, 1990). Provisions in three of these treaties raised important constitutional issues in their own right, and these issues were soon to make their way to the Federal Constitutional Court, Germany's highest and most prestigious tribunal. Empowered to decide constitutional disputes within the framework of specified procedures, the Constitutional Court serves as the principal guardian of the Basic Law.[20] Its wide-ranging jurisdiction and enormous power remained undisturbed in the wake of German unity,[21] and so the Court would retain the last word, as always, on the validity of any law or treaty, including provisions of the treaties marking the pathway to German unity.

Amending Procedure

The ink had barely dried on the Unification Treaty when eight members of the Bundestag challenged the constitutionality of provisions changing various clauses of the Basic Law. Petitioners claimed that by agreeing to consent to the treaty as a whole, parliament had interfered with their right, as members of the Bundestag, to debate each of the respective changes separately and to offer amendments thereto.[22] They also argued that the GDR's accession to the FRG could only be achieved by direct legislation under Article 23, not by means of an international treaty.

A unanimous Court rejected these arguments, holding that the federal government enjoyed broad maneuverability in deciding what procedures would be most feasible for bringing about German unity. Given the primacy of the constitutional goal of reunification, said the Court, the federal government had the authority to achieve unity by means of a treaty so long as the process of parliamentary consent observed the requirements of Articles 59 (2) and 79 (2). Under the former provision, treaties regulating the political relations of the federation require the consent of both Bundesrat and Bundestag, whereas the latter requires amendments to the Basic Law to be approved by a two-thirds vote of all members of the Bundestag and by two-thirds of all votes in the Bundesrat. Because both parliamentary bodies approved the treaty by a two-thirds vote, said the Court, these constitutional requirements were satisfied.[23]

Electoral Unity

The Unification Treaty decision was only the first of a long list of cases that the unification of Germany would bring to the Federal Constitutional Court. Another important case challenged the constitutionality of the East-West German Election Treaty, an agreement laying down transitory regulations for the first all-German election scheduled for December 2, 1990.[24] Under this agreement the entire country—East and West—would constitute a single voting area subject mainly to the terms of West Germany's Federal Election Act. Unlike the GDR, which for its March 18, 1990, election adopted a system of pure proportional representation, the FRG had always employed a two-ballot system of single-member constituencies and proportional representation that awards legislative seats only to parties—that is, political parties eligible to appear on the second or "list" ballot—that obtain 5 percent of the national vote. When a party reaches the 5 percent goal under this system, it is entitled to a number of parliamentary seats proportionate to its total second-ballot vote.

The treaty makers knew that the nationwide application of the 5 percent rule to the December 2 election would hurt the chances of small regionally based parties to win parliamentary representation. To offset this disadvantage, and sensitive to the plight of smaller parties in the GDR, they permitted them to form joint lists with a major party so long as the major and minor parties did not oppose each other in any *Land*. Dissatisfied with this "piggyback" arrangement, the Greens, Republikaner, and the Party of Democratic Socialism attacked the validity of the 5 percent clause on the ground that it violated Articles 38 and 21 of the Basic Law.[25] The Constitutional Court agreed. In a unanimous opinion, the Court held that the nationwide use of the 5 percent clause for the first all-German election would deny these parties equal protection.[26] The court reaffirmed the general validity of the 5 percent rule, but felt that in this particular election its application to Germany as a whole would tend to underrepresent significant segments of public opinion, especially in view of the dominance of the major parties in both East and West.[27]

At issue in the case too were stringent rules governing party eligibility and ballot access. These rules would disqualify loosely knit political groups in East Germany such as New Forum and Democracy Now, associations well known for the crucial role they played in facing down the ruling Communist Party and its hardline leaders.[28] Because these groups were just beginning to emerge in the embryonic democratic states of the old GDR, said the Court, they should be given the opportunity to compete and form alliances for electoral purposes in the first all-German election.[29] Additionally, in a companion case, the Court held that small western parties should be allowed access to the ballot in the eastern states since they had so little time to develop and expand their organizations there.[30] The Court made clear, of course, that these rulings were to be regarded as one-time exceptions to electoral rules otherwise permissible under the Basic Law.

The Bundestag acted immediately by incorporating the Court's rulings—even its suggestions—into the Federal Election Act. In response to its main decision, the Bundestag retained the 5 percent rule but applied it separately to East and West Germany, as the Christian Democrats had originally proposed. (Alternatively, and consistent with the Constitutional Court's opinion, the Bundestag might simply have eliminated the 5 percent rule for the December election.) The dual voting system, a one-time exception to the nationwide application of the 5 percent rule, did its work; its effect on the outcome of the election was profound. Having won 9.9 and 5.9 percent of the vote in the old GDR, the PDS and the Greens (listed jointly with a number of groups called Bündnis90) acquired seventeen and eight seats respectively in the all-German parliament.[31] Nationwide, the two parties received only 2.4 and 1.2 percent of the vote, figures that would otherwise have disqualified them from holding any seats in the new parliament.

Abortion

As mentioned earlier, one reason the Unification Treaty amended the Basic Law to permit the new eastern *Länder* to deviate from its provisions was the issue of abortion. West Germany permitted abortions to be performed by licensed physicians only for specified medical, genetic, ethical, and social reasons duly certified by a panel of doctors and other counselors. In the absence of these indications (*Indikationen*), abortion was, as a general principle, a criminal offense when performed at any stage of pregnancy. East Germany, by contrast, permitted abortion on demand within the first trimester of pregnancy. Stalemated, the two German states agreed to retain their respective abortion policies until an all-German legislature could work out a satisfactory compromise, the Unification Treaty having laid down a December 31, 1992, deadline for the enactment of an all-German law acceptable to both sides.[32]

This short-term solution, with different laws being enforced in the eastern and western *Länder,* implicated the Constitution because in 1975 the Federal Constitutional Court held that the "human dignity" and "right to life" clauses of the Basic Law obliged the state affirmatively to protect and safeguard "unborn life" at every state of pregnancy.[33] In doing so, the Court nullified a liberalized abortion statute enacted in 1974 that would have removed abortion from punishment under the criminal code during the first three months of pregnancy, allowing a woman to make that choice herself after a counseling session required by law.

When considered in the light of the abortion case, Article 4 (5) [1] of the Unification Treaty appeared to stretch the limits of the Basic Law. This provision of the treaty inserted Article 143, a new amendment, into the Constitution, which permitted the eastern *Länder* to "deviate" from the Constitution for a transitional period of two years, but stipulated that any such deviations "must not violate . . . principles set out in Article 79 (3)" of the Basic Law. In addition, Article 79 (3) makes "inadmissible" any constitutional amendment incompatible with the Basic Law's human dignity clause.[34] The issue thus posed was this: Was Article 143 unconstitutional for having breached a fundamental value of the Basic Law—here the value of human dignity—as defined by the Federal Constitutional Court? Equally important was whether a treaty amending the Basic Law may authorize the eastern *Länder* to ignore, even temporarily, an authoritative judicial ruling interpreting the concept of "life" within the meaning of the Constitution. More important still was whether any all-German abortion policy would survive constitutional analysis if it conflicted with the Constitutional

Court's 1975 decision. All of these queries were open to dispute. Beyond dispute was the Federal Constitutional Court's authority to decide them with finality in a proper proceeding, an opportunity that would soon arise.

On June 26, 1992, after months of sturdy debate and hard work, a slim majority in the Bundestag passed a "compromise" bill effectively legalizing abortion during the first three months of pregnancy.[35] During this period, the law would leave the abortion decision up to the woman after compulsory submission to nonbinding counseling and a two-day waiting period. Interruption of pregnancy after the twelfth week would remain punishable by imprisonment unless performed by a licensed physician for compelling reasons specified by law. Even though the bill allowed the woman to choose in the early stages of pregnancy, it included a supplementary package of social welfare measures designed to encourage her to make a pro-life choice. The package included childbearing costs, job training for the woman, provisions for day-care centers, and a monthly child allowance, the costs of which were to be borne by the various *Länder*. In the Bundesrat the bill won the approval of all the *Länder* except Bavaria.[36] With the federal president's signature, it became law.[37]

The parliament appeared to have done its duty under the Unification Treaty. The treaty committed the two German states to work out a new all-German policy that "would ensure better protection of unborn life and provide a better solution, in conformity with the Constitution, of conflict situations faced by pregnant women, notably through legally guaranteed entitlements for women—first and foremost to advice and public support— than is the case in either part of Germany at present."[38] All hands among the contending parliamentary groups were well aware of the Constitutional Court's 1975 ruling that the state is obligated to protect unborn life at all stages of pregnancy. Few contested this view. The legislative debate thus centered on whether the value of unborn human life could be more effectively protected by punishment under the criminal code, except where indications are present, or by a term solution that would allow the woman to decide by a certain date within a caring and supportive social context.

As expected, the law was immediately challenged in the Federal Constitutional Court. Two-hundred-and-forty-eight members of the Bundestag—the one-third necessary to institute the proceeding—petitioned the Court for a temporary injunction against the enforcement of the statute. On the day before it was to enter into force, and to the surprise of many observers, the Court's Second Senate unanimously issued the injunction,[39] pending a full determination of its constitutionality. The injunction restored the status quo, with separate policies remaining in force in eastern and western Germany respectively.

In the ensuing months, both sides geared up for the main proceeding. In two full days (December 8–9, 1992) of hearings before the Constitutional Court, the petitioners advanced the view that the new law contravened the 1975 abortion ruling and in any event was a constitutional-ly insufficient means of protecting unborn life. Respondents, on the other hand, argued that the new law was the best policy that could be hoped for in the light of social and political realities and that out of respect for these realities, as well as the spirit of the Unification Treaty, the Court ought to accept the legislative judgment that the statute adequately discharges the state's responsibility to safeguard the human fetus.[40]

There were three possible decisions. First, the Court could sustain the statute as written. Second, it could nullify the satute outright, resting on its 1975 decision, in which case the Court would nullify Article 31(4) of the Unification Treaty, thus imposing West Germany's abortion policy on all of Germany. Finally, the Court could sustain the statute but require more restrictions on abortion. The Court handed down its decision on May 28, 1993, choosing the second option, and thereby recriminalizing abortion for the whole nation. But the Court also seemed to seek a middle ground, by ruling that women who undergo an abortion during the first trimester would not be prosecuted.

Property

The deviation clause of the new Article 143 was also designed to deal with the problem of property rights. On June 15, 1990, the two German govern-ments issued the Joint Declaration on the Settlement of Open Property Issues, an agreement to return expropriated property in the GDR to its orig-inal owners or their heirs. Incorporated into the Unification Treaty as Exhibit III,[41] the agreement covered seized businesses and real estate—nearly all the industrial and landed property in the GDR. Other property lost as a consequence of forced emigration, renunciation, flight to West Germany, nonconsensual sale and conversion into people's property, or appropriation by the state was also to be restored to former owners under the general policy of *Rückgabe vor Entschädigung* (restitution before com-pensation).[42] Compensation, however, was available as an option.

Former owners were legally entitled to file claims for property seized or taken between January 30, 1933, the beginning of Nazi rule, and October 2, 1990, the day before unification. The joint resolution included two exceptions to the policy of restitution. First, real estate and buildings urgently needed for investment and property unable to be returned in its original form would not be restored to their former owners;[43] they would receive compensation instead for the value of their lost property. Second, property seized during the Soviet occupation period (May 8, 1945, to October 6, 1949) was altogether exempt from the restitution and compensa-tion requirements of the Joint Declaration, except for any payment that a future all-German parliament might, in its discretion, confer on the owners of lost property as a way of indemnifying them for burdens sustained in the war.[44]

The exemption for Soviet occupation expropriations was the most controversial of the Unification Treaty's property settlement provisions. The Soviet Union and GDR absolutely refused to undo these takings, which for the most part involved the uncompensated seizure of large industrial concentrations as well as agricultural holdings over 250 acres, the latter having been broken up, distributed to poor farmers, and organized later into agricultural production cooperatives. The Soviet Union would not have signed the Two-Plus-Four Treaty without this concession on the part of the Allies and the FRG. Former owners of land in the East, however, claimed that the exemption clauses violated their constitutional right to property within the meaning of Article 14 (3), their right to equality under law (Article 3 [1]), and the rule of law, one of the Basic Law's unamendable principles (Article 79 [3]). They took these complaints to the Federal Constitutional Court as soon as the treaty entered into force.

On April 23, 1991, the Constitutional Court affirmed the validity of the exemption clauses.[45] The decision was an exercise in judicial pragmatism. Faced with the Soviet Union's nonnegotiable stance against any roll back of properties expropriated during the occupation, the Court accepted the government's argument that the exemption was a compromise necessary to achieve the higher constitutional goal of reunification.[46] Equally important, the Court sustained the validity of Article 143 over the objection that it amounted to an unconstitutional amendment to the Basic Law.[47] (Petitioners claimed that Article 143 eroded the "core" values of Articles 1—protecting human dignity—and 20—the rule of law.) In point of international law, finally, the Court noted that Germany was not responsible for the takings between 1945 and 1949, that the properties were subject to a legal system other than that of the FRG, and that in any event the Basic Law did not enter into force until after the property had been taken.[48]

Regulations emerging out of other provisions dealing with the settlement of open property would produce another round of constitutional challenges. Such matters as controls on buying and selling of property, determinations of legal ownership, denials of restitution claims, and trust agency investment decisions would produce these challenges, all stemming from efforts to achieve a socially acceptable balance between the claims of property owners and the needs of economic justice. The sudden switch from a state-directed to a free-market economy was bound to disrupt the lives of East Germans and to weigh heavily on various constitutional guarantees. Many of these guarantees, especially the right to property, are subject to reasonable regulation so long as the "core" of such rights remains protected. The Basic Law protects private enterprise and private property, but it also sanctions the social welfare state. So long as lawmakers reasonably balance these competing interests, their rules and regulations are more than likely to withstand constitutional review.

Other Proceedings

The various treaties on reunification extended to subjects, apart from property and abortion, that would also implicate fundamental rights and constitutional values. For example, the dissolution of certain public institutions in eastern Germany and the restructuring of the civil service, including the judiciary and the universities, resulted in a flood of constitutional complaints. In a leading case, the Federal Constitutional Court upheld the validity of rules terminating the employment contracts of hundreds of public employees and summarily dismissing those formerly engaged by the secret police (Stasi) or accused of human rights violations.[49] The Court found a basis for these terminations in Article 130 of the Basic Law, a provision it sought to balance against the constitutional right to choose one's trade or profession (Article 12). As applied to pregnant women and mothers, however, the termination rule violated the state's constitutional duty, pursuant to Article 6 (4), to confer special care and protection on mothers.[50]

Two additional constitutional decisions involved similar issues. In the first, the Constitutional Court sustained treaty provisions permitting the eastern *Länder* to dissolve some fifty institutes employing some 24,000 workers, among them 15,000 scientists and their assistants.[51] The importance of the case stems from the protection accorded by the Basic Law to freedom of research and teaching (Article 5 [3]). This freedom, however, said the Court, attaches to individuals, not to the institutions in which they work. But once again, the Court qualified its holding by rejecting the wholesale dismissal of women with children. In a second case, the Court nullified a law, enacted by Saxony, conferring jurisdiction on that state's disciplinary court to review decisions, pursuant to a provision of the Unification Treaty, dealing with the reappointment or recertification of former GDR judges. Holding the statute incompatible with Sections 71 and 78 of the Federal Judges Act,[52] the Court's decision would surely foreshadow other similar conflicts likely to emerge in the years ahead as the eastern *Länder* continue the process of harmonizing their institutions and procedures with those of the West.

Constitutional conflict over various provisions of the Unification Treaty, together with regulations seeking to implement them, will continue unabated into the future. Controversies surrounding compensation for the victims of political oppression, the legal status of civil servants, the relationship between the new *Länder* and the federation, the dismissal and relicensing of legal and other professionals, and the prosecution of human rights violations, not to mention the pending trials of former GDR leaders, will indubitably furnish additional chapters in the continuing saga of reunification as it pertains to the Basic Law.

Prospects for Constitutional Renewal

As noted earlier, the Unification Treaty recommended that both GDR and FRG governments consider, within two years, additional amendments to the Basic Law to reflect the reality of reunification and a changed Germany. They were to pay particular attention to a new set of federal-state fiscal relations, to the introduction of state objectives into the Constitution, and to the possibility of revising the Basic Law itself under the terms of Article 146. The new all-German parliament honored this pledge by setting up a Joint Commission on Constitutional Revision, its membership to consist of sixty-four parliamentary delegates, half of them from the Bundestag and half from the Bundesrat. Its final report, after extended consultations behind closed doors during much of 1992, would be ready in late 1993.[53]

The Joint Commission's work has gone beyond the items singled out for special attention in the Unification Treaty. In recent months it has solicited recommendations involving such topics as local self-government, parliamentary practices and campaign finance, term lengths for certain elected officials, the federal postal and railway systems, and readjustments in the federal system prompted by the requirements of European unity.[54] Other proposed amendments, some of which seek to fulfill the promise of the Two-Plus-Four Treaty,[55] deal with military affairs, including a controversial proposal to allow the deployment of German military forces beyond the area covered by NATO. Although many of these proposals, including suggestions for reordering the relationship between the federation and the *Länder,* would tinker with numerous articles of the Basic Law, they would not alter the fundamental character of the German Constitution.

Proposals to extend the list of constitutional rights and insert state objectives into the Basic Law would, however, impose additional responsibilities on the state and, in some cases, on individuals. These proposals include guarantees of full employment, a clean environment, adequate housing, security against eviction from housing quarters, comprehensive medical and welfare assistance, and democracy in the workplace, placing an affirmative duty on the state to create jobs during periods of unemployment and to enact laws to ensure the realization of other basic needs. In addition, education and culture would be defined as "public functions" that the state must undertake and promote. Protection of the environment has been pushed with particular vigor. Its strongest proponents propose adding the words "and creation" to the preambular declaration acknowledging the German people's "responsibility before God and men." They would also make protection of the natural environment a "special duty of the state" and even charge individuals with this burden by "obliging everyone to contribute to [this goal] by his [or her] own behavior."

The values of sociality and equality reflected in these state goals also inform suggested amendments for expanding individual and group rights. Some proposals would reinforce the equality of men and women and ban discrimination against nonmarital families as well as national, linguistic, and religious minorities. A related proposal would place these groups under the state's special protection. Another would subject women as well as men to the military draft and equalize the length of time that draftees and conscientious objectors spend, respectively, in the military and substitute civilian service.[56] Still another would protect the individual against the disclosure of personal information collected by or stored in official or unofficial data processing centers.

Are these changes necessary? For constitutional scholars who feel that the Basic Law is sufficiently flexible to meet the problems of reunited Germany as well as the needs of a society about to enter the twenty-first century, the answer is "no." As for state objectives, they argue that most of the proposals are already implicit in the Basic Law's concept of human dignity (Article 1) and its principle of the social welfare state (*Sozialstaatlichkeit*) (Article 20). They add that proposals for additional rights— for example, those based on equality and the right to "informational self-determination"—have already been vindicated by the Federal Constitutional Court. Others, however, believe that in the light of the state's increasing reach over the lives of individuals and the unpredictability of judicial protection, certain rights ought to be frozen into the Constitution itself.

Proposals likely to generate the most scrutiny are those favoring the introduction of plebiscitary elements into the Basic Law—to give Germans the opportunity, at the national level, to employ the mechanisms of direct democracy. Any such reform would, of course, seriously modify the representational character of Germany's governing system. Elements of plebiscitary democracy such as the initiative and referendum are favored mainly by left-wing parties and groups that see in these devices a means of circumventing political party oligarchies and of breaking down patterns of authority allegedly removed from the influence of public opinion. Apart from the problems of how and when such devices would be employed and to which issues they would extend, certain conservative interests see them as threat to the kind of political integration that a responsible and responsive government is supposed to achieve.

A related proposal would give the Bundestag the right to dissolve itself and call for new elections, an effort to overcome the political gridlock ostensibly caused by an entrenched and ossified party system. The Basic Law in its present form allows for no power of self-dissolution. In addition, the "constructive vote of no confidence" prescribed by Article 67 prevents the removal of the chancellor unless parliament elects his successor when the no-confidence vote takes place. The original purpose behind Article 67 and related provisions of the Basic Law was to create a strong chancellor and to keep the political system from splintering into polarized groups. The system has worked much as the founders intended and, contrary to those who would wish to further democratize parliamentary politics, its defenders will fight to maintain constitutional arrangements that in their view have helped to create a stabilized and balanced political order.

Last, and perhaps most important of all, the Commission may propose a popular referendum on the Basic Law itself. Indeed, as suggested earlier, this appears to have been the main reason for the Unification Treaty's retention of Article 146. As amended, it provides for the Basic Law's termination on the day the German people freely adopt a new constitution. The intent behind these words, however, as the Unity Treaty itself suggests, is to allow the German people, finally, to vote on the Basic Law itself. A powerful argument could be marshaled in support of such a vote. The Basic Law was drafted originally by a constituent assembly—the Parliamentary Council—elected by the *Länder* parliaments and then ratified by those same parliaments. Any fundamental law that is supreme and designed originally for the permanent governance of a whole people ought to be sanctioned, so the argument runs, by a constituency far broader than the body responsible for proposing and drafting it—in short, and if possible, by the people themselves.

Considerable confusion would attend any effort to hold a national referendum on the Basic Law. For one thing, the Basic Law lays down no procedures for conducting such a referendum. For another, it is not clear what the voting population would be asked to approve. Would it be the entire Basic Law or certain provisions or sections thereof? Would approval be required in all the *Länder*? In the East as well as in the West? What type of majority would be required? Each of these issues would be the subject of fierce debate. On the other hand, if approved by large majorities in both eastern and western *Länder,* a national referendum would eliminate any lingering doubt about the Basic Law's legitimacy, no matter what the fate of present proposals to amend the Constitution.

German constitutionalism would have been more deeply affected by a decision to hold a new constitutional convention and rewrite the Basic Law as a whole. This would have been a reasonable response to German unity. As just noted, the Basic Law had not been ratified by popular referendum. Nor were western Germans given the opportunity to approve either the fact or mode of reunification. Many East Germans, on the other hand, particularly those educators, artists, and churchmen who led the fight for the "bloodless revolution" early on, had no intention of unifying Germany, at least not immediately. Rather, they set out to put an end to the police state, to make the system more democratic, and above all to humanize it. With the help of a former justice of West Germany's Federal Constitutional Court, these early revolutionaries actually drew up a new draft of an East German constitution, one designed to capture what many believed was an impressive tradition of peace and solidarity.[57] A constitutionally reformed GDR was not to be, however; the election of March 18, 1990—the day on which East Germans voted to end the division of Germany—put an end to this dream. The speed with which unity occurred within the framework of the Basic Law dismayed the idealists among the revolutionaries. In their view, the election expressed envy or greed more than freedom or self-determination; for them, East Germans succumbed to the temptation of Western consumerism. In short, the blitz westward manifested only crass materialism. In the less charitable version of this thesis, a West Germany capitalist steamroller overpowered East Germans in a moment of acute vulnerability, depriving citizens of a future in which a new Germany, combining the values of East and West, might have become a force for peace, justice, and internationalism in the world.

Still, the arguments for instant unity under the Basic Law were also strong. Although not conceived in perpetuity, the Basic Law had taken on the character of both permanence and legitimacy: permanence because it had stood the test of time, having nurtured a stable and durable political order marked by respect for liberal values and limited government; legitimacy because an overwhelming majority of West Germans—between 70 and 90 percent of the voting-age population—had given its tacit consent to the Basic Law in eleven federal elections over a span of forty-one years. Indeed, a new constitutional convention may well have brought on a constitutional crisis in its own right, unsettling the delicate balances painfully crafted into the Basic Law in 1949, not to mention throwing into question forty years of constitutional practice and interpretation by a supreme tribunal whose role in the protection of rights rivals that of the United States Supreme Court.

Few expect the Basic Law to undergo significant alteration. A constitutional revision commission made up of legislators with a vested interest in the existing political and legal order is unlikely to propose radical changes in the Basic Law. The most important changes will probably occur in the area of federal-state fiscal relations. Here compelling reasons exist for adjustments in the distribution of tax resources, given the backward political economies of the eastern *Länder*. Other changes, however, are likely to be more cosmetic than substantial, with perhaps two exceptions: a change in Article 16 (2) limiting the right of asylum, and changes in Article 24 and 87a (1) allowing the military forces to be deployed for purposes other than the defense of Germany and outside the area of NATO. Interestingly enough, these two changes are being proposed and debated in the country as a whole, largely outside the framework of the constitutional reform commission. Once again, however, the changes wrought by the debate will not touch the vital core of the Basic Law. In short, reunification will most surely result in significant political change but only within the framework of the existing constitutional order.

Notes

1. See, for example, Häberle 1990. The argument for a new beginning was even made by two justices of the Federal Constitutional Court. See Ernst-Wolfgang Böckenförde and Dieter Grimm, "Nachdenken über Deutschland," *Der Spiegel,* March 5, 1990: 72–77.

2. See Preamble of the Basic Law of the Federal Republic of Germany (hereafter cited as GG). The Preamble envisioned "a new order of political life for a transitional period [until] the entire German people are called upon to achieve in free self-determination the unity and freedom of Germany."

3. For an excellent description of these procedures and a discussion of the arguments for and against their use, see Quint 1991.

4. The Basic Law was never ratified by popular vote. It was approved by the legislatures of the then existing *Länder.* The Parliamentary Council that drew up the Basic Law consisted of delegates also chosen by the *Länder* legislatures. See Merkl 1963, 58–59.

5. See Judgements of April 22, 1953, 2 Entscheidungen des Bundesverfassungsgerichts 226, 277 (hereinafter cited as BVerfGE); February 26, 1954, 3 BVerfGE 288, 319; August 17, 1956, 5 BVerfGE 85, 126; March 26, 1957, 6 BVerfGE 309, 336; July 31, 1973, 36 BVerfGE 1, 16; and October 21, 1987, 77 BVerfGE 150–151.

6. Constitutional experts, legal scholars, and other academicians were far from unanimous, however, in preferring Article 23. More than 100 academicians, among them sixty legal scholars and social scientists, came out in favor of Article 146 as the preferred route to unity. See *Frankfurter Rundschau,* March 30, 1990. Their statement followed a declaration in favor of Article 23 by 100 public law professors, including many of the Basic Law's leading commentators. See *Die Welt,* March 30, 1990. See also the statements of Christian Starck (preferring Article 23), *Frankfurter Allgemeine Zeitung,* April 5, 1990; Jürgen Habermas (preferring Article 146), *Die Zeit,* March 30, 1990; and Josef Isensee (favoring Article 23), *Frankfurter Allgemeine Zeitung,* April 6, 1990.

7. See Dolzer 1990. Other scholars, however have contested this view. See Frowein 1990; Giegerich 1991.

8. *Badische Zeitung,* March 31, 1990.

9. 36 BVerfGE 1, 29. See also Frowein, supra note 10, at 12.

10. Constitutional Act of July 22, 1990, Gesetzblatt der DDR, Teil I (1990): 955. In addition, the twenty-three districts of Berlin were to be combined to form a single city-state. See Unification Treaty, infra note 15, Article 1 (2).

11. Representatives of France, Great Britain, the United States, the Soviet Union, and the two German states concluded the Two-Plus-Four Treaty on the Final Settlement with Respect to Germany, Bundesgesetzblatt, Teil II (1990): 1,318. The Treaty Between the Federal Republic of Germany and the German Democratic Republic on the Establishment of German Unity (August 31, 1990) is the official title of the Unification Treaty. See Bundesgesetzblatt, Teil II (1990): 889. The official English translation of both treaties appears in *The Unification of Germany in 1990: A Documentation,* supra note 5. Unless otherwise indicated, quotations from the treaties are taken from this source.

12. Two-Plus-Four Treaty, Article 1 (4).

13. Ibid., Article 4, § 2.

14. Ibid., Article 4, § 1.

15 The new formula continues to give a political advantage to the smaller states. The five new *Länder,* together with Berlin, have twenty-three votes, equal to

34 percent of the sixty-eight votes represented by all sixteen states. See Unification Treaty, ibid., Article 4, § 3.

16. See Umbach and Clemens (eds.) 1992. The right to civil service employment was also implicated in the new Article 143. Article 131 of the Basic Law, which deals with employment and pension rights of persons who were employed in the public service on May 8, 1945, would not be applicable at all to the eastern *Länder*. See Unification Treaty, Article 6. However, Annex I of the treaty provided for a number of transitional arrangements to govern the legal status of persons in the public service at the time of accession. In addition, Article 20 (2) of the treaty reads: "The exercise of public responsibilities (state authority as defined in Article 33 [4] of the Basic Law) shall be entrusted as soon as possible to professional civil servants. . . . Article 92 of the Basic Law [dealing with the judiciary] shall remain unaffected."

17. Unification Treaty, Article 4, § 5 (2).

18. Ibid., Article 4, § 5.

19. For a discussion of the meaning of this language, see infra, pp. 35–36.

20. See Kommers 1989, 11–17.

21. The Unification Treaty did, however, amend two sections of the Federal Constitutional Court Act, the organic statute that spells out the Court's organization, authority, and procedures. See Gesetz über das Bundesverfassungsgericht (hereinafter cited as BVerfGG) in der Fassung der Bekanntmachung vom 12 Dezember 1985. One change provided that an East German lawyer or judge appointed to the Federal Constitutional Court need only possess the qualifications of a Diplomjurist, an east German law degree representing a lower level of training than required of judges in western Germany. See Unification Treaty, Annex I, chap. III, Section F, Par. 1 (a), BGBl (1990): 963. The other change, also designed temporarily to accommodate eastern Germany's different standards of academic achievement, permits an eastern *Land* or one of its constitutional organs to be represented by their officials in proceedings before the Court, regardless of the latter's legal educational backgrounds. Ibid., Par. 1 (6).

22. In their defense petitioners invoked Articles 38 (concerning parliamentary representation), 42 (concerning voting procedures in the Bundestag), 76 (concerning proper procedures for the submission of bills), and 79 (concerning procedures for amending the Basic Law). Their main arguments rested on Article 79 (1), which declares in part that "[t]his Basic Law can be amended only by statutes which expressly amend or supplement the text thereof."

23. Judgment of September 18, 1990, 82 BVerfGE 316, 320–321.

24. Vertrag zur Vorbereitung und Durchführung der ersten gesamtdeutschen Wahl des Deutschen Bundestages zwischen der Bundesrepublik Deutschland und der Deutschen Demokratischen Republik, Bundesgesetzblatt I (1990): 822.

25. Article 38 provides for the election of representatives in "general, direct, free, equal, and secret elections" whereas Article 21 secures the right of political parties to "participate in forming the political will of the people." The 5 percent clause is anchored in § 6 (6) of the Federal Election Act. See Bundesgesetzblatt (hereafter BGBl) I: 2059 (September 21, 1990).

26. Judgment of September 29, 1990, 82 BVerfGE 322.

27. Ibid., 340–341. See also von Beyme 1991, 163–177.

28. See Wolle 1992, 97–103.

29. 82 BVerfGE 322, 341.

30. Judgment of October 17, 1990, 82 BVerfGE 353.

31. See Wallach and Francisco 1992, 85–89.

32. Unification Treaty, Article 31 (4).

33. Judgment of February 25, 1975, 39 BVerfGE 1.

34. GG, Article 1 (1).

35. *Frankfurter Allgemeine Zeitung,* June 27, 1992, 1.

36. *Frankfurter Allgemeine Zeitung,* July 3, 1992, 1.

37. Das Schwangeren- und Familiengesetz vom 27 Juli 1992, BGBl. I: 1398.

38. Unification Treaty, Article 31 (4).

39. *Frankfurter Rundschau,* August 5, 1992, 1. For details of the decision and the public reaction to it, see *Die Welt,* August 6, 1992, 5, and *Deutsches Allgemeines Sonntagsblatt,* August 7, 1992, 11.

40. Written briefs for petitioners (dated August 25, 1992) and respondents (dated September 14, 1992) prepared respectively by Professors Peter Lerche and Fritz Ossenbühl (counsel for petitioners) and Professors Erhard Denninger and Winfried Hassemer (counsel for respondents).

41. Unification Treaty, Article 41 (1) in tandem with Exhibit III, Einigungsvertrag, Bulletin Nr. 104. Bonn: Presse-und Informationsamt der Bundesrepublik, September 6, 1990, 1,119–1,120.

42. For more detailed discussion of these issues in English, see Quint 1991; Horn 1991.

43. Unification Treaty, Annex III, § 3 (a).

44. Ibid., § 1.

45. 84 BVerfGE 90.

46. Ibid., 127–128.

47. Ibid., 117–121.

48. Ibid., 122–125.

49. Judgment of April 24, 1991, 84 BVerfGE 133. The Court sustained the validity of regulations promulgated pursuant to Article 13 of the Unification Treaty. See Anlage 1, Kapitel XIX, Sachgebeit A, Abschnitt III, Nr. 1 (BGBl. II: 1140).

50. 84 BVerfGE 133, 145.

51. Judgment of March 10, 1992 (1 BvR 454 [1991]) (mimeographed).

52. Judgment of July 8, 1992 (2 BvL 29 [1991] and 2 BvL 31 [1991]) (mimeographed).

53. The following discussion draws on the Joint Commission's reports and discussions. Most helpful in this regard have been the stenographical reports of several sessions in the Bundestag. (Gemeinsame Verfassungskommission, Stenographischer Bericht.) These records will not become generally available until after the publication of the Commission's final report.

54. Many of the proposed amendments would strengthen local units of government, including the *Länder,* whose representatives fear that European political and economic union may diminish their authority. Other proposals call for the privatization of the federal railroad and postal service. Suggested parliamentary and election reforms include enhancing the rights and prerogatives of legislative investigating committees and opposition parties, allowing the Bundestag to dissolve itself, lengthening the terms of office for members of the Bundestag, and confining the federal president to a single seven-year term of office.

55. Under one such amendment Germany would renounce the possession or production of nuclear, biological, or chemical weapons. Another proposal would ban the exportation of weapons from German soil.

56. The proposal for equalizing the time spent in civilian and military service is an effort to nullify a law that requires a person doing compulsory civilian service to spend twenty months on duty, whereas military conscripts serve for only fifteen months. The Federal Constitutional Court sustained this law over the objection that it offended the equal protection clause of Article 3. See 69 BVerfGE 1 (1985).

57. The Preamble, written by the East German author Christa Wolf, looked toward the creation of a new state inspired by "revolutionary renewal" and rooted in the "humanistic tradition" created by "the best women and men of all sections of the [East German] population." The draft constitution copied numerous provisions of the Basic Law, including many of its individual rights provisions, but it added substantially to the list of socioeconomic rights. These included the right to education, social security, full employment, welfare assistance, a clean environment, and a woman's "right to pregnancy in self-determination" as well as absolute equality between men and women. The list also included the right to strike as well as bans on company lockouts, cartels, and monopoly restraints on trade.

References

von Beyme, Klaus. 1991. *Das Politische System der Bundesrepublik Deutschland nach der Vereinigung*. Munich: Piper.

Böckenförde, Ernst-Wolfgang, and Dieter Grimm. 1990. "Nachdenken über Deutschland." *Der Spiegel,* March 5, 72–77.

Dolzer, Rudolf. 1990. *The Path to German Unity: The Constitutional, Legal and International Framework*. Washington, DC: The American Institute for Contemporary German Studies.

Frowein, Jochen A. 1990. "Die Verfassungslage Deutschlands im Rahmen der Völkerrechts." *Veröffentlichungen der Vereinigung der Deutschen Staatsrechtslehrer* 49:25–26.

Giegerich, Thomas. 1991. "The European Dimension of German Reunification: East Germany's Integration into the European Communities." *Zeitschrift für ausländisches öffentliches Recht und Völkerrecht* 51:408–409.

Häberle, Peter. 1990. "Verfassungspolitik für die Freiheit and Einheit Deutschlands." *Juristenzeitung* 45:358–363.

Horn, Norbert. 1991. "The Lawful German Revolution: Privatization and Market Economy in a Re-Unified Germany." *The American Journal of Comparative Law* 39: 725–746.

Kommers, Donald P. 1989. *The Constitutional Jurisprudence of the Federal Republic of Germany*. Durham, NC: Duke University Press.

Merkl, Peter H. 1963. *The Origin of the West German Republic*. New York: Oxford University Press.

Quint, Peter E. 1991. "The Constitutional Law of German Unification." *Maryland Law Review* 50:506–516.

Umbach, Dieter, and Thomas Clemens (eds.). 1992. *Mitarbeiter Kommentar zum Bundesverfassungsgerichtsgesetz*. Heidelberg: C.F. Müller Verlag.

Unification of Germany in 1990: A Documentation, The. 1991. Bonn: Press and Information Office.

Wallach, H.G. Peter, and Ronald A. Francisco. 1992. *United Germany*. New York: Praeger.

Wolle, Stefan. 1992. "Der Weg in den Zusammenbruch: Die DDR von Januar bis zum Oktober 1989." In Eckhard Jesse and Armin Mitter (eds.), *Die Gestaltung der deutschen Einheit*. Bonn: Bundeszentrale für politische Bildung, 97–103.

Chapter 8

The Future of Federalism in the Unified Germany

Arthur B. Gunlicks

It is interesting to reflect today on the euphoria in Germany and elsewhere that accompanied the fall of the Berlin Wall in November 1989 and the generally high expectations and rosy predictions that seemed to prevail as a result of the spectacular developments that occurred during 1990. These developments ranged from the first free elections in East Germany on March 18 and the economic, monetary, and social union of East and West on July 2 to the unification of Germany on October 3, the elections in the five new East German *Länder* on October 14, and the first free all-German elections since 1933 on December 2. The future of the united Germany looked bright indeed.

Since at least the beginning of 1991, however, there has been a far more sober assessment of the future of a united Germany, especially for the Germans in the East. Even a brief listing of the many reasons for the changes that have occurred since the heady days of 1990 would take too much space in this chapter. Its more modest focus examines some of the changes that have affected the *Länder* and the federal system in Germany since the fall of the Wall, and it takes note of several current and emerging controversies resulting from these changes.

Federalism was a crucial component of the political system introduced in West Germany in 1949, and, in contrast to its largely reactionary features in the Bismarck Reich, it has become closely identified with the success of West German democracy (Gunlicks 1986, 3–5). Federalism has had an immense impact on German domestic and even foreign affairs, and several books, mostly but not all in German, have been written about the subject from a variety of perspectives.[1] The purpose of this chapter is to select and discuss briefly four topics that I believe will be among the most important, not only for German federalism but also for the German political system in general. They are *Neugliederung,* or the redrawing of boundaries and consolidation of smaller into larger *Länder*; fiscal equalization among the *Länder*; revisions of the Basic Law (constitution); and the relationship of European Community to the *Länder*.

How Many *Länder*?

Although it was clear from the beginning that a united Germany would be a democratic and federal state, a requirement of Article 79 of the Basic Law that is not subject to amendment, it was not clear what this meant for the former GDR. Soon after the Wall came down, many people in the West were reminded that the East Germans had established five *Länder* between December 1946 and February 1947: Mecklenburg (to which West Pomerania was added in 1990), Brandenburg, Saxony-Anhalt, Thuringia, and Saxony. The first three were artificial creations with little or no history, whereas Thuringia had existed as a *Land* since 1920, and Saxony was a former kingdom with a long history of independence. They owed their creation to the Potsdam agreement, in which the Allies had called for decentralized political structures and local self-government in postwar Germany. The 1949 constitution of the newly established GDR also provided for a federal system with five *Länder*; however, by the early 1950s it was clear that the SED and the Soviets preferred a highly centralized unitary state, and in July 1952 the five *Länder* were reconstituted in *Kreise* (counties) and fifteen *Bezirke* (districts), including East Berlin. During the first months of 1990, various citizen roundtables created in the districts took up the issue of recreating the *Länder,* for they found that many East Germans no longer wanted to be identified with the GDR but rather with Saxony, Thuringia, Mecklenburg–West Pomerania, etc. It became clear that the restoration of the *Länder* could help reestablish a sense of legitimacy for the emerging political system that was replacing the old regime (*Das Parlament* 1991, 7).

Nevertheless, a number of proposals were considered for the old GDR, ranging from retaining the GDR as one *Land* that would still be slightly smaller in size of population than North Rhine–Westphalia in the West, to creating two, three, four, or five *Länder* (Blaschke 1990, 39–50). In July 1990 the East German parliament, elected in March, passed a law that provided for five new *Länder*. Following certain boundary adjustments made in the late summer after the parliament considered the results of a number of nonbinding referenda, the five new *Länder* came into being on October 3, 1990; they did not include East Berlin, which was joined with West Berlin.

While attention centered on reestablishing the five *Länder* in the East, there was also some discussion of combining a number of territories in the East and West, for both sentimental and economic reasons. For example, one proposal would have formed three new *Länder* by joining Schleswig-Holstein and Hamburg with Mecklenburg–West Pomerania; Hesse with Thuringia; and Lower Saxony with Saxony-Anhalt. There was also discussion of minor territorial adjustments, such as uniting the city of Heiligenstadt and its surrounding territory in Thuringia with Duderstadt in Lower Saxony; and, more recently, returning eight villages east of the Elbe River in Mecklenburg–West Pomerania to a region in Lower Saxony.[2]

The creation of five new *Länder* in the East has revived an old and divisive debate in Germany regarding a *Neugliederung,* or reordering and reorganization of the *Länder.* In general, the restructuring of *Land* boundaries in Germany has occurred only under severe pressure from the outside and/or as the result of war. Thus Napoléon was directly and indirectly responsible for reducing the number of German states from more than 300 to thirty-nine by 1815. Some states, for example, Hanover, were annexed by Prussia in the 1860s during the Austro-Prussian War. There were twenty-five states when Bismarck formed his Reich, eighteen (later seventeen) in the Weimar Republic. We have already seen that Thuringia and Saxony were *Länder* in the East before 1933. In the West only Bremen, Hamburg, and Bavaria had histories as *Länder* before Hitler. In their occupation zone, the British formed North Rhine–Westphalia by combining two Prussian provinces and Lippe. They turned Schleswig-Holstein, once a Prussian province, into a *Land.* And they created Lower Saxony by combining the Prussian province and former state of Hanover with the old *Länder* Oldenburg, Braunschweig, and Schaumburg-Lippe. In the U.S. zone, the Americans created the Rhineland-Palatinate by combining some Prussian provinces and the Bavarian Palatinate, and Hesse resulted from a combination of Prussian provinces and old, small *Länder.* The Saarland, of course, was returned without enthusiasm by France in 1957. Only Baden-Württemberg is a German creation; it was formed after the fact that the northern parts of Baden and Württemberg had been placed in the U.S. zone and the southern parts had been placed in the French zone created the necessary conditions for serious thinking about boundary reform.

In the late 1960s much discussion about territorial reform took place in West Germany, including boundary reforms for the villages, towns, cities, counties, and, of course, the *Länder.* Major territorial reforms were enacted at the local level in the eight territorial *Länder* (Gunlicks 1986, 1981), and a commission was formed to look at the *Land* boundaries. This commission, called the Ernst Kommission, recommended major boundary changes (Ernst Kommission 1973). It proposed that the Federal Republic have either five or six *Länder*: North Rhine–Westphalia; Baden-Württemberg; Bavaria; a combination of the Saarland, Rhineland-Palatinate, and Hesse; and a combination of Schleswig-Holstein, Hamburg, and part of Lower Saxony on the one hand, and Bremen and Lower Saxony on the other hand;

or a joining of all of these *Länder* into one very large *Nordstaat*. Nothing ever came of these proposals, due in part to the Finance Reform of 1969 and the rise of "cooperative federalism."

Since early 1990 discussions concerning a reordering of boundaries and a reduction in the number of *Länder* have continued unabated. There is relatively little controversy over the proposal to combine Berlin and Brandenburg into one *Land,* but proposals to incorporate the smaller and weaker *Länder* in the West, especially Bremen and the Saarland (Hamburg has indicated a willingness to consider consolidation with one or more of its neighbors), into their larger neighbors and to reduce the number of *Länder* in the East have led to heated debate. An alternative arrangement also discussed was cooperation between *Länder* to promote common goals.

The arguments for a *Neugliederung* are numerous and persuasive.[3] They often start with Article 29 of the Basic Law, which provides for a reorganization of the federal territory "to ensure that the *Länder* by their size and capacity are able effectively to fulfill the functions incumbent upon them" (official translation). Reform advocates argue that sixteen *Länder* are too many. Perhaps the most compelling argument concerns the impact of the economically weak *Länder* on the system of fiscal equalization, which will be discussed further below. Weak *Länder*—including all five new ones—place strains on this system, because the wealthier *Länder* are required to share their tax revenues with them. To the extent that the poorer *Länder* complain about the funds they receive from the wealthier ones—and they are never satisfied—they will turn to the federal government for grants-in-aid and demand more federal participation in activities traditionally left to the *Länder* (this happened under the Finance Reform of 1969 discussed below). Such demands would simply reinforce centralizing trends already existing in the system, thus weakening federalism further.[4]

A second major argument in favor of *Neugliederung* concerns the Bundesrat. Before unification there were ten *Länder* with forty-one votes in the Bundesrat, not counting West Berlin's four consultative votes. Each of the largest West German *Länder*—North Rhine–Westphalia, Bavaria, Baden-Württemberg, and Lower Saxony—had five votes; Hesse, Schleswig-Holstein, and the Rhineland-Palatinate had four; and the Saarland, Hamburg, and Bremen had three. If each of the new *Länder* received four votes (except Mecklenburg–West Pomerania, which would get three votes), the ratio between West and East would have been 41 to 19. Even if Berlin were added to the West, the ratio for the East would have been very favorable in proportion to the populations of the former West and East Germany. For this reason, and also because of the disproportionate weight that the small and medium-sized *Länder* would have, the Unification Treaty of August 31, 1990, increased the number of votes for the largest *Länder* to six. This has increased the number of votes in the Bundesrat to sixty-eight. Although they constitute only 21 percent of the total population of Germany, the five new *Länder* have 28 percent of the votes. Given their severe economic problems, they can be expected to join with the weaker *Länder* in the West in promoting measures in the Bundesrat that will ask the federal government to increase its share in the financing of *Land* activities. In any case, sixteen *Länder* will complicate the decisionmaking process in the Bundesrat and make the federal system less transparent than it was with only eleven.

A third major argument has to do with the European Community, a subject to which I shall turn below. I simply note here that there has been considerable discussion about a future Europe of regions, but it is not clear what the definition of region will be. It is in the interest of the Germans to have strong regions, that is, *Länder,* that will serve as models for others to emulate.

Finally, this is an opportune time to restructure the *Länder*. It is clear that there are too many, that at least half are too small in population, that they lack economic viability, and that reform must come now before the status quo becomes too institutionalized and entrenched.

Of course there are counterarguments. Why, it is asked, is it so unacceptable to have sixteen *Länder* when the United States has fifty? Although Germany is only the size of Montana, Switzerland, a country much smaller than Germany, has twenty-six cantons. Luxembourg, a sovereign country and member of the EC, has only 350,000 inhabitants. Why is it intolerable for Bremen to have only 650,000 or the Saarland 1.2 million inhabitants? How will the uniting of two or three weak *Länder* lead to a strengthening of the new whole? Whether there are sixteen or eight *Länder* will make no difference to the EC, which is increasingly ignoring even national boundaries. The focus on administrative efficiency and effectiveness and fiscal autonomy is basically a technocratic perspective that ignores the more important psychological identification with, and legitimacy of, the *Länder* as they now exist. In any case now is not the time to attempt a reform of *Länder* boundaries. There are too many other pressing problems that have priority, and, in any case, Article 29 of the Basic Law prohibits changes without the consent of the citizens of the individual *Länder*. Given their probable reluctance to consent to the reforms being advocated, the Basic Law would have to be amended to permit changes with less public input. That may not be so easy.

Fiscal Equalization

In the United States, there is a system of financing in which more or less separate tax sources can be identified for each level of government. The federal level is identified with income taxes, the states with sales taxes, and the local governments with property taxes; however, this does not preclude other levels from applying the same tax. Most states, for example, have some form of income tax. In Germany the rule is that any one revenue source may be taxed by only one level of government. Instead of different levels of government competing for revenues from the same source, in Germany one level collects the taxes and shares the revenues with another level.[5]

Although the federal government has exclusive jurisdiction over various monopolies and customs duties, it has concurrent powers over all other taxes. In keeping with the German federal tradition, however, the *Land* governments do have some separate taxes, and they are responsible for the laws concerning traditional local taxes. Taxes shared by the different levels of government are regulated at the federal level, but the political process at this level includes the participation of the Bundesrat, which represents the *Land* governments. The shared taxes in Germany are those placed on income, corporations, and sales of services and products (value-added taxes, or VAT), which together are called joint taxes (*Gemeinschaftssteuern*). These account for more than two-thirds of all tax revenues in the Federal Republic. Since 1980 the municipalities have received 15 percent of the income taxes derived from the payments of local citizens. The remaining 85 percent of the income taxes and all of the revenues from the corporate taxes are divided equally between the *Land* and the federal governments. The VAT, which is less sensitive to economic conditions than the income and corporation taxes, was added to the shared taxes by the Finance Reform of 1969. It is now 15 percent, having been raised from 14 percent in January 1993. The *Länder* received 35 percent of the VAT before, and 37 percent after January 1993.

One of the most important changes made in the Basic Law as a result of the Finance Reform of 1969 was the insertion of a new section (VIIIa) and two new articles (Articles 91a and 91b) concerning joint tasks (*Gemeinschaftsaufgaben*) involving both the federal and *Land* governments. This new section on joint tasks has legally formalized the system of "cooperative federalism," a concept often used to describe federal relationships in the Federal Republic.

In addition to the funds it furnishes for the joint tasks, the federal government provides grants-in-aid to the *Länder* for a variety of tasks, including investments that are designed to counter disturbances in the economic balance, to contribute to an equalization of economic differences in the federal territory, or to promote economic growth. Federal grants for investment purposes are program-oriented and directed especially at important investment initiatives that are considered essential by the federal government but that probably could not be completed without federal assistance. The federal government may not itself assume responsibility for the program; it and all costs that follow after completion remain the responsibility of the *Land* or local government (which may have received federal assistance via the *Land*).

Separate taxes, shared or common taxes, and federal grants to the *Länder* are all a part of what is called in Germany "vertical fiscal (or tax) equalization." In order to provide a more equitable distribution of tax revenues than vertical equalization alone can produce, a "horizontal fiscal equalization" among the *Länder* and municipalities has been added as an important feature of the *Land* and local tax systems. This virtually uniform tax system does not produce the differences among the *Länder* that are found among the U.S. states, and the systems of vertical and horizontal tax equalization are designed to assist the *Länder* still further in providing something approaching "uniform living conditions."

The first goal of the fiscal equalization procedures among the *Länder* is to increase the tax need indicator of those with deficits to 92 percent of the average for all of the *Länder*. The remaining deficit of 8 percent is supplemented only up to 37.5 percent. This brings the revenues of *Länder* with deficits up to at least 95 percent of the average tax revenue for all *Länder*. Those with above-average revenues may retain their surpluses up to 102 percent; thereafter, 70 percent of the surplus between 102 and 110 percent and all of the surplus above 110 percent goes to the equalization fund.[6]

Although the German system of vertical and horizontal fiscal equalization has had the intended effect of dramatically diminishing fiscal disparities among the *Länder,* it has not been without cost. Part of that cost has been in the centralizing effects of the system and in the controversies it has led to among the *Länder* (Bulmer 1991, 108–109). Provisions concerning "uniform living conditions," which are found in the Basic Law in Article 72, Para. 2 (3) and Article 106, Para. 3 (2), and underlined by Article 104a, Para. 4, have encouraged the poorer *Länder* in particular to demand sizable federal grants for their activities and investments as well as more support from the richer *Länder*. This frees them from assuming responsibility for any higher taxes or lost revenue. Some critics have argued that a price has also been paid in the equalization system's discouragement of cost-efficient administration by both poor and rich *Länder* (Tretner 1991). In any case the receiving *Länder* become more dependent on outside sources, which weakens self-initiative, fiscal responsibility, and therefore the federal system.

In 1988 the revenues shared by the Länder reached DM 3.4 billion. Federal grants to the poorer *Länder* contributed another DM 2.5 billion. Baden-Württemberg was the main contributor to the equalization funds (DM 2 billion). Only Hesse and Hamburg made more modest contributions. Lower Saxony was the main recipient.

For more than a decade there has been increasing reference to a North-South division in the FRG, with the northern Länder suffering a relative or even real economic decline in comparison to those in the south. The problems associated with coal, steel, and shipbuilding in the northern rustbelt industrial regions have led to increasing expenditures for social programs, especially public assistance payments that are granted by the municipalities to those whose unemployment benefits have expired, thus placing a great burden on the municipalities and, indirectly, the *Länder*. The unequal burdens carried by the poorer, mostly northern *Länder* have resulted in increasing demands for more money from the equalization funds and for more federal grants. The richer *Länder* and the federal government have not been eager to provide additional funds. After long discussions, the federal government and a majority of the *Länder* agreed to a compromise: a new law designed to equalize the different capacities of the *Länder* (*Strukturhilfegesetz*). This law, which went into effect in January 1989, allocated an additional DM 2.45 billion annually to the weaker *Länder* for important investments. This law did not end the controversy among the *Länder* or between them and the federal government, in part because the law's provisions clearly favored what were then CDU-governed *Länder*. Four *Land* governments challenged the law in the Federal Constitutional Court, which had overturned the previous fiscal equalization system once before in 1986.

Though it was clear even before the unification of Germany on October 3, 1990, that the system of fiscal equalization needed reform, a political solution did not seem to be in sight. With unification approaching suddenly and unexpectedly, the situation changed dramatically.[7] Unless a temporary separate regulation for the five new *Länder* could be found, the former West German fiscal equalization system would be overwhelmed. Equalization funds would rise from DM 3.5 billion to DM 20 billion. All of the West German *Länder*, with the exception of Bremen and perhaps the Saarland, would become paying *Länder*, and they would all have to give up their supplementary federal grants. Because this scenario was unacceptable to the old *Länder*, provisions were made for a special set of arrangements for the new *Länder* in the Unification Treaty that was signed on August 31, 1990. In May the old *Länder* and the federal government had agreed to share the projected East German deficit on the basis of the ratio of one-third old *Länder*, one-third federal government, and one-third East German *Länder*. The West German share was set at DM 115 billion through 1994, to be paid through a specially created "Fund for German Unity." Twenty billion Deutsche Marks were to be raised by the federal government from savings gained from costs once attributed to the division of Germany (e.g., aid to West Berlin, aid to border regions). The rest was to be divided between the federal and *Land* governments and raised by borrowing. This would leave the old *Länder* with bills of DM 47.5 billion.

The Fund for German Unity was established by the old *Länder* as compensation for excluding the new *Länder* until January 1, 1995, from the vertical and horizontal fiscal equalization schemes provided by the Basic

Law. Special provisions were also made for sharing the VAT. Thus separate regions were created, with the old *Länder* receiving their regular share of the VAT in the former western areas, the new *Länder* receiving 55 percent of the West German average in 1991, 60 percent in 1992, 65 percent in 1993, and 70 percent in 1994. According to some experts, this provision was clearly at odds with the intent of the law, which was designed to have the *Länder* share in the general revenues.

Certain corrections were made in February 1991. Experience soon showed these arrangements to be completely unsatisfactory. The new *Länder* received their full share of VAT funds as of January 1991, although some division between East and West was retained. The federal government also gave up the 15 percent of the German unity funds that it had intended to use for central purposes. These changes increased aid to the new *Länder* by an additional DM 10 billion in 1991 and an additional DM 31 billion by 1994. Another special fund allocated DM 12 billion to the East in 1991 and 1992 for investments and work programs. In spite of earlier assurances by Helmut Kohl that taxes would not be increased to finance unification, certain taxes were raised in 1991 after it became clear that unification would cost more than anticipated. These tax increases were to provide an additional DM 46 billion to the East.

In addition to these measures, serious partisan controversy emerged toward the end of 1991 concerning an increase in the VAT from 14 to 15 percent and an increase in the *Land* share in the VAT revenues from 35 to 37 percent. The proposal passed in the Bundestag, but the SPD threatened to use its new majority in the Bundesrat to defeat the measure. The only *Land* in the East governed by the SPD, Brandenburg, deserted the national party, however, and voted with the Bonn government coalition parties in February 1992 to uphold the change. Consequently the new *Länder* will receive DM 23.4 billion in 1993 and 1994 from this change, and they will benefit as well from a 31-billion-Deutsche-Mark-increase in the Fund for German Unity between 1992 and 1994 (BNA 1992, 172).

Taken together, various transfers to the East amount to very large sums indeed, and such large transfers will continue in the coming years. In 1991 they amounted to DM 153 billion (almost $100 billion). The federal government, the Fund for German Unity, and the *Treuhandanstalt,* which is responsible for privatizing the approximately 8,500 businesses in East Germany, contributed DM 128 billion, the Federal Labor Office DM 19 billion, and various West German *Länder* and municipalities DM 6 billion. About 62 percent of these funds were spent for various social measures (unemployment compensation, subsidized wages), and about 38 percent for investments (*Bundestag Report,* October 12, 1991, 12).

In the meantime widespread dissatisfaction and pessimism in the East have resulted from high unemployment and underemployment, the relentless closing down or shrinking of whole industrial branches, and a feeling that the East Germans are misunderstood by their often arrogant and contemptuous "big brother" in the West. The expected rush by West Germans and other Westerners to invest in the East has not materialized as hoped: a largely neglected and decaying infrastructure (highways and roads, railways, telephone systems), outmoded industrial equipment, the collapse of markets in Eastern Europe, catastrophic environmental pollution, inadequate and decaying housing, continued uncertainties regarding property ownership, and other serious deficiencies, in some cases not recognized or anticipated sufficiently in the West before unification, have too often discouraged would-be investors. A Bundesbank report published in March 1992 noted that although the East had 20 percent of the population, it produced only 3.5 percent of the German GDP. In spite of the massive investments now taking place and planned for the near future, some observers now suggest that with luck the East Germans may produce goods and services at 55 percent of the per capita rate in the West by the end of the century (Christ 1992, 7–8). Others have suggested that the East is about forty years behind the West in economic development (Julitz 1992, 15).

Given the economic conditions in the East and the realization by the old *Länder* that admitting the new *Länder* to the West German system of fiscal equalization would have devastating consequences for them, it seems safe to predict that the federal government and *Länder* will have to devise a new system before 1995, when the new *Länder* are now scheduled to join the equalization system as regular members. This will probably result in a growing dependence of the poorer *Länder* (including all five of the new *Länder*) on the federal government and a weakening of German federalism. At least one prominent German political scientist has suggested that it would be better to create one *Land*—Prussia-Saxony—to represent East German interests, because it is doubtful that the five new *Länder* can exist economically and administratively without becoming overly dependent on the federal government (Lehmbruch 1990, 480–481). The contradiction or at least tension between the demand for "uniform living conditions" on the one hand and a strong federal system on the other hand has become more apparent than ever (Lehmbruch 1990, 479; Blumer 1991, 112). This has led one financial expert to urge elimination of the fiscal equalization system altogether, to grant the *Länder* autonomous taxing powers, and to accept—as people do in the United States—the resulting differences that will develop among the *Länder* in their per capita revenues (Tretner 1991; Grunenberg 1992).

Constitutional Reform

This discussion of fiscal equalization leads to a third major challenge facing the *Länder*: constitutional reform. This will surely include revision of the Basic Law's provisions regarding fiscal relations among the *Länder* on the one hand, and between them and the federal government on the other hand. Article 7 of the Unification Treaty regulates the finances of the new *Länder* and their local governments until January 1, 1995, when the tax provisions of the Basic Law will be made applicable to the East. Few people believe, however, that this will occur, for reasons presented in the preceding section. The five new *Länder* will still have such high fiscal needs in 1995 that meeting these needs under the current equalization system will simply be unacceptable to the old *Länder*.

Not only will the *Länder* be under pressure to revise the Basic Law's provisions regarding fiscal relationships; they will also have to deal with a large number of other proposals for constitutional reform. Some changes have already occurred as a result of the provisions of Article 4 of the Unification Treaty: Article 23, under which the five new *Länder* joined the Federal Republic, has been repealed. The Preamble of the Basic Law was changed to add the five new *Länder* to the list of *Länder* in Germany and to state that the Basic Law now applies to all Germans. The four largest *Länder,* all located in the West, were given six rather than five votes in the Bundesrat. And, in addition to other changes, Article 146 of the Basic Law was revised to read: "This Basic Law, which applies to the whole German people following the realization of unity and freedom, will lose its validity on the day on which a new constitution goes into effect which has been freely accepted by the German people."[8]

Article 5 of the Unification Treaty "recommends" that the Bundestag and Bundesrat take up the issue of constitutional revision, especially provisions affecting the relationship between the *Länder* and the federal government and the possibility of consolidating Berlin and Brandenburg under conditions that would be exceptions to the normal constitutional requirements. It also suggests that lawmakers consider the issue of adding certain goals of the state (*Staatszielbestimmungen*) to the Basic Law, as well as the question of the application of the revised Article 146 and its framework for a constitutional referendum.

During the debate in the Bundestag in May 1991 concerning these recommendations, it became clear that the governing and opposition parties had different views on how implementation was to proceed. The CDU/CSU-FDP coalition advocated the creation of a constitutional committee with thirty-two members, sixteen each from the Bundestag and Bundesrat. The SPD urged the formation of a much larger constitutional council with 120 members, including not only politicians but also representatives from the sciences, the arts, economics, labor, and other walks of life. These proposals symbolized significant differences over the nature of the changes to be made; that is, whether to effect minor adjustments or a thoroughgoing review. Not surprisingly, the Greens and Bündnis90 called for a "total revision," whereas SPD spokespersons have indicated their commitment to the major points of the Basic Law but also their support for numerous changes. The CDU/CSU-FDP objected to a general review and to participation by persons outside of parliament. The governing parties also rejected the proposal of the SPD to hold a referendum on the revised Basic Law (*Bundestag Report,* May 29, 1991, 2–4).

On January 16, 1992, a constitutional commission composed of thirty-two members of the Bundestag and thirty-two representatives from the Bundesrat (i.e., from the sixteen *Land* parliaments) met to begin deliberations. The commission will have to decide how and where the Basic Law should be amended, and whether the final package should be voted up or down by a popular referendum (*Das Parlament* 1991, 9; *Bundestag Report* 1992, 1–3).

Controversy over constitutional issues had begun in early 1990 with a draft for a new GDR constitution, which, while never getting beyond a brief discussion stage, did receive some attention, especially for certain state goals, which many observers in the West thought were naive and utopian. Later in the spring, a heated debate began among jurists over the issue of how the GDR should join the Federal Republic. Article 23 of the Basic Law provided by far the easiest method, since it merely called for the East to "accede." Article 146, on the other hand, called for a new constitution for the united Germany, to be approved by popular referendum. The new GDR government formed after the elections of March 18 quickly agreed to accession under Article 23, but demands persisted that the Basic Law be amended to include certain state goals and that a popular referendum be held on the revised Basic Law. These demands were encouraged and further promoted by the process of drafting new constitutions in the five new *Länder* in 1991 and 1992.

Article 5 of the Unification Treaty calls for a constitutional commission to consider amendments—including state goals—and the issue of a referendum. In the meantime it has become clear that a number of practical proposals for amendment will have to be considered, concerning such subjects as fiscal equalization, federal-*Land* relations, EC-federal-*Land* relations, asylum-seekers and refugees, the right of foreign residents to vote in local elections, abortion rights, plant lockouts in labor-management disputes, the role of German military forces in international peacekeeping actions, a revision of the provisions concerning parliamentary dissolution, and so on. There is also a demand from the SPD, Greens, and PDS for state goals such as the right to employment, the right to living quarters, and the right to a clean environment. They have also urged that referenda be introduced for a variety of questions, and that the revised Basic Law be approved by referendum. The CDU and FDP have indicated support for a provision concerning environmental protection, but there is no agreement on the wording of such an amendment. It should be noted that amendments require a two-thirds vote of both the Bundestag and the Bundesrat, which means that only those proposals that receive the approval of the two large parties, CDU/CSU and SPD, will have a chance to succeed.[9]

The *Länder* and the European Community

As indicated above, one of the issues the constitutional commission will consider is the relationship between the *Länder,* the federal government, and the European Community. One of the most important issues in this regard is Article 24 of the Basic Law, Paragraph 1 of which states that "the Federation may by legislation transfer sovereign powers to inter-governmental institutions." This means that the federal government can transfer not only its own but also *Land* powers to the EC without the approval of the *Länder,* in spite of Article 79, which guarantees federalism in Germany. In addition, Article 235 of the EC treaty grants "implied powers" to the EC, including education, broadcasting, and media, that is, powers exercised by the *Länder*. Because of the growing influence of the EC in European policymaking in general, the *Länder* fear increasing marginalization.[10]

The *Länder* have been concerned about the effect of the European Community on their autonomy from the beginning, and initial efforts by the Bundesrat to protect *Land* interests proved ineffective (Nass 1989, 175–176). In 1979 the chancellor and the *Land* prime ministers agreed to improve communications regarding projects of the EC Commission and Council of Ministers. The individual *Länder* could present views from which the federal government could deviate only for compelling reasons, if the matter concerned the powers of the *Länder*. The federal government agreed to include two representatives from the *Länder* in negotiations on such matters if possible. But this agreement did not have the desired results, either (Nass 1989, 177).

When parliamentary deliberations on the Single European Act (SEA) took place in 1986, a heated debate led to a disappointment for the *Länder*: The Bundesrat, not the *Länder,* was given the right to express its views to the federal government before the government made a decision on EC matters that affect *Land* interests. The federal government may deviate from the Bundesrat views only for "unavoidable" reasons (Nass 1989, 178; Hrbek 1991, 94–95). To help anticipate issues that need to be raised in the Bundesrat and to keep informed generally about EC matters, the *Länder* opened their own information offices in Brussels (Hrbek 1991, 96–97).

It should be noted that the *Land* governments, not the *Land* parliaments, participate in the Bundesrat deliberations. These parliaments have requested that in some cases their governments inform them of their plans before going to the Bundesrat to express a view on EC matters. However, it is the *Land* government that decides on the vote in the Bundesrat, and the *Land* government is not bound by any decision of the *Land* parliament. The

Bundesrat decides on the basis of majority rule, which means that a particular *Land* government can be outvoted. In addition, the federal government is not bound by the decisions of the Bundesrat. Finally, the EC Council of Ministers may also take a majority decision against the Federal Republic, or a situation may arise in which the federal government will not obtain unanimous approval from the Council of Ministers for the policy line the Bundesrat supported (Nass 1989, 98–99).

The end result is that the political situation of the *Länder* is not very strong. The FRG, not the *Länder,* is a member of the EC, and only the member nations participate in the Council of Ministers and the EC Commission. The *Länder* execute European law, of course, as they do federal law. But in the latter case they do so on their own responsibility and influence the legislative process in the Bundesrat. In contrast, the Council of Ministers can assign to the EC Commission the task of executing European law "even in those cases in which the German federal government would not be able to establish an executive agency due to the administrative powers of the *Länder*" (Nass 1989, 181; Hrbek 1991, 98–99). There are also inherent limits on the degree of *Land* participation. The federal government cannot allow a *Land* prime minister to represent Germany in EC councils. Thus *Land* participation is limited in the final analysis to the national decisionmaking process (Nass 1989, 182–183).

On October 17, 1991, a working group of the Bundesrat Commission on Constitutional Reform urged that the Bundesrat be given a stronger role in the integration process of Germany into the EC. The *Länder* agreed to propose amendments that would change Article 24 of the Basic Law: by providing for participation of the *Länder* in the decisionmaking of the federal government (when it engages in intergovernmental decisionmaking that affects the *Länder* directly) and by ensuring that the *Länder* could send their own delegations to intergovernmental institutions to represent their interests. The commission also proposed an amendment to Article 36 that would ensure appropriate consideration for the *Länder* when siting decisions are made for new federal, European, and international agencies (*Das Parlament* 1991, 11).

Another dimension of the EC-federal-*Land* relationship is the strong interest of the *Länder* in the regionalization of Europe (Burgess and Greß, n.d.). In October 1987 the *Land* prime ministers agreed to "Ten Munich Theses on Policies Regarding Europe," which included the goal of a federal Europe that protected the cultural, social, economic, and other peculiarities of member states and that encouraged citizens to participate. The most important theses were subsidiarity, that is, the idea that local or regional responsibility for policy issues should be passed on to national or European levels only when effective solutions require action by higher levels; "federalism instead of centralization"; and "protection of the educational and cultural autonomy of the *Länder*" (Borchmann 1991, 340–341).

Following the meeting in Munich, the *Länder* have reemphasized these concerns. In June 1990, shortly before the semiannual meeting of the European Council in Dublin, the Bundesrat made a number of proposals concerning the importance of regions. In August the Bundesrat agreed to a resolution containing four demands: (1) to anchor the subsidiarity principle by treaty; (2) to amend treaty provisions to include in meetings of the Council of Ministers a second representative from *Länder* or regions when policies falling under their responsibilities are on the agenda; (3) to provide by treaty for a "regional organ" consisting of 152 delegates from the various regions and *Länder* of Europe with the right of consultation and of appeal to the European Court of Justice; and (4) to grant the *Länder* and regions the right to bring cases before the European Court of Justice.

In November 1990, in one of the first meetings of the Bundesrat with the new *Länder* governments, a resolution was passed that demanded that European political union incorporate three levels, to be confirmed by treaty: the European level, for dealing with problems that transcend national borders; the level of the nation-state; and the regional level. These demands and the ones made in August were repeated in December 1990 (Borchmann 1991, 341–342).

Recognizing that Germany is the only federation in the EC at this time, the *Land* governments want to drum up support from regions in other parts of Europe in order to have their concerns taken seriously by other EC member states. They have looked especially at regions in Spain, Belgium, and Italy as potential allies, and, of course, they can expect help if and when Austria and Switzerland join the EC. As early as October 1989 Bavaria invited leaders from thirty-six regions in nine member states to a conference in Munich on "Europe of the Regions." A resolution was passed calling for a pluralistic Europe in which regions and regional associations would be guaranteed certain rights. A second conference with the same title was held in Brussels in April 1990, and it was attended by representatives of twenty-seven *Länder,* regions, and autonomous organizations located in seven EC member states and Austria, Switzerland, and Yugoslavia. The second conference confirmed the resolutions of the German *Länder* concerning the protection of regional rights and the clear division of Europe into three levels. A third conference took place in Italy in October 1990 with similar results. The four demands made by the Bundesrat were accepted on December 5, 1990, by the more than 100-member Assembly of the Regions of Europe in Strasbourg (Borchmann 1991, 343–344).

To avoid having to repeat the charges made by the *Länder* that the federal government had not included them in the negotiations leading to the Single European Act, the Bundesrat insisted in 1990 in several resolutions that the *Länder* be consulted by the federal government regarding its position on European union and that they be represented in upcoming discussions in the European Council of Ministers on achieving this goal. At first the German federal government was reluctant to accept the demand for a regional "third level" in the EC. But the federal and *Land* governments did agree on a proposal regarding subsidiarity and, after some delay, on a common position regarding education and the establishment of a regional committee. They were unable to agree, however, on participation of the *Länder* in meetings of the EC Council of Ministers and on the right of the *Länder* to bring cases before the European Court on the grounds that these issues fell under the federal responsibility for foreign affairs (Borchmann 1991, 343–344).

For the European negotiations concerned with political union, the *Länder* pushed for two representatives in the German delegation from Baden-Württemberg and North Rhine–Westphalia; for the meetings concerned with economic and currency union, they recommended representatives from Hamburg and Bavaria. In spite of some initial problems, the federal government acceded to the request from the *Länder* and included representatives from the four *Länder* at the December 1990 meeting of the European Council of Ministers in Rome.

After the Rome meeting there was little conflict between the federal government and the *Länder* over participation of the latter in EC negotiations. In December 1990 the conference of *Land* prime ministers organized a European Commission consisting of European experts in the *Land* prime ministers' offices. These experts met with the *Land* representatives participating in the negotiations regarding political union and economic and currency union, respectively, and subsequently worked out positions to present to the federal government, in part with the participation of federal bureaucrats. However, the federal government remained adamant in its opposition to *Land* participation in Council of Minister meetings and in bringing cases before the European Court (Borchmann 1991, 345–346).

At the European Council meeting in Maastricht on December 9–10, 1991, some of the goals—though in modest form—were realized. The principle of subsidiarity was included in the agreement, which could affect to some extent the centralizing tendencies in the EC, as was the creation of a 189-member regional committee in which Germany, like France, Italy, and Great Britain, will receive twenty-four seats (Borchmann 1991, 345–346). Chancellor Helmut Kohl praised these two achievements in his speech before the Bundestag on December 13 (*Das Parlament* 1991, 3; *Europa Archiv* 1992, 114), but an opposition spokesman for the *Länder* noted that although the principle of subsidiarity and a regional committee were included in the Maastricht agreement, it remained to be seen what this would mean in future practice. He also pointed to the successful Belgian— not German—proposal to include in Council of Minister meetings representatives of *Länder* and regions when their interests are directly involved (for example, education, culture, science, and electronic media). Of course, the effect of this provision will depend in part on member-state legislation and implementation (*Das Parlament* 1991, 8). The demand that the regions be given the right to sue in the European Court of Justice was not accepted at Maastricht.

In the meantime the prime ministers of the *Länder* reviewed the Maastricht Treaty and demanded changes regarding both the political union and the economic and currency union. They believed that the treaties gave the EC too much power to interfere in their affairs. They were disappointed that the European Parliament was not granted more power than it was, and they insisted that the new German *Länder* receive their eighteen parliamentary seats by the end of 1992 rather than later. The *Länder* wanted to participate in EC negotiations on financing for the poorer regions of Europe, and they wanted to see federalism strengthened in the German Basic Law in order to compensate the *Länder* for losses in the EC treaties. They assumed that the *Länder* would participate in the decision based on the Maastricht Treaty to extend voting rights for local government elections to all citizens of EC member states living in the locality. They also insisted on a revision of Article 24, as noted above, so that the Bundesrat must consent to the transfer of any sovereign rights to intergovernmental organizations. Several other demands concerning amendments to the Basic Law were made as well. The *Länder* also agreed to negotiate with the federal government concerning their representation in the new regional committee of the EC.

Conclusion

Federalism is a well-established feature of the political system of the Federal Republic, and it is protected in perpetuity by Article 79 of the Basic Law. Federalism was the subject or a major focus of attention in numerous symposia,[11] books,[12] and special issues of journals that celebrated the first forty years of the Basic Law.[13] Ironically, federalism and the Basic Law now both seem threatened following the long-sought unification of Germany. These threats are not so direct or immediate as to raise serious questions about the future existence of either. It is clear that federalism will remain a feature of the German political system, and the current controversy over amending the Basic Law will not change in any significant way the general institutional outline or functioning of the previous political system.

Nevertheless, German federalism, about the future of which there was much discussion in Germany even before the fall of the Wall, is now being blown in a number of directions by the winds of dramatic change in Germany and Europe. It is not clear at this time how long these winds will blow, what their effects will be, or how lasting the effects will be. There can be little doubt, however, that federalism in Germany will be a major topic of discussion in the current decade, and that by the year 2000 a different federal order will have evolved.

Notes

1. For two recent publications in English, see the special issue of *Publius* 19, 4: Fall 1989; also Jeffery and Savigear 1991.

2. See, for example, *Frankfurter Allgemeine Zeitung,* March 3, 1990, 1; March 21, 1990, 4; and April 21, 1990, 6; also German Information Center, Deutschland Nachrichten, January 10, 1992, .7.

3. See, for example, Ulrich Penski (1991), "Die Vereinigung beider deutscher Staaten als Problem und Herausforderung für das föderalistische System in Deutschland," in Arthur B. Gunlicks and Rüdiger Voigt (eds.), *Föderalismus in der Bewährungsprobe: Die Bundesrepublik Deutschland in den 90er Jahren* (Bochum: Universitätsverlag Brockmeyer), 265–271; for the case in favor of *Neugliederung* in English, see Uwe Lombardy (1991), "Into the 1990s: Federalism and German Unification," in Charlie Jeffery and Peter Savigear (eds.), *German Federalism Today* (New York: St. Martin's Press), 144–147.

4. For a very pessimistic assessment of the financial condition of the new federal order in Germany, see Nina Grunenberg, "Deutsches Muster ohne Wert?" in *Die Zeit,* North American Edition, March 20, 1992, 3.

5. The most recent discussion of German public finances in English is Rüdiger Voigt (1989), "Financing the German Federal System in the 1980s," in *Publius* 19, 4:99–113. See also Arthur B. Gunlicks (1986), *Local Government in the German Federal System* (Durham: Duke University Press), Chapter 7; and Arthur B. Gunlicks (1986), "Financing Local Governments in the German Federal System," in J. Edwin Benton and David R. Morgan (eds.), *Intergovernmental Relations and Public Policy* (New York: Greenwood Press), 77–92.

6. For details in English, see Hans Zimmermann (1981), *Studies in Comparative Federalism: West Germany* (Washington, DC: Advisory Commission on Intergovernmental Relations), 35–38.

7. The following discussion is based on Wolfgang Renzsch (1991), *Finanzverfassung und Finanzausgleich* (Bonn: Verlag J.H.W. Dietz Nachf.), 274–281.

8. The text of the Unification Treaty of August 31, 1990, can be found in *Europa Archiv,* October 25, 1990, D515–D536.

9. For a discussion of the numerous legal and political questions raised by the issue of constitutional revision, see Dieter Blumenwitz, "Wie offen ist die Verfassungsfrage nach der Herstellung der staatlichen Einheit Deutschlands?"; Ulrich K. Preuss, "Die Chance der Verfassunggebung"; and Peter Badura, "Staatsaufgaben und Teilhaberechte als Gegenstand der Verfassungspolitik." All in *Aus Politik und Zeitgeschichte,* B49/91; see also Chapter 7 in this volume.

10. Michael Burgess and Franz Greß, "German Unity and European Union: Federalism Repulsed or Revitalized?" in Michael Burgess and Franz Greß (eds.), *Regional Politics and Policy* (forthcoming); for a list of policy areas in which the *Länder* see EC interference, see Rudolf Hrbek (1991), "German Federalism and the Challenge of European Integration," in Charlie Jeffery and Peter Savigear (eds.), *German Federalism Today* (New York: St. Martin's Press), 86–87.

11. For example, "Federal Republic of Germany—40 Years of the Basic

Law—Experience and Prospects," sponsored by the American Institute for Contemporary German Studies and the Dräger Foundation, Washington, D.C., October 23–25, 1989.
    12. For example, see Peter H. Merkl (ed.) (1989), *The Federal Republic of Germany at Forty* (New York: New York University Press).
    13. For example, see Arthur B. Gunlicks (ed.) (1989), "Federalism and Intergovernmental Relations in West Germany: Fortieth Year Appraisal." Special Issue of *Publius: The Journal of Federalism* 19, 4.

References

Badura, Peter. 1991. "Staatsaufgaben und Teilberechte als Gegenstand der Verfassungspolitik." *Aus Politik und Zeitgeschichte,* November 29, 1991.

Benton, J. Edwin, and David R. Morgan (eds.). 1986. *Intergovernmental Relations and Public Policy.* New York: Greenwood Press.

Blaschke, Karlheinz. 1990. "Alte Länder—Neue Länder: Zur territorialen Neugliederung der DDR." *Aus Politik und Zeitgeschichte,* June 29, 1990.

Blumenwitz, Dieter. 1991. "Wie offen ist die Verfassunsfrage nach der Herstellung der staatlichen Einheit Deutschlands?" *Aus Politik und Zeitgeschichte,* November 29, 1991.

Bulmer, Simon. 1991. "Efficiency, Democracy, and West German Federalism: A Critical Analysis." In Charlie Jeffery and Peter Sanigear (eds.), *German Federalism Today.* New York: St. Martins Press.

Bundesnachrichtenauf. 1992. *Eastern Europe Reporter* 2, 5:172.

Borchmann, Michael. 1991. "Doppelter Föderalismus in Europa: Die Forderung der deutschen Länder zur Politischen Union." *Europa Archiv* 46, 11:340–341.

Bundestag Report. 1991. May 29, 1991, 2–4.

———. 1991. October 12, 1991, 12.

Burgess, Michael, and Franz Greß. *Regional Politics and Policy.* (Forthcoming).

Christ, Peter. 1992. "Der Osten schreibt rot." *Die Zeit,* March 6, 1992, 7–8.

Ernst Kommision. 1973. *Bericht der Sachverständigenkommision für die Neugliederung der Bundesgebietes.*

Grunenberg, Nina. 1992. "Deutsches Muster ohne Wert?" *Die Zeit,* March 20, 1992, 3.

Gunlicks, Arthur. 1981. *Local Government Reform and Reorganization: An International Perspective.* Port Washington: Kennikat Press.

———. 1986. *Local Government in the German Federal System.* Durham: Duke University Press.

Gunlicks, Arthur, and Rüdiger Voigt (eds.). 1991. *Föderalismus in der Bewährungsprobe: Die Bundesrepublik Deutschland in den 90er Jahren.* Bochum: Universitätsverlag Brockmeyer.

Hrbek, Rudolf. 1991. "German Federalism and the Challenge of European Integration," in Charlie Jeffery and Peter Sarigear (eds.) *German Federalism Today.* New York: St. Martin's Press.

Jeffery, Charlie, and Peter Savigear. 1991. *German Federalism Today.* New York: St. Martin's Press.

Julitz, Lothar. 1992. "Die Investionslücke schließen." *Frankfurter Allgemeine Zeitung,* March 13, 1992, 15.

Lehmbruch, Gerhard. 1990. "Die improvisierte Vereinigung: Die dritte deutsche Republik." *Leviathan* 18, 4: 480–481

"Mchr Mitwirkungsrechte für die Länder." 1991. *Das Parlament.* October 25, 1991, 11.

Merkl, Peter. 1989. *The Federal Republic of Germany at Forty.* New York: New York University Press.

Nass, Klaus Otto. "The Foreign and European Policy of the German Länder" *Publius: The Journal of Federalism* 19, 4 (Fall 1989).

Das Parlament. 1991. December 20–27, 1991, 3.

Preuss, Ulrich K. 1991. "Die Chance der Verfassungsgebung." *Aus Politik und Zeitgeschichte,* November 29, 1991.

Publius: The Journal of Federalism. 1989. Special Issue, 19, 4 (Fall 1989).

Renzsch, Wolfgang. 1991. *Finanzverfassung und Finanzausgleich.* Bonn: Verlag J.H.W. Dietz.

Tretner, Carl-Heinz. 1991. "Vielfalt von Aachen bis Zittau." *Frankfurter Allgemeine Zeitung,* September 28, 1991.

Zimmerman, Hans. 1981. *Studies in Comparative Federalism: West Germany.* Washington, DC: Advisory Commission on Intergovernmental Relations.

Chapter 9

The Reconstruction of Organized Labor and Employer Associations in the Former GDR

M. Donald Hancock

Accompanying the dramatic political events that culminated in German unification in 1990 was the fundamental reconstitution of interest group representation in the former German Democratic Republic. This process entailed, first, the dissolution of socialist trade unions in the GDR and, subsequently, the extension of West German structural patterns and programmatic principles on behalf of both labor and capital to the five new *Bundesländer*. The creation of an all-German system of industrial relations raises important questions concerning the future relations between Germany's principal social partners. Will the West German pattern of largely sustained cooperation between capital and labor persist in the unified nation? Conversely, will the formation of all-German trade unions with an expanded membership that includes some four million ideologically conscious and politically motivated East German workers lead to greater confrontation on the labor market? Or will the unexpectedly high economic costs of unification result in decreased efficacy on the part of organized labor with respect to the collective bargaining process and its role in the political system as a whole?

This chapter seeks to explore these alternatives on the basis of empirical trends during the early 1990s and plausible projections through the remainder of the decade. My thesis is that the future course of industrial relations in the unified Germany will depend primarily on the course of economic development (including employment trends) and strategic political choices by government officials in the decisive years ahead.

Division and Acrimony

The history of the postwar German trade union movement, like that of Germany as a whole, is one of division and long-term ideological acrimony.[1] The capitulation of the Third Reich in May 1945 witnessed the emergence of non-Fascist union organizations at the regional level, as formally sanctioned at the Potsdam conference of July–August 1945, and the largely spontaneous revival of Weimar-era works councils at numerous factories throughout occupied Germany. In subsequent years, as the ideological divide between the two parts of Germany deepened, competing national trade union organizations were established in the form of a Confederation of German Trade Unions (Deutscher Gewerkschaftsbund, or DGB) in the Federal Republic and the Marxist-Leninist Free Confederation of German Trade Unions (Freier Deutscher Gewerkschaftsbund, or FDGB) in the German Democratic Republic.

From their parallel formation during the occupation era until the onset of the mass demonstrations in October 1989 that triggered the ultimate demise of the GDR, the DGB and the FDGB proved mutually antagonistic entities. The DGB was established in 1949 as a unitary organization (*Einheitsgewerkschaft*) that combined previously competing traditions of social-democratic, Catholic, and liberal unionism. From the outset the DGB emerged as a relatively weak peak association; the effective capacity to assert labor demands in day-to-day industrial relations resides primarily in the hands of its largest and strongest unions (notably the Metal Workers' Union, or IG Metall, with 2.7 million members, and the Public Sector Union, Öffentliche Dienste, Transport und Verkehr, or ÖTV, with a membership of nearly 1.3 million largely lower-income salaried employees and blue-collar workers).[2] The DGB itself provides programmatic guidance and supportive research to its member unions (and indirectly to the SPD) through its Economic and Social Science Institute and advises the Federal Government in a variety of formal and informal policy consultative arenas.[3] Similar to the Trade Union Congress (TUC) in the United Kingdom, the DGB plays at most an indirect role in wage negotiations— serving as a conduit for information exchange during wage negotiations rather than as an active partner in the process itself. Instead, the individual trade unions that belong to the DGB bargain over collective wage agreements and other terms of employment with counterpart employer associations in the public and private sectors of industry and services on a regional or *Land* basis.[4]

As key pillars of the pluralist economic and political order that characterized West German society after World War II, the DGB and its member unions played a constructive role in promoting legislative initiatives during the formative years of the Federal Republic's institutionalization and legitimation; this legislation accorded workers extensive legal rights of representation and consultation at both the plant and company levels of economic decisionmaking. Among the key reforms were the Codetermination Act of 1951 (*Mitbestimmungsgesetz*), which established parity representation of workers on the supervisory boards of the iron, coal, and steel industries; the Works Constitution Act of 1952 (*Betriebsverfassungsgesetz*), which defined the consultative rights of elected works councils in plants and accorded workers and salaried employees one-third representation on the boards of West Germany's remaining industries; the Works Constitution Act of 1972 (*Betriebsverfassungsgesetz*), which strengthened the status of works councils and extended consultative rights of workers; and the Codetermination Act of 1976 (*Mitbestimmungsgesetz*), which extended worker representation to near-parity status on the supervisory boards of all limited companies employing more than 2,000 employees.[5] The cumulative effect of these legislative enactments was to provide West German workers extensive opportunities, through their elected representatives, to participate in plant and company decisions affecting personnel matters and social problems (though not "general policy decisions of the company, such as the production and pricing policy" [Berghahn and Karsten 1987, 104]).[6]

In contrast, FDGB officials swiftly consolidated power after 1946 to create a centralized system of party-state control over the GDR's twenty-seven national trade unions and their 9.6 million members (1989).[7] Politically, the FDGB and its member unions functioned as a political-bureaucratic extension of the monopolistic SED in helping control and manage East German industrial production and services. In the process, FDGB unions sought to mobilize and motivate workers on behalf of the socialist cause while providing auxiliary benefits in the form of group vacation outings and other collective activities. To the profound disgruntlement of many trade unionists, the FDGB negotiated wage agreements directly with cabinet ministers and other government functionaries without prior consultation with rank-and-file workers.

The people's revolution of 1989 fundamentally altered the contextual framework of trade unionism in the GDR and set into motion a process of internal renewal that culminated in the dissolution of the FDGB, the reconstitution of East German trade unions along West German lines, and the creation of all-German trade unions. In parallel steps, employer associations were reestablished at the local and regional levels as counterpart organizations to the reconstituted trade unions.

Organizational Renewal

According to the interview responses during a research visit to key East German trade union offices in Berlin in early July 1990,[8] lower-level trade unionists claimed to be among the most vocal critics of the former Honecker regime during the mass protests of October/November 1989. Their anger was directed not only at the practice of centralized wage negotiations, but also at the institutional and ideological rigidity of the FDGB's Stalinist leadership. Following Erich Honecker's forced resignation as head-of-government and party chief in October 1989—and especially the

SED/PDS's precipitous fall from power in the aftermath of the March 18, 1990, election—a counter-elite of union activists replaced the previous leaders in a sweeping reform of the East German trade union movement.[9] Larger unions reorganized as equivalent organizations to West German industrial unions: the Metal Workers' Union (IG Metall), the Chemical and Paper Workers' Union (IG Chemie, Papier, Keramik), the Construction Union (IG Bau, Steine, Erden), and the Mining and Energy Union (IG Bergbau und Energie), among others. Service-oriented unions were also established according to West German precedents, among them the Public Sector Union and the Teachers' Union (Gewerkschaft Unterricht und Erziehung). Temporarily, some unions that had no West German counterparts, such as the Union of Scientific Workers (Gewerkschaft Wissenschaft), retained an autonomous existence until their subsequent dissolution during the winter of 1990 and the absorption of their members into larger all-German organizations.

The FDGB itself effectively ceased to function in May 1990 when it was displaced by a *Sprecherrat* (speakers' council) made up of the chairmen of the various East German unions. It was formally dissolved at a special East German trade union congress convened in Berlin in September 1990. The official justification for this move, according to an FDGB spokesman, was that the "union members' loss of confidence in the organization and the need for a break with the past necessitated the disbanding of the organization."[10]

An immediate imperative for reconstituting East German trade unions along democratic lines was the need to establish new structures and recruit a new cadre of leaders to represent the material and social interests of workers under increasingly chaotic economic conditions in the wake of the economic and monetary union on July 2, 1990. East Germany's economic opening to the West, which began incrementally during the fall of 1989 and abruptly accelerated during the summer of 1990, brought a surge of unemployment caused by the inability of East German firms to compete effectively with Western goods and agricultural produce. In early August 1990, the number of unemployed workers in the GDR had climbed to 1.8 million (out of a work force of 9.2 million), and by the end of the year it had risen to nearly 2 million. A simultaneous crisis affecting the GDR's 3,500 agricultural cooperatives, half of which were reportedly near collapse in late August, only exacerbated the acute adaptation problems in the industrial sector of the new federal states.

Thus, during the summer and fall of 1990 the new East German union leadership needed to preserve jobs while seeking equitable wage settlements in response to inflationary increases in the cost of food and consumer goods. To these ends, unions—led by IG Metall—pursued a dual strategy of negotiations and selective strikes (the latter to dramatize their claims publicly and to mobilize rank-and-file support for the revitalized union movement). A preliminary problem confronting the unions was that ministerial officials—whose predecessors had unhesitatingly concluded wage agreements with the now-defunct FDGB—were reluctant to conclude agreement on behalf of what was obviously a caretaker government. Interim wage settlements were nonetheless reached, then reviewed, and, in some cases, renegotiated following Germany's political unification on October 3, 1990. Although union officials were unable to prevent a continuing rise in unemployment throughout the summer and early fall, they did succeed in mitigating some of its effects by pressing their public and private negotiating partners to increase the number of part-time jobs (*Kurzarbeit*) in industry.

Simultaneously, the East German trade union movement faced the formidable task of adapting institutionally and programmatically to the West German pattern. The principal initiative to achieve structural equivalence appears to have come from the East German side.[11] DGB officials proved singularly reticent in instigating or coordinating a grand strategy of union integration from their headquarters in Düsseldorf, preferring instead to encourage individual unions within their umbrella embrace to respond to East German requests for organizational assistance. The most visible action by the DGB to establish a presence of its own in the GDR was to allocate DM 15.5 million to open regional offices during the summer of 1990 in Erfurt and Magdeburg. Accordingly, institutional reconstitution occurred on a piecemeal and union-specific basis from March 1990 onward, typically with financial and personnel assistance from leading West German unions such as IG Metall and ÖTV. Initially, this took the form of structural reorganization on a local and regional basis and joint meetings of executive committee members representing labor in the two parts of Germany. Subsequently, the newly formed East German unions merged with their West German counterparts during the fall and winter of 1990 by integrating institutions and members.

The Restoration of Employer Associations

While trade unions reconstituted to correspond to existing structures in the Federal Republic, representatives of East German industry and services began to establish regional industrial and employer associations to represent their own economic interests in March 1990. In contrast to organized labor, spokesmen for private ownership and capital began from a relative tabula rasa. Powerful national employer organizations had emerged after the turn of the century in the form of the Central Association of German Industry (Centralverband der Deutschen Industrie), the Association of German Employers (Vereinigung Deutscher Arbeitgeberverbände), and the National Association of German Industry (Reichsverband der Deutschen

Industrie). During the imperial and Weimar eras, they had engaged Germany's trade unions in alternately confrontational and constructive dialogue with respect to collective bargaining rights and labor's efforts to promote economic democratization on the basis of works councils that were constitutionally sanctioned in 1920. Early during the National Socialist interregnum, the employer associations merged to form the Reichsstand der Deutschen Industrie (RDD).

Allied occupation officials ordered the RDD's dissolution at the end of World War II, and successor associations were quickly established in western Germany in the form of the German Federation of Industry (Bundesverband der Deutschen Industrie, or BDI) and the Federal Association of German Employers (Bundesvereinigung der Deutschen Arbeitgeberverbände, or BDA).[12] No equivalent organizations were sanctioned in the GDR, given the SED's collectivization of most means of production, distribution, and services. Hence, with the SED regime's impending demise and the first moves toward privatization in early 1990, East German employers were compelled to act in an institutional vacuum.

An initial step toward the reintroduction of employer groups in the GDR was the creation of an Industrial Forum (Industrieforum) on March 9, 1990, which was composed of the top management of East Germany's industrial conglomerates (*Kombinate*). When it quickly became apparent that members of the Industrial Forum were more interested in narrow economic interests than broader sociopolitical issues, BDA officials in the West intervened to assist East German managers in the formation "from the top down" of local- and state-level associations (*Fachverbände* and *Landesvereinigungen,* respectively) equivalent to those in the Federal Republic. Among the first to be established was Metall, with regional headquarters in Thuringia. Its executive officers promptly entered into a personal union with their West German counterparts in the neighboring state of Hesse. In rapid order, employer associations representing chemical industries, construction, printing, commerce, energy, textiles, and other key industrial branches were created.

By early July 1990, twenty-two such associations were either already established or in the process of formation.[13] Simultaneously, five state-level employer associations formed in tandem with the reestablishment of *Länder* governments in Mecklenburg–West Pomerania, Saxony-Anhalt, Thuringia, Saxony, and Brandenburg as a prelude to Germany's political unification in October.

Consequences

The reconstitution of East German trade unions and the reintroduction of employer associations during 1990 proved crucial in the extension of West

German pluralist structures to the former territory of the GDR. Clearly, German unification has involved much more than the economic, social, and political merger of the two German states under the Basic Law of the FRG. It also constitutes an organizational transformation of East German society as a necessary (if insufficient) condition for both the establishment of a functioning all-German system of industrial relations and the long-term social integration of workers and citizens into the new capitalist-democratic order.

An immediate consequence of social and economic unification was the extension of West German labor legislation—including laws affirming "new opportunities for workers' interest representation" (Jürgens, Klinzing, and Turner 1991)—to the five new federal states. Among them are parity (or near-parity) representation of workers on the supervisory boards of larger firms under the terms of the Codetermination Acts of 1951 and 1976 and consultative rights of works councils under the 1952 and 1972 Works Constitution Acts. Although the exercise of these rights has yet to be sufficiently analyzed on the basis of survey research, field interviews, and documentary evidence, East German workers have at least formally achieved the same degree of industrial democracy as their West German colleagues. In light of the denial of participatory opportunities to workers in company decisions under the former SED regime, this is no mean achievement.

Simultaneously, economic and social union has brought the extension of West German laws and practices governing wage agreements to the new *Länder*. The result has been an orderly transition to a national system of sector-wide collective accords, in which East German workers automatically receive a larger percentage of annual wage increases than those accorded their western colleagues to compensate them for their lower incomes when compared with those in the old federal states. (In 1992, East German wage levels averaged approximately 46 percent of those in western Germany, due primarily to lower productivity within the boundaries of the former GDR. Unions and employer associations have pledged to achieve East-West wage convergence by 1994.)

The West German system of industrial democracy and collective bargaining procedures, however, was immediately subjected to unanticipated and severe strains of economic dislocation. The most pressing challenge confronting federal and *Länder* government officials and the principal labor market partners was the wholesale reconstruction of the former East German economy. This has involved a concerted effort to privatize industry, services, and agriculture while maintaining and/or creating as many jobs as possible. The technological obsolescence of most companies in eastern Germany, an inadequate transportation and communications infrastructure, and widespread environmental damage inherited from the East German regime seriously complicate these formidable objectives (see Chapter 10 in this volume).

Privatization of some 12,515 "people-owned firms" (*Volkseigene Betriebe*) was entrusted by the GDR's last government to a newly formed Trust Agency for the People's Property (the *Treuhandanstalt,* or the *Treuhand* as it is popularly known), with headquarters in Berlin. Political authority over the *Treuhand* was transferred after political union to the Federal Ministry of Finance and the Federal Ministry of Economics in Bonn. The *Treuhand* had responsibility for the sale or closure of firms and decisions concerning which companies would remain in operation through government subsidies. For these purposes, the *Treuhand* was initially allocated DM 25 billion from federal funds.

Treuhand executive officials, their veritable army of staff assistants, and outside consultants have struggled valiantly to implement the trust agency's economic mandate—but with decidedly mixed results. On the one hand, the agency successfully disposed of a majority of firms in its care during the first two-and-a-half years of its existence. By the end of November 1992, the *Treuhand* announced that 10,669 previously state-owned enterprises (over 85 percent of the total) had been sold to German or foreign buyers.[14] The remaining 1,846 firms together employed approximately half-a-million workers out of a total work force of over six million.

Yet privatization has extracted enormous individual and social costs, including a surge in unemployment caused by plant closings and the elimination of redundancies in companies confronting economic penetration by West German firms and the loss of traditional export markets in Eastern Europe. In the first year following unification, the East German work force shrank a full 25 percent—from 9.2 million in 1990 to 6.75 million by December 1991. By November 1992, the number of registered unemployed workers rose to over 1.1 million. The latter total—representing 13.5 percent of the work force—is but the tip of the proverbial iceberg, in that 1.7 million workers employed in part-time work, hundreds of thousands engaged in job training or job creation programs, and those who elected early retirement were not numbered among the officially unemployed. In isolated cases, 70 percent or more of workers in single-industry towns or villages were without jobs. Those most severely affected by East Germany's depressed economic conditions are women, who comprised nearly two-thirds of the registered unemployed in June 1992.

East German workers responded to worsening economic conditions with a series of protest strikes and demonstrations throughout the former GDR. In February 1991, some 30,000 employees took to the streets to protest the planned closure of the shipbuilding industry in Rostock. In March, an estimated 100,000 metal workers stopped work to voice their discontent over the threat of increased unemployment and to articulate simultaneous demands for higher wages. Through April 1991, tens of thousands of workers staged demonstrations in Leipzig, Erfurt, Halle, and other cities in response to appeals for direct action by IG Metall, various citizen groups, and Protestant church officials. Overt protests subsided in subsequent months, but latent discontent remained high among both organized and unorganized workers in the face of continued economic uncertainty.

A year later, increased labor militancy spread to western Germany as well. Incensed that a tax increase in 1991 unfairly burdened Germany's industrial and service employees with a disproportionate share of the financial costs of unification, union leaders pressed public and private employers for substantial wage hikes during the winter and spring of 1992. Warning strikes in the banking sector in March presaged a massive walkout of 250,000 public sector workers in late April, which provoked Germany's largest strike in thirty-seven years. The strike ended when employers and the Public Sector Union (ÖTV) agreed on a 5.4 percent average increase in wages (plus a single payment to the lowest-paid and mid-level workers). Following a series of warning strikes in May, a national strike in the metalworking industry was narrowly avoided when IG Metall and employer representatives agreed to a similar 5.4 percent wage hike for a period of twenty months.

Wage demands subsequently moderated through the remainder of the year and into 1993, but a continuing sense of relative economic deprivation in both parts of Germany—among *Ossis* because of increased unemployment and lower wage levels than in the West and among *Wessis* because of the heavy tax burden of unification and a prospective reduction of social services announced by the federal government in November 1992 to help finance a "solidarity aid package" for the new *Länder*—may conceivably lead to further conflicts on the labor market in the years ahead.

Prospects

Thus, an important social consequence of German unification is that worker discontent over wages and the government's fiscal policies has already resulted in a discernible departure from the largely harmonious postwar pattern of industrial relations that had characterized collaborative interaction between organized labor and employers. Paradoxically, a longer-term consequence of increased labor militancy—not in response to militancy per se but to lessen the probability of its recurrence—is increased political efficacy on the part of organized labor. This could occur as federal and *Länder* officials seek to mitigate conflict by enlisting the support and resources of private capital, employer associations, and the DGB and its principal unions in a coordinated effort to rebuild the East German economy. Such efforts—reminiscent of the institutionalization of democratic corporatist policymaking lineages in the Federal Republic from the mid-1960s through the mid-1970s—would signal a shift in national economic management from a social market approach to a more centrally directed, coordinated market approach to investments and job creation programs.[15]

Economic imperatives, however, may determine an alternative industrial relations scenario. A postunification economic slump in western Germany, which commenced in 1992 with a slowdown in the annual economic growth in the old federal states and an accompanying increase in the unemployment rate from 5.4 percent in September 1991 to over 6 percent by the end of January 1992, has imposed formidable constraints on potential union activism. By early 1993, Germany was virtually in a recession, with the nation's leading economic experts projecting an annual growth rate of only 0.5 percent for the year in western Germany and 1 percent for the nation as a whole.[16] An immediate result was a further increase in the unemployment rate to 7.4 percent in January 1993.

Sluggish economic performance in both western and eastern Germany has led both individual firms and IG Metall (e.g., at a new Opel automobile manufacturing plant in the East German city of Eisenach) to negotiate separate local agreements on wages and working conditions outside the framework of sectoral collective bargaining agreements.[17] While such "rogue agreements" on the enterprise level are technically illegal, union officials have felt compelled to quietly go along with them because of their unwillingness "to drive [such] firms out of business. . . ."[18] But if such practices multiply, the result would be a weakening of the capacity of Germany's unions to act as an authoritative institutional instrument of worker representation in the labor market. The result could be a gradual erosion of the Federal Republic's postwar pattern of sectoral collective bargaining.

Thus, Germany's system of industrial relations has entered a new period of flux and uncertain outcomes. Whether conflict, cooperation, or weakened trade unionism will prevail depends on the political vision and determination of the nation's public and private officials in managing Germany's social integration and economic transformation.

Notes

1. Useful accounts of the history and politics of German trade unionism include Helga Grebing (1969), *The History of the German Labour Movement* (London: Oswald Wolff); and especially Andrei S. Markovits (1986), *The Politics of the West German Trade Unions: Strategies of Class and Interest Representation in Growth and Crisis* (New York: Cambridge University Press). See also M. Donald Hancock (1989), "The Ambivalent Insider: The DGB Between Theory and Practice," in Peter H. Merkl (ed.), *Forty Years in West German Politics* (New York: New York University Press).

2. Statistisches Bundesamt (1990), *Statistisches Jahrbuch für die*

Bundesrepublik Deutschland 1990 (Wiesbaden: Statistisches Bundesamt), 699. The membership totals are for December 1990.

3. Unions and employer associations are represented formally on the governing boards of key industrial agencies such as the Federal Office of Employment, located in Nuremberg, and are regularly consulted on pending policy matters by administrative officials representing the federal ministries of labor, economics, and others. Informal contacts exist at multiple levels of government, including the Federal Chancery (Kanzleramt). From 1967 until the summer of 1977, trilateral economic consultations involving government, employer associations, and the DGB were held on a regular basis in the form of "concerted action" *(konzertierte Aktion)*, as mandated by the 1967 Law to Promote Economic Growth and Stability. I recount the rise and fall of concerted action as an institutionalized form of corporatist policymaking in M. Donald Hancock (1989), *West Germany: The Politics of Democratic Corporatism* (Chatham: Chatham House Publishers).

4. An excellent descriptive overview of the DGB, unions, employer associations, and wage bargaining is Volker R. Berghahn and Detlev Karsten (1987), *Industrial Relations in West Germany* (New York: Berg Publishers).

5. The participatory rights of federal civil servants are governed by the Personnel Representation Act of 1955 *(Personalvertretungsgesetz)*, which allows for representation and consultation on lines broadly similar to the works councils. The various state governments have enacted legislation of their own regulating the consultative rights of state-level civil servants.

6. See also Helga Welsh's perceptive assessment of codetermination, with a primary emphasis on the effects of the 1972 Works Constitution Act: Helga Welsh (1991), "Workplace Democracy in Germany," in M. Donald Hancock, John Logue, and Bernt Schiller (eds.), *Managing Modern Capitalism: Industrial Renewal and Workplace Democracy in the United States and Europe* (New York: Praeger).

7. Staatliche Zentralverwaltung für Statistik (1989), *Statistisches Jahrbuch der Deutschen Demokratischen Republik* (Berlin: Staatsverlag der DDR), 41.

8. With the indirect assistance of the DGB and academic colleagues in East Berlin, I visited the GDR headquarters of IG Metall, ÖTV, Gewerkschaft Wissenschaft, and Handel, Banken und Versicherung (Trade, Banks, and Insurance). Prior and subsequent interviews were conducted at the SPD-Ost in Berlin, the central DGB office in Düsseldorf, and the BDI and the BDA in Cologne.

9. An account of early moves toward union reconstitution in 1989 and during the first half of 1990 can be found in Manfred Wilke (1990), "Unification of German Trade Unions: Reorganizing East German Labor," *German Comments: Review of Politics and Culture* 19: 71–78.

10. Quoted in *The Week in Germany,* September 21, 1991.

11. This was the view expressed by interview contacts in both eastern and western Germany during the summer of 1990.

12. A brief discussion of the historical development of employer associations in German can be found in Berghahn and Karsten 1987, 145–169.

13. Bundesvereinigung der Deutschen Arbeitgeberverbände (1990), *Übersicht über die Verbandsgründungen in der DDR* (Cologne: BDA [photocopy]).

14. German Information Center, *The Week in Germany,* January 7, 1993, 4.

15. Conceptual and empirical aspects of contrasting "social market" and "coordinated market" approaches to economic management are presented in chapters dealing with industrial policy in Hancock, Logue, and Schiller 1991.

16. German Information Center, *The Week in Germany,* October 29, 1992, 4.

17. "Germany Labours On," *Economist,* January 23, 1993, 63.

18. Ibid., 64.

References

Berghahn, Volker R., and Detlev Karsten. 1987. *Industrial Relations in West Germany.* New York: Berg Publishers, 1987.

Bundesvereinigung der Deutschen Arbeitgeberverbände. 1990. *Übersicht über die Verbandsgründungen in der DDR.* Cologne: BDA (photocopy).

Grebing, Helga. 1969. *The History of the German Labour Movement.* London: Oswald Wolff.

Hancock, M. Donald. 1989. *West Germany: The Politics of Democratic Corporatism.* Chatham: Chatham House Publishers.

Hancock, M. Donald, John Logue, and Bernt Schiller (eds.). 1991. *Managing Modern Capitalism: Industrial Renewal and Workplace Democracy in the United States and Europe.* Westport, CT: Greenwood-Praeger.

Jürgens, Ulrich, Larissa Klinzing, and Lowel Turner. 1991. "Scrapping the East German Industrial Relations System. Risks and Opportunities in a New Beginning." Paper presented at the Annual Meeting of the American Political Science Association in Washington, DC, September 1991.

Markovits, Andrei S. 1986. *The Politics of the West German Trade Unions: Strategies of Class and Interest Representation in Growth and Crisis.* New York: Cambridge University Press.

Merkl, Peter H. (ed.). 1989. *Forty Years in West German Politics.* New York: New York University Press.

Staatliche Zentralverwaltung für Statistik. 1989. *Statistisches Jahrbuch der Deutschen Demokratischen Republik.* Berlin: Staatsverlag der DDR.

Statistisches Bundesamt. 1990. *Statistisches Jahrbuch für die Bundesrepublik Deutschland 1990.* Wiesbaden: Statistisches Bundesamt.

Wilke, Manfred. 1990. "Unification of German Trade Unions: Reorganizing East German Labor." *German Comments: Review of Politics and Culture* 19: 71–78.

Chapter 10

Coping with the Legacy of East German Environmental Policy

Karl Kaltenthaler

The tragic state of the environment in the five new eastern *Länder* of the Federal Republic of Germany is becoming increasingly evident. Environmental data, hitherto considered state secrets, validate the East German populace's sense of concern. Opinion research in the eastern *Länder* has shown that only one-third of the populace feels healthy.[1] The environmental situation in the GDR played a significant role in the mass flight of its citizens to the West. In fact, East German physicians often encouraged those suffering the effects of environmentally related illness to leave the GDR. Demographic statistics also betray the dangerous nature of the situation. The GDR registered an alarming decline in life expectancy after the mid-1960s (Busch-Lüty 1981, 29). Equally disturbing is the fact that 50 percent of the working populace has suffered from work-related illnesses, such as bronchitis and other respiratory problems (Melzer 1985, 4).

The environmental burden is not distributed equally. The worst problems are endemic to the southern portion of the former GDR. The areas around Leipzig and Dresden are highly industrialized and likewise suffer the worst air pollution. The GDR, as a country, had the dubious honor of having the highest concentration of sulfur dioxide in its air of any country in Europe. This poor air quality was, of course, not limited to the territory of the GDR and was a source of ill health for West Germans as well as other Europeans. The Elbe, Werra, and Weser rivers, all shared by East and West Germany, received up to 80 percent of their pollutants from East German sources.[2]

The most pressing query that arises from the environmental situation in the former GDR is, What caused such an advanced state of environmental damage? The most relevant factors are the East German policymaking framework, a set of ideological principles, economic priorities, and the eastern portion of Germany's indigenous resources. These variables are not of equal importance, but taken together they provide an explanation of the former GDR's environmental problems. As the East German environment was largely a product of economic policy, it is prudent to view the environmental situation as an outcome of policymaking processes. Each of the aforementioned variables will be discussed separately in the sections to follow.

Due to the persistent seriousness and complexity of East Germany's environmental situation, both German states had been in the process of creating the necessary institutions to facilitate inter-German environmental cooperation since the early 1970s. West Germany had a shared concern for the East's environmental problems, not so much out of a sense of national responsibility but because of damage done to its own environment by spillover from the East. Polluted water, flowing into West Germany from rivers shared with the East, has been a perennial source of contention. Every year East German industry dumped some 10,000 tons of poisonous pollutants into the Elbe River, which flowed directly into the FRG.[3] Air pollution was also a source of mutual concern. The East's brown coal-dependent industries produced some of the worst air pollution in the world, a good portion of which subsequently plagued the western portion of Germany. All of these problems have yet to be solved and are now the responsibility of the unified German government.

This chapter will examine why the East German environmental protection measures were so unsuccessful in coping with advanced industrialization and how the subsequent environmental problems of the eastern *Länder* are being dealt with now that Germany is unified. The measures being taken to rectify the dismal state of the East German environment must be viewed in the context of how environmental policy was formulated and implemented in the former GDR. I will argue that East German environmental policy was weakened or made ineffective by the demands of East German economic priorities, the ill-defined responsibilities of policymaking institutions, and a closed policymaking process. The combination of these factors largely explains the causes of the environmental problems in the eastern portion of Germany. The solutions to these environmental problems are found in establishing rational economic policies, replacing ill-defined East German institutions, opening the environmental policy agenda to public scrutiny, and cleaning up the pollution that already exists. But before I address these solutions I will look more closely at the causes of the present problems.

The Ideological Setting

What Marx, Engels, and Lenin had to say about the environment would comprise a very slim volume indeed. Yet the ideological aspects of man's relationship with nature were of great importance in the GDR. East German scholars and policymakers made frequent reference to the difference between a socialist and a capitalist economic system and its consequences for the environment. A detailed set of rationalizations was developed by the East German government to explain away environmental problems in the GDR and to demonstrate the superiority of socialism in coping with environmental problems.

The basic premise of East German critiques of market-based environmental measures pointed to the contradictions in the capitalist economic system. For example, capitalists' endless striving for profit provides no motivation to protect the environment because no profit can be gained from such endeavors (Kosing 1989b, 121). In a socialist society, on the other hand, the lack of class conflict precludes this contradiction between man and nature. Claiming that environmental problems are an expected by-product of advanced industrialization, capitalists try to hide the nature of the environmental crisis they cause (Kosing 1989a, 1,020). The Marxist-Leninist reply is that environmental damage is not the result of industrialization but of system-specific deficiencies.

The means for overcoming environmental problems are found in socialist planning. Planning eliminates the contradictions between man and nature. The superiority of socialism is predicated on its ability to make society function in a unified and contradiction-free manner (Horsch 1989, 2). Socialism provides a unity of action that eliminates those societal forces that cause environmental damage (Kosing 1989b, 119).

Considering the claims for the systemic superiority of socialism, it would seem that the environmental problems that the GDR admitted having would be quite difficult to explain away. Yet an elaborate set of reasons was developed, which once again points toward capitalism as its source.

First, environmental problems were viewed as an inheritance of the old capitalist society because the contradictions inherent in capitalism do not disappear immediately with the adoption of socialism (Raestrup and Weymar 1982, 836). Socialist society must try to cope with this environmental inheritance as it advances toward communism. Thus, environmental problems in the GDR were not to be viewed as products of its socialist system, but as residue from the former bourgeois state (Gruhn 1982, 45).

A second, although less-cited reason, was that the GDR had to use "capitalist-deformed technology" (Raestrup and Weymar 1982, 836). Economic realities forced the GDR to buy much of its technology from the West, and this technology, the GDR ideologues claimed, maximized production regardless of environmental consequences. Capitalist competition leads to the development of such environmentally hazardous technologies because of its constant pursuit of profit (Gruhn 1982, 45).

A third reason for the persistence of environmental problems in the GDR was found in the need to secure "the power of the socialist state." The "imperialist encirclement" of the GDR meant that funds that could have been spent on the environment were diverted to military purposes (Reichelt

1984, 1,011). The competition with capitalism extended to the economic arena, thereby preventing resources from being allocated to environmental concerns (Gruhn 1981, 431). The solution to this problem was to be found in the demise of capitalism. Only when capitalism was gone would the worldwide class struggle cease and the environment become a priority (Kosing 1989a, 1,023).

Despite a rather rigid environmental dogma, the GDR did experience scholarly contention over the Marxist interpretation of several key concepts. One such controversy dealt with the designation of environmental expenditures as "productive" or "unproductive." In short, productive labor contributes to economic growth, whereas unproductive labor either makes no contribution to economic growth or inhibits it (DeBardeleben 1985a, 207). The East German political economist Johann Koehler argued that environmental protection measures were unproductive labor because they distract labor from the production of material goods (Gruhn 1981, 432). The Humboldt University economist Günther Streibel argued that environmental measures were at least partially productive because they may lead to the retrieval of resources. Koehler argued that environmental expenditures were a luxury that the GDR could ill afford. Streibel and more environmentally minded academics posited that environmental expenditures were a positive long-term investment.

A similar argument centered on natural resource pricing. According to Marx, value only results from the addition of labor. Resources are inherently worthless until labor is added. They are viewed as free gifts of nature (DeBardeleben 1985b, 241–242). This view, though dominant, was challenged by scholars who saw the wanton exploitation of resources as a potential source of economic decline in the long run.

One can see that there was by no means anything like a scholarly consensus on environmental issues in the GDR, but a series of questions appear when one examines that debate. How relevant were ideological debates to actual policymaking? Did ideological arguments function merely as rationalizations for policy decisions motivated by other factors? The answers to these questions lie in the patterns of policy choices made by GDR elites.

The Economy Versus the Environment

Upon examination, it becomes clear that economics held a much more important place in terms of national priorities than did environmental protection. The GDR devoted only 0.4 percent of its gross social product (GNP minus services) to environmental matters, compared to the Federal Republic of Germany's 1.07 percent outlay (*Information* 1990, 1).

It is the Soviet-style economic model that provides the best explanation of GDR economic priorities. This economic model placed economic growth as its first priority. Thus, the optimal growth of production was the primary concern for GDR policymakers (Gruhn 1986, 98). This "growth mania," combined with centralized planning, led to extreme pressures on economic units to fulfill ambitious plan targets. Fulfilling the plan left little for environmental concerns from already scarce resources (Raestrup and Weymar 1982, 839). The GDR's impressive rates of yearly economic growth were achieved in part because of a lack of attention to the externalities of the production process. Economic growth through fulfillment of the plan was seen as a means of achieving a living standard comparable to the West's, thus placating the populace, as well as a means of fulfilling certain ideological duties. It was through the development of the productive processes that the Communist society was to be achieved.

The concept of the scientific-technical revolution, which gained popularity in the early 1970s, called for an advanced role for science in all spheres of life, and was naturally welcomed by the growth-oriented GDR elites (McCauley 1979, 137). The quickly advancing sciences of cybernetics and computers were seen as means of achieving greater productive potential and therefore higher rates of growth. The early 1970s saw the GDR leadership strengthen its commitment to high-growth economic policies.

Events in the West in the early 1970s led to what may be considered a serious challenge to the GDR's growth-oriented principles. In 1972 the Club of Rome's report *The Limits to Growth* attacked the notion that neverending economic growth and industrialization would lead to a better life.[4] This study argued that ever-increasing industrialization would have disastrous effects on the environment.

The debate that resulted in the West pertaining to these studies had its counterpart in the East. The official East German response was a sharp dismissal of the Club of Rome argument. The GDR ideologues pointed to the general crisis of capitalism as the cause of mounting environmental problems in the West (Pauke 1985, 209). The limits-to-growth argument did, however, spark a rather heated discussion among GDR scholars. But the acceptance of the premises of the Club of Rome would have entailed the rejection of the ideological orthodoxy. Few were willing to go that far.

The official East German reply to the limits-to-growth argument was that growth was possible without overly negative consequences by means of closed production cycles (Busch-Lüty 1981, 23). Closed-cycle production refers to the use of recycling as much as possible to ensure the most ecologically safe means of production. Growth is made possible by recycling the by-products of industrialization (Schubert 1984, 1,029). The concept also demanded the persistent development of new technologies to achieve the best methods of saving scarce resources. This process was referred to as the "ecologicalization of production" (Busch-Lüty 1981, 23).

In fact, the GDR did maintain a rather impressive system of recycling. Some 14 percent of its material needs from 1986 to 1990 were supplied through the use of recycled materials (Streibel 1989b, 654). Naturally, this was of tremendous economic benefit to the resource-poor GDR, but it was not enough to make up for the resource deficiencies and scarcity of hard currency endemic to the GDR economy.

The Soviet-style economic model that the GDR adopted was by no means the solitary source of environmental damage in the GDR. The existence of advanced environmental problems in both capitalist and socialist societies lends credence to the argument that environmental problems are an inherent concomitant of industrialization (Busch-Lüty 1981, 18). But the degree of environmental degradation may possibly be linked to the economic system. The Marxist labor-value theory has also been considered by some a system-endogenous impediment to environmental protection. Yet ideology, by itself, probably explains little in this context.

The most parsimonious explanation of the environmental catastrophe in the former GDR lies in the persistent goal of growth at all costs. Any economy, regardless of ideological slant, that hopes to achieve tremendous economic growth rates with inefficient economic units, a lack of modern technology, and a lack of available capital, must a fortiori consider environmental protection to be too financially burdensome. The GDR's hard currency deficit only exacerbated its economic situation, putting further pressure on policymakers to divert capital to more profitable enterprises than environmental protection (Raestrup and Weymar 1982, 839). The GDR's economic paradigm, based on the Soviet Stalinist economic model, proved itself a key factor in the destruction of the East German environment because of its obsession with industrialization, regardless of the human or environmental consequences.

Environmental Protection Policy in the GDR: Institutions and Outcomes

The GDR was one of the first nations in Europe to initiate environmental legislation. Its Environmental Protection Law of 1970 precedes both West and East European measures. The GDR's constitution mandated in Article 15 that natural resources and the environment be protected.[5] In terms of legal measures the GDR was quite progressive.

The institutional body that bore the foremost responsibility for environmental protection in the GDR was the Ministry for Nature Protection, Environmental Protection, and Water Management.[6] This institution formulated the GDR's basic environmental policies, which were crafted in cooperation with the State Planning Commission as well as the Subcommittee for Environmental Protection of the Council of Ministers of the GDR. The coordination of policy among these bodies was meant to eliminate potential discrepancies between the plan and environmental policies. These coordinated policies manifested themselves in the "plan of environmental protection," which was to be an integral part of each five-year plan (Streibel 1989a, 708). The Environmental Inspectorate, founded in 1985, was intended to oversee the implementation of the "plan of environmental protection." But the unwritten rule of the relationship between the aforementioned institutions gave primacy to the plan. Thus, the institutions that could have forestalled the completion of plan targets and had an impact on environmental damage, such as the Environmental Inspectorate, were relegated to a very limited role.

Rather paradoxically, in light of the Marxist value theory, the GDR established a set of resource user fees. Theoretically, user fees should not have been a part of enterprise plans because of the Marxist dogma that resources have no intrinsic value. Yet reality prevailed over theory, and in 1968 user fees were established for land, with water fees following in 1971 (DeBardeleben 1985a, 159).

Similarly, the GDR established pollution fees in the early 1970s. These fees were assessed by the amount of emissions put out above the legal limits. The financial penalties were so meager that most enterprises found it more economical to pollute and pay the fees than to observe the limits and risk not fulfilling their plan targets (Raestrup and Weymar 1982, 839). The consequences for not heeding plan targets were foremost on the minds of most enterprise managers, save a few ecologically minded mavericks.

How is it that the GDR, with its advanced system of environmental legislation, compiled such a dismal record of environmental damage? Aside from the factors discussed above, the answer also lies in the contradictions between the legislation and the priorities of the economic planning agencies. The aforementioned relations between the various state organs were by no means clearly defined (Fuellenbach 1977, 26). Furthermore, what appears on paper to be a pattern of policy processes was in reality something quite different. The primary factors in the policy process were not legal stipulations pertaining to the environmental policy area but the avenues by which policy preferences were actually channeled.

The Politics of the East German Environment

In any political system, policy feedback plays a role in influencing, to one degree or another, future policy decisions. In an open political system, popular reaction to policy can play a major role. Two important variables involved in this political equation are (1) avenues of influence to policymakers, and (2) the availability of information to the public.

The GDR could have been characterized as a closed political system, largely unresponsive to public opinion (Zimmermann and von Beyme 1984, 11). The political system itself, based on the uniform concentration of power, precluded the formation of autonomous political bodies that could have exerted influence on political elites. Without viable challenges to its policies, the SED leadership was largely immune from the type of political pressure exerted by interest groups in its capitalist sister state.

The ideological underpinnings of the GDR policy process stemmed from the Leninist concept of democratic centralism. Democratic centralism, in its practiced form, sets up a one-sided policy process. Directives came from above, leaving little or no room for change from subordinate organs. This also implies that directives from the politburo, once released, were bound to be implemented without significant change. Despite the appearance that there was a sharing of power among various levels of planning and control organs, the practice of GDR policymaking revealed a much different picture.

Although the policy process appeared impenetrable to many, the East German populace did have legal recourse against unpopular policies in the form of petitions (*Eingaben*). The petitions were an individual's means of expressing displeasure with government policies. These petitions could be presented to the Volkskammer, or a state official. But overall, petitions rarely resulted in changes in policy, despite assurances that they were given consideration (Mallinkrodt 1987, 119).

The pattern for environmental policy conformed to the general policy pattern in the GDR. Environmental policy was largely immune to public reaction. Yet that does not imply that GDR policymakers were not cognizant of public displeasure with environmental policies. The SED regime reacted in two ways to the environmentally conscious in the GDR: cooptation and repression (Fricke 1984, 203–204). Cooptation was achieved by means of the Society for Nature and the Environment (Gesellschaft für Natur und Umwelt). This organization was founded in 1980 and achieved a membership of approximately 50,000 (Fiedler 1984, 1,024). This official organization was meant to channel environmentally aware citizens' energies toward beautification projects and similar activities and away from criticizing government environmental policies.

But creation of the society did not quell critical voices in the GDR. In fact, the GDR's ecological movement, although by no means as organized or developed as its counterpart in West Germany, was a persistent source of dissent against SED environmental policy. The movement saw its conception primarily within the evangelical church during the early 1970s (Knabe 1985, 170). The church served as an umbrella for those who had no means of organizing otherwise. Whenever the regime felt that critics had outstepped their bounds, and those were often quite narrow boundaries, it would clamp down. Perhaps the most famous example was the raid in 1987 on the environmental library located in the evangelical Zionsgemeinde in

Berlin. This church was a center of environmental activism that had attracted the wrath of the SED regime by serving as an alternate source of environmental information.

Intellectuals, both scientific and artistic, did, on occasion, express their displeasure with the environmental policy in the GDR. Writers such as Hanns Libulka, Christa Wolf, and Erik Neutsch injected environmental themes into their works, thereby risking the censor's ban (Knabe 1985, 201–250). Scientific intellectuals were also forced to maintain the party line on environmental policy or face censorship.[7] Thus, intellectuals debating topics such as natural resource pricing or the critique of progress were always constrained not to stray too far from the official position. Many intellectuals, expelled to the West for their views, were never exactly aware where the boundaries for dissent stood.

The dearth of challenging and innovative views on the environment in the GDR can be viewed as a primary factor in the SED regime's response to environmental problems. The lack of organized pressure on the regime to change its destructive environmental policies only provided the regime a freer hand to continue policies that led to the present environmental catastrophe. The following sections of this chapter will deal with the consequences of East German environmental policy and with the measures being undertaken to rectify the situation.

Overview of East German Environmental Concerns

Water Pollution

The GDR had the smallest water supply per capita in Europe (*Information* 1990, 16). The GDR's natural water potential comprised some 17.7 billion cubic meters, which came out to a per capita water availability of 1,086 cubic meters/year. The world average for available water per capita is 12,000 cubic meters/year (Fuellenbach 1977, 19). In dry years the GDR's water supply dropped as low as 8 billion cubic meters (Melzer 1985, 71). These conditions created a particularly difficult problem in the GDR. Drinking water use per capita rose from 114 liters/day in 1975 to 138 liters/day in 1988 (*Information* 1990, 20). This trend only exacerbated the water problem as increasing industrialization demanded more water. It has been estimated that the available water was used up to five times in the more industrialized areas of the GDR (Fuellenbach 1977, 20). It is also worth noting that only 20 percent of the GDR's water was usable as drinking water (*Information* 1990, 17).

The GDR made serious efforts to rectify the critical water situation. The Water Law of 1982 attempted to save water through a comprehensive "intensification" of water management (Voigt 1984, 1,039). Yet the efficacy of this measure was strictly limited by the lack of new technology to clean used water. The GDR's hard currency deficit made the acquisition of new technology all the more difficult.

The most serious pollutants in East German waters were nitrates and heavy metals. Although both industry and agriculture contributed to the polluting of the water supply, the highly industrialized areas around Leipzig, Dresden, Erfurt, Gera, Halle, and Chemnitz (Karl-Marx-Stadt) were the most heavily polluted (*Information* 1990, 20).

Air Pollution

Whereas the lack of available water put the GDR in first place in Europe in water scarcity, its dependency on lignite (brown coal) gave it the equally dubious distinction of having the worst air pollution in Europe (*Information* 1990, 4). The GDR's energy needs were based up to 70 percent on brown coal, with natural gas covering 10 percent and oil a further 12 percent of the remainder of the GDR's energy needs. Brown coal is a particularly pernicious energy source because it releases great amounts of sulfur dioxide and dust when burned.

The GDR was beset by a set of factors that made its energy needs particularly problematic. First, the GDR had an extremely high demand for energy: the third highest per capita in the world behind the United States and Canada. Through its subsidization of energy use, the GDR encouraged energy waste and actually was ranked the world's worst in that category. This wasteful use of energy was carried out in a country whose only plentiful energy source was brown coal.

Several occurrences in the early 1980s led to the SED regime's renewed and strengthened commitment to brown coal. Political unrest in Poland led to the disruption of anthracite coal shipments to the GDR, thus curtailing the GDR's major supply of that fuel. Equally disruptive was the rise in the cost of oil and the USSR's new policy that the GDR pay for part of its oil in hard currency, coming at a time when the GDR was facing a severe currency shortage (Schwartau 1985, 9). The GDR's nuclear potential was not developed enough to make up for the losses of other sources of energy. As a consequence, the GDR created the largest brown coal industry in the world. This emphasis on brown coal, born of economic necessity rather than of an ideological predilection, has had a disastrous effect on air as well as water and soil quality. As the GDR mined more and more land for brown coal, it destroyed much-needed water supplies and poisoned the soil in the process. But the most damaging effect on the brown coal industry was its contribution to air pollution. Table 10.1 demonstrates the incredible burden brown coal placed on the East German environment.

These enormous amounts of sulfur dioxide and dust were many times the average of these pollutants found in West European states. They

Table 10.1 Sulfur Dioxide and Dust Emissions in the GDR

Year	kilotons	SO_2 tons/km^2	tons/ capita	kilotons	Dust tons/km^2	tons/ capita
1980	4,262.3	39	0.26	2,456.4	23	0.15
1985	5,339.6	49	0.32	2,335.1	22	0.14
1986	5,358.3	50	0.32	2,322.7	21	0.14
1987	5,559.7	51	0.33	2,335.2	22	0.14
1988	5,208.7	48	0.31	2,198.5	20	0.13

Source: Information zur Analyse der Umweltbedingungen in der DDR und zu weiteren Massnahmen. Berlin: Institut für Umweltschutz, 1990: 4.

Table 10.2 Percentage of Forest Damaged in the GDR

Year	Percentage
1987	31.7
1988	44.4
1989	54.3

Source: Information zur Analyse der Umweltbedingungen in der DDR und zu weitere Massnahmen. Berlin: Institut für Umweltschutz, 1990: 14.

affected not only the urban centers but have reached into the countryside as well. The destruction of forests increased dramatically in the 1980s, as Table 10.2 clearly shows.

The areas with the worst air pollution were around Bitterfeld, Leipzig, Cottbus, and Görlitz (*Information* 1990, 5). Up to 75 percent of the forests around Leipzig are classified as damaged (*Information* 1990, 14).

GDR vehicles also contributed to air pollution. The two-stroke motors used in the Trabant automobile emit up to 100 times the pollution that an automobile with a catalytic converter would emit. However, speed limits and a fourteen-year wait for the car served as a means of keeping them from adding too substantially to the air pollution crisis.

Nuclear Energy

The GDR began its nuclear program in 1966 with the construction of a nuclear power plant at Rheinsberg. The Rheinsberg plant had a relatively weak capacity of 80 megawatts (MW) and was followed in the 1970s by the Lubmin plant with its 3,520 MW capacity (Bischof 1986, 435). These two together produced some 10.5 percent of the GDR's energy needs (Bischof 1986). These plants were to be followed by two more at Stendal and Dessau, but progress on their completion was slow, despite the SED regime's commitment to nuclear energy.

The GDR's nuclear program suffered from the effects of a negative image domestically because of the growing antinuclear sentiments in the neighboring Federal Republic. In fact, the East German media did its best to ignore the antinuclear movement in the FRG in order to avoid antinuclear sentiments in the GDR (DeBardeleben 1985b, 246). The East German populace was, therefore, given very little information about its own nuclear program; the SED regime merely reassured the populace that the GDR's nuclear plants were perfectly safe.

The catastrophe of Chernobyl in 1986 had a serious effect on the GDR public's trust in its own Soviet-designed nuclear plants. The GDR media initially downplayed the disaster. When the news finally came out in its entirety, the SED regime made it clear that the focus should not be on hedging away from nuclear power but on making it safer (Bischof 1986, 433). Actually the GDR's legal measures toward safe nuclear energy were not the problem.[8] The problem lay in a lack of practical measures such as safety backup systems. In order to allay fears that its own nuclear plants were unsafe, officials implied that safety measures in the USSR were not as stringent as they were in the GDR (Gruhn 1986, 676).

In fact the GDR's nuclear safety record was anything but reassuring. A serious fire in 1975 almost led to the meltdown of the reactor at the Lubmin plant near Greifswald. Save for the functioning of a single safety system, a catastrophe at least on the order of Chernobyl would have resulted. This fact was held from the East German public until January 1990 (*Der Spiegel* 6, 1990, 115). The fact that it took events such as the Greifswald disaster and Chernobyl to spur the SED leadership to implement safety measures approaching Western standards reflected the SED regime's reluctance to act except in time of crisis (Gruhn 1986, 676).

The "Wende" and the GDR's New Environmental Politics

The events of October and November 1989 destroyed the SED monopoly on power and all that it entailed. In the months between October 1989 and the election in March 1990, the SED made radical efforts to revamp its tarnished image. Not the least of those efforts was the attempt to "ecologize" the party. The past record of environmental abuse under the SED leadership made this a difficult task, yet the now freely expressed concerns of the public demanded that the party attempt to do something about it or lose votes in the coming elections.

Hans Reichelt, the long-serving minister of the environment, resigned on December 19, 1989, under criticism for the state of the East German environment. The newly won press freedoms of the GDR media made it increasingly difficult to conceal the extent of environmental degradation in the GDR. Reichelt's successor, Peter Diederich, promised to tackle the critical environmental situation in an aggressive manner.[9] One of the most important tasks Diederich promised to undertake was to make previously classified environmental data public.[10] Immediately, measures to halt environmentally damaging economic practices were implemented. First, some 210 firms that were operating with special permission to pollute had that right revoked. Second, Reichelt promised that the GDR would reduce its brown coal use by 50 percent by 1995. And perhaps his most bold promise was to curtail the eight billion Ost Marks a year paid out in energy subsidies, which produced so much waste in the GDR. Likewise the SED (now renamed the PDS) also promised environmental controls independent of the economy, which was now to be market-based.[11] These promises, along with those of the Ministry for Nature Protection, Environmental Protection, and Water Management, ignored (or hoped the voters ignored) the fact that the GDR simply did not have the resources to complete these well-intentioned plans. The GDR was bankrupt, economically broken by years of mismanagement.[12] The alternative, and a particularly viable one in light of the growing political convergence of the two German states, was to turn to the Federal Republic of Germany for help.

The "Wende" and the Convergence of German Environmental Policies

Erich Honecker's fall from the leadership of the East German state in October 1989 and the subsequent opening of the GDR by his successor Egon Krenz prompted a rapid rapprochement of the two German states. The new SED/PDS leadership, in its scramble to gain legitimacy, made determined efforts to reform its relations with the FRG. Part of the reform effort went hand-in-hand with its startling new commitment to environmental protection and request for immediate West German aid for the environment. The result was a series of eleven pilot projects agreed upon on November 17, 1989. The projects focused primarily on the Elbe and on various air pollution measures.

The continuing momentum of the inter-German convergence finally opened the door to the formation of a "Joint Environmental Commission" in early 1990. This commission, first proposed in 1984, would oversee the inter-German environment with particular emphasis on transnational problems. At its first meeting in February 1990, the commission called for the immediate shutdown of all East German concerns that caused significant damage to the environment. This was a particularly radical declaration, seeing as it came one month before the East German elections. The East German candidates now had to weigh the effects of environmental improvement against the cost of jobs. Few politicians in the GDR spoke of the "ecologization of the environment" in terms of mass shutdowns and unemployment. Most promised a better way of life and a better environment. The question became: Which would the electorate find most important?

German Unification and Environmental Protection

The trade-off between economic development and environmental protection is not as stark as it appears. In actuality, as the process of German political and economic integration progresses, much of the economic distortion in the eastern portion of Germany will fade away. The factors involved in the equation of East German environmental problems, such as economic priorities, institutional ambiguity, and the closed nature of East German policymaking, have been overtaken by German unification, thus easing some of the burden on the strained East German environment.

The central issue in the rectification of the East German environment concerns finances. As the eastern portion of Germany plans to adopt West German environmental standards in its environmental union with the western portion of the FRG, the reality of the East German economy sets in. Not only does East German industry have very limited capital, but to immediately achieve West German environmental standards it would have to virtually cease to function. Conservative estimates have stated that 50 percent of East German industry would have to shut down immediately to match western environmental standards.[13] Of course the currency union and subsequent economic developments have forced many inefficient (and likewise environmentally damaging) enterprises to close, but the political repercussions of that are being felt strongly throughout the Federal Republic. The unification of the German states has only heightened the awareness that the environmental problems in the eastern *Länder* are now more than ever an all-German problem.

The federal government will have to provide the eastern *Länder* with generous financial assistance in its attempt to remedy the economic and environmental crises. Many East German power plants will have to close as the region frees itself from its reliance on brown coal, and the disgraced nuclear power industry will have to wait until it can be brought into line with West German nuclear safety standards before it can contribute to the East's energy needs. The Greifswald nuclear power plant (Lubmin) has already closed. Considering the negative popular feelings in both parts of Germany toward nuclear power, it seems doubtful that nuclear power will play a major role in replacing the antiquated coal-fired power plants.

West German firms are slowly stepping in to fill the vacuum that the revamping of the East German energy industry will create. Estimates place the cost of bringing the East German energy industry into line with western German standards at DM 100 billion.[14] Already 400 million DM have been promised by the federal government as part of *Gemeinschaftswerk Aufschwung Ost* (Operation Upswing in the East) to aid in the environmental cleanup in the eastern part of Germany (*Sozialpolitische Umschau* 162, 1991, 1). This enormous sum is to be covered both by private investment and government grants, but as investment in the new *Länder* has been slower than the government had hoped, it may find itself footing more of the bill than it had anticipated. The FRG's energy surplus will play a large role in supplying the eastern portion of Germany with power as it revamps its own energy network. However, this does not provide a complete solution. The energy network in the eastern *Länder* will have to be rebuilt eventually to cope with the revitalization of the eastern economy.

The institutional problems that beset East German environmental policy have been partially overcome by the dissolution of East German environmental institutions and the usurpation of their powers by the western German Ministry of Environmental Protection and Reactor Safety. This ministry has rather well-defined environmental responsibilities and is responsive to public pressure because its policies are an important aspect of the government's reputation and electoral strength and because of the saliency of environmental issues in public opinion. Environmental issues have been important electorally in West Germany, and therefore West German institutions developed a responsiveness to public opinion that their East German counterparts lacked. Thus, the unified German government approaches the environmental problems in the eastern portion of Germany with institutions that have been tempered by the effects of democratic politics and have evolved in a political environment in which environmental issues frequently made the public agenda. The effectively organized West German environmental bureaucracy, which has now taken over the responsibility for the environment of unified Germany, will alleviate part of the problem of dealing with environmental damage in the eastern portion of Germany caused by the ineffective GDR environmental bureaucracy.

The time frame for achieving environmental parity with the western portion of Germany was referred to in 1990 in terms of a ten-year period (*Pressemitteilung der Bundesregierung*, October 9, 1990). A key variable in attaining that goal is the willingness of Germans to pay for a cleaner environment, in terms of taxes in the West and unemployment in the East. The reality of unsubsidized living for Germans in the East could well dampen their enthusiasm for paying for a better environment.

Conclusion

This chapter was an attempt to tie together the environmental policy process of the GDR, its failure in maintaining healthy environmental standards, and recent policies established for rectifying the environmental situation in the former territory of the GDR. Despite the disappearance of many facets of the East German environmental situation, some will persist for years to come. Because the eastern portion of Germany's environmental problems are the sum of an aggregation of factors, it will require a medley of remedies to deal with them.

As the process of German economic, political, and social integration gains momentum and the two portions of Germany struggle to create a common society, the issue of living standards will play an important role. Because environmental conditions are an intrinsic part of a society's standard of living, it is certain that environmental issues will command an important place in the politics of the unified Germany.

The legacy of years of East German environmental mismanagement cannot be overcome in a short time span. It took years to develop into its present state, and it will take years to remedy it. The most important factors in determining the scope and pace of the cleanup effort are the priorities of the German populace and the financial resources available to pay for the job. The German government may be willing to run up deficits in the short run but such spending will not become a habit. Considering the long-term nature of cleaning up the environmental problems in the eastern *Länder*, there is a distinct possibility that the willingness to spend for the East's environmental problems may taper off. But we may remain certain that the environmental problems in East Germany will not disappear as important public policy issues.

Notes

1. *Der Spiegel* 12, 1990: 134.
2. *Rheinische Post*, May 10, 1990, 12.
3. *Der Spiegel* 46, 1989: 48.
4. See DeBardeleben 1985a, 176–182, for a more in-depth discussion of the Club of Rome's position.
5. *Verfassung der DDR 1968*, 17.
6. The ministry was given this name in 1990. It was previously known as the Ministry for Environmental Protection and Water Management.
7. Such instances were related to the author in interviews with environmental experts in the GDR.
8. See *Kommentar zur Verordnung über die Gewährleistung von Atomsicherheit und Strahlenschutz*. 1987. Berlin: Staatsverlag der DDR.
9. *Neues Deutschland*, January 12, 1990, 3.
10. "Interview mit Peter Diederich," *Der Spiegel* 2, 1990: 133.

11. *Neues Deutschland,* January 29, 1990, 3.
12. It became public knowledge in 1989 that the GDR had external debts totaling some 60 billion Ost Marks.
13. *Der Spiegel* 2, 1990: 27.
14. *Deutsches Allgemeines Sonntagsblatt,* March 23, 1990, 14.

References

Bischof, Henrik. 1986. "Nach Tschernobyl Zur Atomenergiepolitik der RGW Staaten." *DDR Report* 8:433–436.

Bundesministerium für Umwelt, Naturschutz und Reaktorsicherheit: Pressemitteilung. 1989. 11/17: 2.

Busch-Lüty, Christiane. 1981. "Zur Umweltproblematik in sozialistischen Systemen: Ideologie und Realität." *Aus Politik und Zeitgeschichte* 27:1–36.

The Club of Rome. 1972. *The Limits to Growth: A Report for the Club of Rome's Project on the Predicament of Mankind.* New York: Universe Books.

DeBardeleben, Joan. 1985a. *The Environment and Marxism-Leninism.* Boulder: Westview Press.

―――. 1985b. "Esoteric Policy Debate, Nuclear Safety Issues in the Soviet Union and the German Democratic Republic." *British Journal of Political Science* 15, 3:244–255.

―――. 1988. "'The Future Has Already Begun': Environmental Damage and Protection in the GDR." *International Journal of Sociology* 18, 3:144–164.

Fiedler, Manfred. 1984. "Initiativen für Natur und Umwelt." *Einheit* 11:1,024–1,030.

Fricke, Karl Wilhelm. 1984. *Opposition und Widerstand in der DDR.* Cologne: Verlag Wissenschaft und Politik.

Fuellenbach, Josef. 1977. *Umweltschutz zwischen Ost und West.* Bonn: Europa Union Verlag.

Gemeinsame Mitteilung der Regierungen der DDR und der BRD. January 17, 1990.

―――. February 23, 1990.

Gruhn, Werner. 1981. "Aktuelle Aspekte der DDR-Umweltpolitik." *Deutsche Studien* 19, 76:424–440.

―――. 1982. *Umweltpolitische Aspekte der DDR Energiepolitik.* Erlangen: Institut für Gesellschaft und Wissenschaft.

―――. 1986. "Reaktionen der DDR auf Tschernobyl." *Deutschland Archiv* 19, 7:676–678.

Haendke-Hoppe, Maria, and Konrad Merkl. 1986. *Umweltschutz in beiden Teilen Deutschlands.* Berlin: Duncker und Humblodt.

Horsch, Gerd. 1989. "Die Einbeziehung von Umweltfordernissen in die Leitung, Planung, und Stimulierung sozialistischer Industriebetriebe." Paper presented at the 23rd Social Science Colloquium at the TU Dresden, December 14 and 15, 1989.

"Interview mit Peter Diederich." 1990. *Der Spiegel* 2:133.

Information zur Analyse der Umweltbedingungen in der DDR und zu weiteren Massnahmen. 1990. Berlin: Institut für Umweltschutz.

Knabe, Hubertus. 1985. "Gesellschaftheher Disseus in Wandel. Ökologisches Diskussion und Umweltengagement in der DDR." In *Umweltprobleme und Umweltbewußtsein in der DDR.* Köln: Verlag Wissenschaff und Politik.

Kommentar zur Verordnung über die Gewährleistung von Atomsicherheit und Strahlenschutz. 1987. Berlin: Staatsverlag der DDR.

Kosing, Alfred. 1989a. "Natur und Gesellschaft." *Einheit* 11:1,018–1,024.

———. 1989b. *Sozialistische Gesellschaft und Natur*. Berlin: Dietz Verlag.

Lambrecht, Horst, and Cord Schwartau. 1987. *Deutschland Archiv* 20, 6:600–608.

"Das Land der 1000 Vulkane." 1990. *Der Spiegel* 2: 27.

Mallinkrodt, Anita. 1987. *The Environmental Dialogue in the GDR*. Lanham: University Press of America.

McCauley, Martin. 1979. *Marxism-Leninism in the German Democratic Republic*. London: Macmillan Press.

Melzer, Manfred. 1985. *DDR Handbuch*. Cologne: Verlag Wissenschaft und Politik.

Pauke, Horst. 1985. "Marx, Engels, und die Ökologie." *Deutsche Zeitschrift für Philosophie* 31, 1985: 207–210.

Pressemitteilung der Bundesregierung. October 9, 1990.

Raestrup, Reiner and Thomas Weymar. 1982. "Schuld ist allein der Kapitalismus: Umweltprobleme und ihre Bewältigung in der DDR." *Deutschland Archiv* 15:830–850.

Reichelt, Hans. 1984. "Die natürliche Umwelt rationell nutzen, gestalten, schützen." *Einheit* 11:1,011–1,013.

Schubert, Manfred. 1984. "Abproduktefreie, abproduktarme Technologien." *Einheit* 11:1,025–1,029.

Schwartau, Cord. 1995. "Die Entwicklung der Umwelt in der DDR. Neue Probleme durch Renaissance der Braunkohle." in *Umweltprobleme und Umweltbewußtsein in der DDR* Köln: Verlag Wissenschaft und Politik.

Sozialpolitische Umschau 162. April 22, 1991: 1.

Streibel, Günther. 1989a. "Leitung und Planung des Umeltschutzes in der DDR." *Wissenschaftliche Zeitschrift der Humboldt Universität zu Berlin* 37, 7:705–711.

———. 1989b. "Ökonomische Probleme der Entwicklung geschlossener Stoffkreisläufe." *Wissenschaftliche Zeitschrift der Humboldt Universität zu Berlin* 37, 7: 652–662.

Umweltprobleme und Umweltbewußtsein in der DDR. 1985. Cologne: Verlag Wissenschaft und Politik.

Umweltschutz in beiden deutschen Staaten. 1980. Bonn: Verlag Neue Gesellschaft.

Voigt, Gerhard. 1984. "Rationelle Nutzung und Schutz des Wassers." *Einheit* 11:1,039–1,040.

Zimmermann, Hartmut, and Klaus von Beyme (eds.). 1984. *Policymaking in the German Democratic Republic*. New York: St. Martin's Press.

Chapter 11

The Transformation of the East German Education System

Lutz Reuter

The West German economic and social system that had been criticized by East German ideologues for decades ironically became part of East Germany's postrevolutionary reality. Among the extensive and ubiquitous changes in economic and social policies resulting from unification, the politics and policies of education are a particularly interesting case. On the one hand, East German education was, for a time, a model for West German reformers. Now the West German education system has been introduced into the eastern *Länder* of the Federal Republic. This chapter will examine the changes taking place in education in the eastern *Länder,* both in terms of their short-term significance and in their long-term implications.

The Education System of the German Democratic Republic

Under the system of democratic centralism, the SED as the "party of the ruling working classes" was the sole political power in state and society as defined in Article 1 of the GDR's Constitution of 1968 to 1974. Consequently, the East German education system was put under a centralized administration, although it was split up into three main branches: the Ministry for Public Education (Ministerium für Volksbildung), the State Secretariat for Vocational Education (Staatssekretariat für Berufsbildung), and the Ministry for Higher and Professional Education (Ministerium für Hoch- und Fachschulwesen). In addition, some specialized colleges and universities were under the jurisdiction of other ministries (e.g., Ministry of Health) or of the SED itself.

Regional and local administrative bodies, consisting of district, county, and city school councils, reported to the control of the central administration, which in turn was also very limited in its ability to act independently because all relevant decisions on education policy and personnel were made by the top circles of the SED, the Politburo and the Central

Committee. Formally, most of these decisions were common statutes issued by the Politburo and the Council of Ministers, whose primary function was their publication and enforcement.

Quantitative planning for the education system was part of the central economic planning process and, as such, subordinate to the various central planning bodies. Vocational education, which was separate from the planning of general and higher education, fell under the jurisdiction of the Central Planning Commission. As a consequence, all jobs within all branches of the economy were subject to planning. Even the numbers of senior high school, college, and university students and of those in apprenticeships and full-time vocational schools were included in the planning process. Teaching was centrally planned through kindergarten, school, and university programs, and curricula were issued by the central departments of the government.[1]

In contrast to West Germany, the GDR had only a few major laws on education. The School Education Reform Acts of 1946, 1950, and 1959 stood for the socialist transformation process of education. The Education Act of 1965 established the comprehensive socialist system of education, from day care nurseries, kindergartens, and day homes for elementary school pupils to adult (general) and continuing (vocational) education. Fundamental goals of socialist education, outlined extensively in the Preamble to the Education Act, included education for Marxism-Leninism; education for the socialist state and its society; and education toward the socialist understanding of humans, which also included early military instruction, love toward the socialist brother nations, and hatred against capitalism and the class enemy. Additionally, there were the Youth Act of 1974 (with similar goals for extracurricular activities and nonformal education of youth), the Decrees on Vocational and Further Education and Their Function for Developing the Societal System of Socialism of the GDR of 1968 and 1970, and the council of ministers' Decree on the Development of Higher Education of 1969 (Anweiler 1990). The policy goals of these decrees differed fundamentally from those of liberal democracies: Party decisions determined the major long-term goals and programs, and laws operationalized and enforced them. The Education Act of 1965 and the government decrees were transformed through numerous detailed instructions. Problems that might have emerged with regard to enforcement, institutional performance, assessment, or other difficulties were connected with education law and not with party decisions. The SED was not bound by the Constitution; it interpreted it. It was impossible to ask for court rulings against educational acts and statutes. Appeals, other than the informal (and mostly irrelevant) complaint, could not be made against administrative decisions such as admission to the *Erweiterte Oberschule* (EOS) or upper secondary school or senior high school. The concept of unlimited and undivided party and state power precluded any kind of independent legislation or jurisprudence (Reuter 1992), although some institutional structures similar to administrative court proceedings emerged in 1988.

Voluntary day care nurseries and kindergartens for children under six, and day care for elementary school students with working parents, were available nearly everywhere in the country. Compulsory general education at the *Allgemeinbildende Polytechnische Oberschule* (POS), a type of mostly undifferentiated comprehensive school and the centerpiece of the socialist school reform of the 1960s, included grades one to ten. Only about 10 percent of the students, depending on school achievement, social activities, political reliability, and social class background, could enroll for a two-year program (grades eleven and twelve) at an EOS, leading to a university preparatory diploma (*Abitur*). Another important route to college or university was enrollment in a three-year vocational program that included high-school graduation. But it was up to the enterprises to grant these young people leave and to send them to college. During the early 1950s, the SED had set up the "worker and peasant faculties." These were special schools within the universities that educated students from the "working classes" without a high-school diploma. For those who could or would not enroll at an EOS, it was compulsory to enroll in a vocational education program, which consisted of an apprenticeship and vocational program, mostly within the same enterprise.

Admission to college or university also depended on individual performance, socialist standing, socialist parentage, and, during the last two decades, on the program-related admission figures of the state planning commissions. As a consequence of strict enrollment limitations, East Germany had a relatively small number of universities and students. All programs included compulsory courses in Marxism-Leninism and premilitary training.

Special secondary schools for the gifted had already emerged during the 1960s (e.g., in mathematics, science, arts, and sports). These were structurally similar to the West German comprehensive schools (*Gesamtschulen*) and were based on course-level differentiation (tracking). Aside from the basic POS principle of teaching all students without tracking, the idea of polytechnical education was central to the GDR school system. Although it did not work very well, the concept attempted to integrate theoretical technical-economic education with practical experience through hands-on training during one weekday.

East Germany also had a wide range of local cultural centers and of continuing education programs (mainly vocational, training, and professional), which were run by the SED, unions, Urania, or the Society for Sport and Technology (*Gesellschaft für Sport und Technik*) with its military-style educational and training programs; the traditional *Volkshochschule* (local and county adult education center) was less common.

The SED, FDJ (SED youth organization), and the unions had unrestricted access to all schools and universities. In fact, a dual structure of specialized administration and SED/FDJ supervision was set up within the educational institutions and the state education administration (Waterkamp 1987; Anweiler 1988, 1990a; Friedrich-Ebert-Stiftung 1989; Hörner 1990).

Education Politics Since the "Wende"

During the first weeks following the peaceful overthrow of the old regime, changes within the educational system began. Even though it was less a matter of educational reform and more a response to the fact that many students were not coming to class on Saturdays, the much discussed five-day school week was formally introduced. The socialist *Staatsbürgerkunde* (civics) was dropped, yet in some schools teachers continued to teach social studies and tried to discuss new democratic concepts. Premilitary education in schools and universities as well as the militarization of the contents of education were abolished. Margot Honecker, head of the Ministry for Public Education and wife of the former secretary-general of the SED, was dismissed. All regulations referring to the superiority of the SED and the role of political organizations in education were dropped. The most outspoken hard-liners among teachers, professors, school principals, superintendents, university rectors, and deans were dismissed or forced into early retirement (DGBV 1991, 47–56). Prime Minister Hans Modrow admitted that the inflexible and indoctrinating education system was in many respects responsible for the social protest. His inaugural speech and government program promised de-ideologization and the end of overregulation, as well as a greater emphasis on differentiation and individualization, although within the bounds of democratized socialism in an independent East German state.

Already in December 1989 the Bund-*Länder*-Kommission für Bildungsplanung (Federal-*Länder* Commission on Educational Planning and Promotion of Research [BLK]) had started to discuss a structural and qualitative equalization of the two German education systems, measures of support for the GDR, and possible exchange programs. Four weeks later, then West German federal minister of education Jürgen Möllemann met his East German counterpart, Hans-Heinz Emons, to arrange for the establishment of a inter-German education committee. They expressed the need for close cooperation in all fields of education and for exchange in higher education, as well as the need to modernize vocational education in East Germany. At its February meeting, the Westdeutsche Rektorenkonferenz, or West German Conference of University Presidents (WRK),[2] adopted a resolution concerning cooperation with GDR universities. The university presidents offered support for modernizing and expanding higher education in the GDR and for increasing its competitiveness. A few days later, the

Kultusministerkonferenz, or Conference of the *Länder* Ministers of Education and Science (KMK), followed these proposals and formally invited the East German representatives to join a common meeting after popular elections were held in March 1990. In a speech, Jürgen Möllemann designed a long-range program of ends and means, thus anticipating policies that should be adopted during the coming months. In April, the Deutsche Forschungsgemeinschaft, or German Science Foundation (DFG), finally proposed to extend its tasks to cover all of Germany as soon as possible.

After Hans Modrow had realized that no chance for any kind of democratically reformed yet socialist GDR existed, and when the central round table that had been set up in December 1990 began to control the transitional government and act as a quasi-parliamentary body, extensive discussions concerning the thorough reform of the education system began. In March 1991, East German minister of education Emons published his "Theses on Education Reform," a program of thorough change and convergence with the West German system, as well as the draft of a new *Gesellschaftskunde* (social sciences) curriculum. But time ran out before Emons was able to achieve any kind of major reform.

After the landslide victory of the conservative Alliance for Germany on March 18, 1990, the process of democratizing and reshaping the eastern German education system was accelerated. Yet before the new East German minister of education was appointed, his West German counterpart published a more detailed program on educational reforms and the equalization of the two systems. He repeated his proposal of establishing a common education commission. At their first meeting, he and the new East German minister of education, Hans-Joachim Meyer (who since December 1990 has held the same office in Saxony), achieved broad agreement on these proposals. The Joint Education Commission was established in mid-May, 1990.

In June, Meyer began his policy of checking teachers, professors, and administrative staff with respect to their responsibilities during the Communist regime and their prospective reliability in terms of democratic attitudes (de-Stasification). Some were dismissed or sent into early retirement. Major system changes were not undertaken because education would be under the jurisdiction of the not-as-yet-reestablished eastern *Länder,* but some important decisions were made: The priority of Russian among the foreign languages was abolished. The program for the seventh grade and up was differentiated between compulsory and optional courses, beginning in August 1990. All students got free access to upper secondary education, dependent only on their performance. New statutes for parent-teacher-student participation were issued. Provisional *Länder* school administration authorities were established on May 30, 1990, and in June new office holders were appointed for all school executive positions.

Within the institutions significant changes also occurred. East German professors and teachers started communicating with their West German peers, sat in on classes, gave lectures, team-taught, or organized conferences and common research programs. On the other hand, some questionable things happened as well. When the Modrow regime was still in power, party officials who had lost government or party jobs got positions in schools, universities, and within the education administration. The central round table and the new education minister failed to stop recruitment. Central round table and reform groups had failed to demand the appointment of new principals and school administration officials. Many teachers complained that old *Seilschaften* (connections) of comrades were already reestablished in May and June when those appointments were finally made. Progressive teachers felt intimidated and voted for old office holders.

Until July 2, 1990, all major West German federal, *Länder,* and corporative education agencies, including the German Academic Exchange Service (DAAD), had developed programs to coordinate and transfer support, funds, equipment, and manpower. There was no doubt that all major forces in East Germany agreed on a comprehensive and thorough reform of the education system. Major driving forces for educational changes and equalization could obviously also be found in West Germany. In fact, the influence from the West continued at least until the summer of 1991 because of the *Land*-to-*Land* partnerships that were set up to help reestablish a workable system of education administration.

The Economic, Monetary, and Social Union Treaty that went into effect on July 2, 1990, did not directly refer to education, which is primarily a responsibility of the *Länder*. But it introduced various West German economic and social laws into East Germany, thus converging selected subject matters of the two German education systems. These laws included the Federal Vocational Education Act, which reestablished the dual system of vocational education and introduced the West German system of occupations, as well as the Federal Labor Promotion Act, which enables the unemployed to get further training or comprehensive retraining benefits. Abolishing the border checks had an impact on students, who began enrolling in educational programs in West Germany and particularly in West Berlin. The government-run *Treuhandanstalt,* whose task is the privatization of the state-run eastern German economy, had the first significant impact on education already in late summer 1990 when company-run day care nurseries, kindergartens, and vocational schools were shut down and not transferred to local jurisdiction.

Since the spring of 1990, numerous private schools were planned in East Germany, many oriented toward the Rudolf Steiner concept of pedagogy. But despite some West German counseling, a lack of experience, a lack of money, and the immobility of the old education bureaucracies were mostly responsible for the fact that only a small number of them actually opened in the fall of 1990.

After the inauguration of the new East German government, an extensive and wide-ranging transfer began of money, equipment, and personnel into the East German education system. It included an ad hoc program worth one hundred million DM for the purchase of new school and college course books funded by the federal government and publishers; a computer support program; and programs to build up new *Länder* education departments and local education administrations, which included staff-lending and training for eastern German administrators as well as exchange programs and DAAD programs to establish part-time and full-time visiting professorships.

Seen from an institutional perspective, the time between March and December 1990 was marked by the absence of administrative authority and by a wide range of activities and experiments within many eastern German educational institutions. Within the departments of Marxism-Leninism at the teacher colleges and universities, groups of (mainly) younger teachers and professors started to actively cope with the democratic change by organizing conferences and developing new programs and retraining courses for teachers. They may have initiated these activities because of a bandwagon effect or a fear of dismissal; nevertheless, it was a harsh set-back for these academics (who had often cooperated closely with their West German peers) when Education Minister Hans-Joachim Meyer suddenly decided to eliminate the renewed social studies programs. He squelched all retraining programs by announcing that no former *Staatsbürgerkunde* (civics) teachers would be reappointed for teaching social studies without a job-performance evaluation. But only a few teachers (some of whom had actively opposed the old *Staatsbürgerkunde*) boldly continued and resolved even to go to court if necessary.

The Transformation of the Socialist Education System and Education Reforms in the New *Länder*

Preschool Education

In the GDR, about 70 percent of all children up to age three were in day care nurseries, because 87 percent of all women between ages sixteen and sixty were employed, including those enrolled in educational programs (Anweiler 1990, 162; Hörner 1990, 12; Friedrich-Ebert-Stiftung 1989, 17). Care was free of charge and parents had to pay only seven to ten Ost Marks per month for meals. Kindergartens for the three to six year olds were not compulsory either (except some programs for five year olds who did not attend any kind of kindergarten program). Of all children ages three to six, 94–98 percent were enrolled (in West Germany only 79 percent were), and the parents' contributions were similar to those for day care institutions. It is probably safe to say that economic pressure and the wish to increase the family's income, and not ideology, were the reasons for the growth of the preschool system.

Despite a growing concern about the problems of early childhood education outside the family, most parents currently depend on these institutions. After economic and political unification, the companies wanted to give up their responsibilities, whereas towns and counties had difficulties taking them over because of their own financial difficulties.

The three-year education programs for preschool teachers have improved during the past decades. They will be transferred into the newly founded *Fachhochschulen,* which are three-to-four-year teaching-oriented professional colleges. For the time being, only a few kindergartens will be shut down because most are still funded by the federal government. This policy has been continued longer than originally planned (December 1991). Like many school teachers and college instructors, preschool educators are afraid of losing their jobs. Because of the much lower degree of ideological indoctrination, most of them were not subject to *Warteschleife* regulations and subsequent dismissals.

In the long run the eastern German *Länder* legislatures will have to introduce kindergarten acts to regulate local and private responsibilities and funding as well as minimum requirements for space and equipment, group sizes, pedagogical programs, and education of the teaching staff. It is possible that the quality of early childhood education will decline significantly and that the number of kindergartens will diminish somewhat as well, either because women are among the first to loose their jobs, or because of an increase of part-time jobs for parents.

Elementary and Secondary Education

The most controversial issue in eastern German education politics and policies, besides the closing of institutions and the dismissal of instructors, scholars, and teachers, is the state of elementary and secondary education. The elementary school systems in East and West Germany do not differ significantly, although most West German *Grundschulen* (elementary schools) were organized and run as independent schools. After 1945, several West German *Länder* introduced six-year elementary education programs that have survived only in West Berlin. The reunited Berlin and the surrounding *Land* of Brandenburg both decided to have the six-year elementary school, while all other *Länder* operate on four-year programs (Max-Planck-Institute 1990, 159).

In contrast to those similarities, the concepts of lower secondary education differ significantly. One can distinguish at least three models that were implemented at the beginning of the 1991/92 schoolyear.

The first model, introduced in Mecklenburg–West Pomerania, follows the traditional tripartite system. Towns and counties are required by the School Education Reform Act to establish *Hauptschulen, Realschulen, and Gymnasien,* but, when demanded by a sufficient number of parents, they may also offer *Gesamtschulen.* Thus, the system is surprisingly close to that implemented by the SPD *Länder* governments in Hamburg, Hesse, and Schleswig-Holstein.

The second model, introduced in Brandenburg, focuses on the *Gesamtschulen,* but also allows for the other two tracks (*Realschulen, Gymnasien*) if requested by parents. Whether this will really make a difference in practice depends on the demands of the parents. One can posit that a dual system of *Gesamtschulen* and *Gymnasien* may emerge. The concept does not have a western German counterpart. In practice, it could be close to Berlin, where the *Gesamtschulen* have a very strong standing, and many of the still-existing *Hauptschulen* are mostly attended by children of foreign guest workers.

The third model is a dual system of *Sekundarschulen* (*Regel-* or *Mittelschulen* in Saxony-Anhalt, Thuringia, and Saxony) and *Gymnasien.* The secondary school is internally differentiated; that is, it has different course levels in subjects like German, foreign languages, math, and science and offers five- and six-year programs.

In these three *Länder* the CDU responded to the reluctance of East German parents, who were used to the "classless" polytechnical high school, to enroll their children in the lowest-ranking *Hauptschulen.* Since the 1960s, the *Gesamtschule* concept was extremely controversial among the major West German parties and was one of the most hotly debated issues of West German domestic politics, denounced by CDU conservatives as the "socialist unity school." Developments in eastern Germany could push the issue back onto the political agenda. The comprehensive secondary school (grades five to ten) with its lack of curriculum differentiation, ideological indoctrination in the humanities, lack of efficiency in teaching foreign languages, instructor-dominated teaching, military instruction, polytechnical education, and vocational orientation, is the focus of demands for reform (Hörner 1990, 13–19; Friedrich-Ebert-Stiftung 1989, 21–34).

The curricula, literally uniform in concept and implementation in all parts of the GDR, had been revised during the late 1980s. Although the heavily theoretical orientation gave way to a greater focus on basic knowledge and abilities, the intensive vocational counseling and the tendency of polytechnical education to orient students away from higher education and academic professions toward skilled workers' vocations remained. The mechanics of manpower planning, which included even the sixth grade in order to balance job supply and demand, was completely dropped in 1990. Reforms of the curricula continue. The history curriculum was not dropped, but the teachers must follow a pluralist approach and deal critically with Stalinism. Other changes affect foreign languages. Students can now choose between English, Russian, and French, but after 80 percent of the fifth-graders chose English as their first foreign language at the beginning of the 1990/91 school year, there were problems with the implementation of these new rules; and the demand for Latin, which had earlier had an extremely marginal position, could not be met.

The often insufficient school equipment and the lack of new school books cause other problems. Old books for the humanities and social sciences could no longer be used and had to be replaced by western material throughout the 1990/91 schoolyear.

The most crucial topics for teacher-student relations and society as a whole are teacher education, attitudes, and behavior; teaching experience before and after the revolution; membership and activities within the socialist party and teachers' union; and teachers' roles in the socialist state and society. The teachers' loss of credibility, their inability to confront the new situation, and their loss of job security have caused serious problems for many. In most eastern *Länder* a significant number of teachers and all principals—those who had been heavily involved in party and Stasi activities (statistics are not available)—were dismissed. East-West German student and teacher exchange programs, in-service training, and further education programs have been set up in the meantime and will be intensified once the *Länder* institutes for continuing teacher education and curriculum development have begun to operate as planned. *Staatsbürgerkunde* (civics) teachers remain excluded from teaching social studies, but not from teaching their second subject. They are expected to become proficient in another second (i.e., third) subject. Based on the existing agreements between the *Länder,* new concepts for teacher education will consider the needs of schools and will follow the lines of the western German models. The *Land* government of Brandenburg decided to keep most teachers by reducing teaching loads and salaries to a level of 80 percent. It appears questionable whether this policy of solidarity can be continued in light of teachers' protests and the legal provisions concerning the civil service.

Changes in the polytechnical school (POS) concept (grades five to ten) were not realized before August 1991, despite the criticism for their lack of structural or achievement-oriented differentiation (tracking). It was agreed that the jurisdiction of the new *Länder* should prevail. While a need for thorough reform toward more differentiated individual options was not questioned, the new concepts, which in fact were more or less imported from western Germany, caused great controversy.

Although political party manifestos of 1990 did not seriously differ on many policy areas, party proposals about secondary school education did. The conservative parties, dominated by the CDU, insisted on a structurally differentiated type of junior high school that would reflect individual interests, abilities, and performance. They called for reintroducing the three-track system of *Hauptschule, Realschule, and Gymnasium,* which they claimed the majority of the electorate demanded. The left parties, whether citizen movement parties, SPD, the SED-successor PDS, or extreme left-wing splinter groups, wanted to use the transformation of the GDR system to reform the school system in all of Germany, demanding an across-the-board introduction of the integrated *Gesamtschule* (comprehensive school).

For the time being, the upper secondary (senior high) schools in all eastern *Länder* except Brandenburg run only two-year programs instead of the three-year programs of the western *Gymnasiale Oberstufe,* or they start them one year earlier. On the one hand, the reason is practical: The POS and EOS had a twelve-year program, and the existing facilities and staffing make an immediate change difficult. On the other hand, this decision is political: It supports those in the West who advocate the eight-year *Gymnasium* and the Europeanization of the national education systems.

In 1991, all new *Länder* adopted school reform acts (Budde 1991), which were already very detailed and resembled the legal typology of western German school legislation. Without a doubt, there was a strong commitment on the part of politicians to follow the existing legal and policy lines. But the decision of the GDR to accede to West Germany unquestionably limited the political options as determined by the Basic Law (Article 7 about schooling); the *Länder* system of equalizing agreements; and the increasing impact of European Community politics, especially on vocational and higher education. Some issues within the new school acts (e.g., the funding of private schools) still remain provisional or lack adequate regulation due to existing conditions and a lack of money.

One of the most persistent problems is the lack of adequate resources available for school reform policies. This means that the eastern *Länder* governments and their policies will remain dependent on federal and state funds and thus be susceptible to western policy interests to a degree that in the long term runs counter to the meaningful functioning of federalism. On the other hand, the demand for equal opportunities and the fear that more young people will move West require speedy and comprehensive policy implementation. For the time being, any estimate of the time necessary for educational reform would be unreliable.

Vocational Education

The GDR vocational education system, which was based on the traditional concept of combining apprenticeship and vocational school, was shaped by the characteristics of the socialist society and centralized planning. East Germany was rather successful in developing an efficient system of vocational education, thus reducing the number of untrained or partly-skilled workers to 15 percent. Its problems came from the bureaucratic manpower planning system, its elements of ideological education, and the fact that the technical and organizational developments within the enterprises did not keep up with worker training, causing dissatisfaction and high fluctuation. Yet the dual system of enterprise and vocational school was actually a combination of practical and theoretical learning for only 70 percent of the students, because most of the vocational schools were run by the enterprises. The new school reform acts put all part-time and full-time vocational schools under the jurisdiction of cities and counties.

Because intracompany education (apprenticeship) falls under the jurisdiction of the federal government, the system of federal vocational agencies, laws, grants, and curricula for about 360 occupations took force in all of Germany in the summer of 1990. Thus, the new *Länder* had little choice other than to set up local part-time *Berufsschulen* (vocational schools). But they also introduced western German full-time vocational and professional schools (three-year *Berufsschulen,* one- to three-year *Berufsfachschulen,* two- to three-year *Fachschulen,* one- to two-year *Fachoberschulen,* and three-year *Fachgymnasien*). The new *Länder* decided to keep open the second route to higher education through vocational education and work experience, even though they no longer restrict enrollment in senior high schools. Major problems have developed regarding new programs unknown under the state-planned economy, including business, banking, auditing, and commerce-related occupations for which qualified teachers are badly needed. Current policies involve importing instructors from the West, exchanging personnel, and retraining teachers.

Enterprises are legally obliged to carry out education contracts that were set up under the old system, and federal money was made available to finish these programs. But due to the closing of many companies, many young people could not continue or did not get apprenticeships, a fact that caused growing public concern and immediate action, such as offering apprenticeship contracts in the West and financial support to small eastern German companies for each new apprenticeship contract they signed.

As in the other areas of educational reforms, transformation policies are very time-consuming. Their success depends on adequate resources for vocational school restructuring, new programs for retraining tenured and educating new teachers, curriculum reforms, and, in the case of the dual system, programs for the reconstruction of the private sector. The strength of the dual system and the close corporatist link between government and business in vocational education appears to be an inherent weakness for vocational education as the East German economy struggles to revive. For the time being, the demise of many enterprises in the new *Länder* seriously limits the vocational educational opportunities for the younger generation.

Higher Education

In 1989, 131,000 students were enrolled at the fifty-five East German institutions of higher education (12 percent of the age group compared with 29.1 percent in West Germany). About 89 percent were full-time students, 51 percent of those were women (West Germany: 38 percent) (Federal Ministry for Education and Science 1990). Typical of the impact of state planning on education since 1970, when the student figure peaked around 143,000, was the continuous decline of enrollment that contrasted with the trends in nearly all other highly industrialized countries (the ratios of East and West German student figures was 1:4 in 1951, 1:3.5 in 1970, and 1:10 in 1987).

The traditional autonomy of the universities was replaced by central guidelines, a strict hierarchy from the minister of education down to the departments and institutes, and the direct influence of the SED/FDJ on all intra-university activities. The major task of the SED/FDJ was to "support" the professors in "ideologically educating" their students, which quite obviously included the control of both. A means to organize this kind of education was the seminar groups of 20–25 students, which were set up at the beginning of their first year and maintained for the entire time of university study. FDJ cadres were in charge of important functions of guidance and control (Anweiler 1990, 414–424; Hörner 1990, 24–33; 40–46).

Several disciplines developed quite differently from their western counterparts or simply vanished over the years. This occurred with most social sciences like political science, business administration, and law (some of these subjects survived under the heading "political economy of capitalism"). Sociology, denounced as an opposition science, came close to extinction.

Over the years the universities lost most of their traditional role in research. As in the Soviet Union, pure research was carried out in the central state institutes and academies. Applied research and development were integrated into the producer combines and enterprises. The universities did not fully lose their research function, but teaching and educating became their primary function. This may explain the often very poor libraries and technical equipment of eastern German universities.

Soon after the beginning of the 1989 revolution, demands emerged to reestablish the traditional autonomy of colleges and universities and the freedom of teaching, learning, and research. A standing conference of college presidents was established for mutual consultation and self-administration. Schools (*Fakultäten*) and departments were reestablished. The institutes of Marxism-Leninism renamed themselves social science departments, afraid that their personnel would be dismissed after the dissolution of the compulsory courses in Marxism-Leninism. Most of them were nevertheless dismissed or retired.

After the aforementioned changes of 1989/90, the process of closing nearly all the central research institutions and social science institutes began, and eastern German universities started to adapt to their western counterparts in summer and fall of 1990. Some of the most serious problems included, or still include:

1. The restructuring of old, and the development of new, programs to help the eastern German universities catch up with their western counterparts and to make them attractive to students in both eastern and western Germany.
2. Improving the equipment of libraries, institutes, and classrooms; upgrading student dormitories and other facilities.
3. Qualification and tenure of the old and the hiring of new professors. The ratio of university staff to students was 1:5 compared with 1:15 in West Germany. The teaching load of the professors was significantly lower in the East. It appears to be undesirable to reduce the eastern German figures down to the western level, although *Länder* budgets may leave no other choice. On the other hand, the academic qualifications of some instructors remain significantly below western standards, and scholars of Marxism-Leninism and other fields are qualified for subjects no longer needed.
4. Regional imbalances in the eastern German higher education system. Over 40 percent of all students, among them 55–65 percent of all students in mathematics, science, and engineering came from Saxony, a *Land* that will be financially unable to fund all of these institutions of higher education. The reshaping of a more balanced regional structure of higher education has begun. New universities were founded or refounded in Potsdam, Frankfurt an der Oder, and Erfurt. But they are also under severe budget restraints. The basic problem of structural imbalance remains.
5. Increasing educational capacities. The problems of transition drove educational capacities down, but the demand is growing, even if it might take some years until the student-age cohort ratio will be at the former western level.

Interestingly, in 1991 some programs and institutions of higher education in eastern Germany (e.g., mathematics, computer science, the sciences) attracted significant numbers of western German applicants. The question of how to deal with the old university personnel proved to be the most complicated and most controversial issue during 1990–1991, because questions of loyalty, qualification, and need were inseparably intertwined. At least three different approaches were discussed:

1. Former GDR professors and other teaching personnel, except those already dismissed in winter 1990, would remain in their positions. From a social point of view, a wholesale dismissal appeared to be unacceptable. Experiences and qualifications that might still be useful would be wasted. Qualifications that were formerly lacking could be acquired within a limited time frame. Finally, most of them might be unable to find any other suitable job after having been dismissed.
2. Only qualified academic teachers and scholars would guarantee the required standards in education and research. Thus closing institutions and departments would be the only way for a really new beginning. Those dismissed and qualified would be able to apply when appropriate positions became available.
3. Neither wholesale releases nor the undifferentiated continuation of labor contracts would solve the problem the eastern German universities confronted. They need to rid the faculties of those who are unqualified, who were unacceptably involved in Stasi affairs, or who got their positions as party protégés, and who continue to work because no immaculate faculty members are available. Even the possibility of transferring scholars and teachers from western Germany would have some obvious limitations, and it would not satisfy the demand that the scientific community of eastern Germany come to grips with its past.

Current *Länder* policies appear to follow along the lines of the third approach, which will raise tricky questions such as, What are the criteria for dismissal? Who is in charge? and What is relevant or can be proven? For those who at least temporarily remained in their academic positions, a dual process of review with regard to ideological and qualifications issues took place in 1991. A crucial point remains: During the summer of 1990, the former GDR minister of education, Meyer, had already obtained reports on both issues, which were the basis for dismissals or new labor contracts. But the Unification Treaty allows dismissals to be based only on need. From a legal standpoint, the current process is rather questionable.

Adult and Continuing Education and In-Service Training

The role of *Volkshochschulen* (adult education centers) had already changed during the early years of the GDR. The centerpieces of the continuing education system were enterprise academies and departments for continuing education at enterprise schools. After a period of raising the general and basic vocational skills of the workers, workplace-oriented additional training became more important.

The system of continuing education is being thoroughly reformed. It is again under the jurisdiction of the *Länder* and local governments and private interests such as firms, business associations, for-profit and nonprofit organizations, political parties, trade unions, and religious denominations. The towns will reestablish local and county *Volkshochschulen*. The current demand for additional vocational and professional qualification courses and full retraining programs for the jobless is high. Many continuing education and retraining firms and organizations from the West opened branches in eastern Germany. Interest in these programs is high, and local labor offices will provide the funds necessary to participate. Nevertheless, the potential success of many of these programs is questionable because of the lack of information about whether and what kinds of jobs will be available. In single-industry areas where unemployment is high because of the demise of the only enterprise, retraining programs are extremely difficult to develop as long as new industries are not introduced.

Consensus on this subject is surprisingly high among governments, political parties, unions, industry, and the business community. It is a policy area of high priority. Updating vocational and professional skills with continuing education and providing training for new occupations are seen as major instruments to overcome unemployment as well as a means to attract new investment.

Conclusion

Quite a few eastern Germans perceived unification as a western German takeover or colonization because of its range and speed, the lack of genuine eastern German concepts, the loss of identity, the western dominance, or the lack of sensitivity (*Besserwessis*). Some of these criticisms are justified, particularly when it comes to the insensitivity and arrogance of some Westerners. Whether relevant policy alternatives really existed or whether the route for change was already paved during the first six months after the revolution will be discussed in the final remarks.

During the mid-1960s, the reformed education system of the GDR was in some respects a challenge to education policies in West Germany. But while various changes occurred incrementally in the West—most conspicuously the increase in the number of students within the more demanding tracks of the lower secondary system and within the senior high school— the East German system ossified. It was only slightly reformed after 1965, became inflexible, and in some respects remained behind, despite some moderate curriculum reforms in the 1980s. The ideologization of the curricula and the teacher-dominated style of instruction remained.

The 1989 revolution started a discussion of how to de-Stalinize learning, teaching, and research. Among the most striking elements that had to be changed were the political indoctrination at all stages of education, the ubiquitous role of the SED/FDJ, the lack of freedom in teaching and educating, and the lack of openness among teachers and students. The practice of instructing from above instead of analyzing and discussing and the impact of central economic planning on general and vocational education had to be reconciled with current realities. The lack of autonomy that universities, students, and professors had to administer, learn, teach, and research, as well as the lack of alternatives and choices in general, vocational, academic, and professional education needed attention. The complicated international situation—mainly the growing instability of the USSR—and domestic expectations did not leave much room for a slower route toward unification. Four elections in eastern Germany in 1990 clearly confirmed the hopes and demands of most East Germans for a speedy reconstruction of their country along the lines of the West German model.

It is questionable whether, and to what extent, voters were aware of the necessity and the scope of changes in the educational system. Above all, the topic of economic and political unification dominated the agenda. But the two elections in the fall of 1990 took place after treaties on the economic union and the political union had been adopted and published. Thus, the scope of the upcoming change was not unforeseen. The October 1990 *Länder* elections focused on regional issues such as education rather than national ones, and, as in March, the conservatives received strong support from the voters.

The number of genuinely eastern concepts were as limited as the number of political players in the new *Länder*. In their absence, social expectations, the Basic Law, the Unification Treaty, the Hamburg Agreement, and other *Länder* and federal agreements will serve as the means of equalizing the *Länder* educational systems in Germany.

The East and West German concepts of egalitarianism were dissimilar; the eastern notion of equality of education was based on a widely uniform school structure, on uniform curricula and teaching practices, and to a certain degree even on egalitarian student assessment. The western model—despite the intense controversies about ideological, theoretical, and practical impacts of equality of educational opportunities—was based on a nationally comprehensive, but structurally differentiated, system of three to four tracks, on individual choice, on curriculum differences and other local and regional variations, and on differences in terms of interests, abilities, and performance. A notion of egalitarianism that does not preclude competitiveness means, for most western Germans, equality of opportunities for students regardless of intellectual talent.

Since the revolution, there has been a consensus on some basic demands for fundamental change. These include freedom of learning, teaching, and research; administrative decentralization; autonomy of colleges and universities; differentiation of the lower secondary schools; de-ideologization and pluralization of the curricula; renewal of teacher education and training; and the need to bring about these goals through measures of thorough change.

Currently, and for the foreseeable future, education in the new *Länder* undoubtedly faces a variety of difficulties: budget constraints, raising qualifications of the teaching personnel, and the restructuring of old or the establishment of new educational institutions and the implementation of new programs. There are insufficient activities and funds for establishing a private sector, particularly in continuing education, similar to that in the West.

In the long run, the all-German system of educational corporatism (with the KMK, BLK, HRK, Science Council, Federal Institute for Vocational Education, and national umbrella organizations of labor, industry, and commerce involved in education) may be changed by the growth in the number of *Länder* and nongovernmental players, a greater variety of new concepts, and perhaps also the impact of what could be called GDR-traditions. But without a doubt, in ten years or so the educational system in the new *Länder* will occupy a highly competitive position in Germany and within the European Community.

Notes

A large part of this chapter was written when the author was a visiting professor of Political Science at Northwestern University, Evanston, Illinois.

1. Curricula were developed by the Academy of Pedagogical Science (Akademie der Pädagogischen Wissenschaften) for elementary and high school curricula and teacher college programs, by the Central Institute for Vocational Education (Zentralinstitut für Berufsbildung) for vocational education curricula and training programs, by the Central Institute for Higher Education (Zentralinstitut für Hochschulbildung) for university programs, and by the Institute for Higher and Professional Education (Institut für Hoch- und Fachschulwesen), as well as some professional commissions that were in charge of different professional institutions.

2. Since unification this body has been renamed the Hochschulrektorenkonferenz (HRK), or Conference of University Presidents.

References

Anweiler, Oskar (ed.). 1986. *Staatliche Steuerung und Eigendynamik im Bildungs-und Erziehungswesen osteuropäischer Staaten und der DDR*. Berlin: Arno Spitz.
―――. 1988. *Schulpolitik und Schulsystem in der DDR*. Opladen: Leske and Budrich.
―――. 1990. *Neuere Entwicklungen im Bildungs- und Erziehungswesen der DDR*. Königswinter: Jakob-Kaiser-Stiftung.

Anweiler, Oskar, et al. 1990. *Vergleich von Bildung und Erziehung in der Bundesrepublik Deutschland und in der Deutschen Demokratischen Republik.* Cologne: Wissenschaft und Politik.

Avenarius, Hermann. 1991. "Die Schulgesetzgebung in den neuen Bundesländern." *Deutsche Lehrerzeitung,* nos. 21, 22, and 23.

"Bildungsprobleme in beiden deutschen Staaten." *Bildung und Erziehung.* 1990. Issue 1/1990.

Ein Bildungsweson im Umbrech—DDR. *Pädagogik und Schule in Ost und West.* 1990. Issue 2/1990.

Budde, Hermann. 1991. "Die Erneuerung des Schulwesens in den fünf neuen Ländern und Berlin (Ost) im Vergleich." *Recht der Jugend und des Bildungswesens* 39:303–307.

Bundesminister für Bildung und Wissenschaft (BMBW). 1990. Grund-und Strukturdaten. Ausgabe 1990/1991. Bonn und Bad Honnef: Bock.

Deutscher Bundestag. Parliamentary Document 11/7820 and Appendix to 11/7820 (Schlußbericht der Enquete-Kommission "Zukünftige Bildungspolitik—Bildung 2000" und Anhangsband). Bonn.

Deutsche Gesellschaft für Bildungsverwaltung (DGBV). 1991. Das Bildungswesen im künftigen Deutschland. Eine Herausforderung für Bildungspolitik und Bildungsverwaltung. Frankfurt/Bochum: DGBV.

Deutscher Juristentag. 1981. *Schule im Rechtsstaat.* Vol. 1: *Entwurf für ein Landesschulgesetz: Bericht der Kommission Schulrecht des Deutschen Juristentages.* Munich: C. H. Beck.

Ein Bildungswesen im Umbruch—DDR. 1990. *Pädagogik und Schule in Ost und West.* Issue 2/1990.

Federal Ministry of Education and Science. 1990. *Basic and Structural Data: Education Statistics for the Federal Republic of Germany.* 1990/1991 Edition. Bonn and Bad Honnef: Bock.

Friedrich-Ebert-Stiftung. 1989. *Bildung und Erziehung in der DDR im Umbruch.* Bonn: Friedrich-Ebert-Stiftung.

Hörner, Wolfgang. 1990. *Bildung und Wissenschaft in der DDR. Ausgangslage und Reform bis Mitte 1990.* Bonn: Federal Ministry for Education and Science.

Max-Planck-Institut. 1990. Arbeitsgruppe Bildungsbericht 1990. Das Bildungswesen in der Bundesrepublik Deutschland. Reinbek bei Hamburg: Rowohlt.

Klemm, Klaus, et al. 1990. Bildungsgesamtplan '90: Ein Rahmen für Reformen. Weinheim/Munich: Juventa.

Reuter, Lutz R. 1992. "Die rechtlichen und administrativen Rahmenbedingungen der bildungspolitischen und pädagogischen Entwicklungen in den beiden deutschen Staaten seit 1945." In Carl-Ludwig Furck and Christoph Führ (eds.), *Handbuch der deutschen Bildungsgeschichte,* Vol. 5: 1945–1990. Munich: C.H. Beck.

Thema DDR. *Pädagogik.* 1990. Issue 3/1990.

Waterkamp, Dietmar. 1987. *Handbuch zum Bildungswesen der DDR.* Berlin: Arno Spitz.

Weishaupt, Horst, et al. 1988. *Perspektiven des Bildungswesens der Bundesrepublik Deutschland: Rahmenbedingungen, Problemlagen, Lösungsstrategien.* Baden-Baden: Nomos.

Chapter 12 ⎯⎯⎯⎯⎯⎯⎯⎯⎯⎯⎯⎯⎯⎯⎯

The Domestic Politics of the Post-Unification Era: Politics, History, and Economy

Karl Kaltenthaler
⎯⎯⎯⎯⎯⎯⎯⎯⎯ *Christopher Anderson*

Writing a conclusion to this book is like writing an autobiography as an adolescent. Although a good deal has happened, we are only beginning to discern the contours of the bigger picture. But what we do know is enormously important for understanding what is yet to come. At this juncture, there are a number of things we know about German unification and the ongoing transition from the pre- to the post-1990 period. In this book we have been able to take a serious look at the foundation that has been laid and bring some order to its various elements.

We find that this book has supplied ample evidence for the view that many of the political developments of the unification process and thereafter have, directly or indirectly, been touched by two overarching issues: economic performance and history. First, many of the current political conflicts in the domestic political arena cannot be understood without reference to the importance of economic performance and economic conditions in the eastern and the western parts of the nation. Second, in order to understand the domestic politics of German unification, we need to recognize the importance of the historical political legacy with which Germans in East and West are saddled. Not only has the end of the Communist regime played a critical role in shaping the political developments of the post-1989 period, but Germans have also had to deal with the legacy of the old Federal Republic as well as the ghosts of Weimar and the Third Reich. Economics and history have touched almost all aspects of postunification German politics, such as the development of electoral politics and the party system and the task of building a new political order in the East and the West.

The Economy: Problems and Prospects

On a practical level, dealing with the East German past has to a great extent meant dealing with the accumulated problems of forty years of "real-socialist" economic management. The reconstruction of the East German economy poses one of the most severe dilemmas for the unified Germany. Creating a viable economy in the five new *Länder* is crucial to the future of Germany as a democratic and prosperous state. There are several fundamental reasons why this will prove a gigantic task.

The major dilemma facing the East German economy has been a lack of investment needed for the modernization of East German firms. The structural similarities of the East and West German economies has meant that the technologically outdated and unproductive East German firms have a serious disadvantage vis-à-vis West German businesses. Their productive capacity has allowed West German firms to claim the East German market without investing in new production facilities there. Yet East German firms need investment in order to be able to gain the technology and productive capacity to become competitive in the German as well as the international market.

The crucial factor in attracting investment to create a competitive productive base for the East German economy, and thus sustained economic growth, is the manner in which political and economic institutions have so far been developed in eastern Germany. Instead of creating new institutions in the former GDR, the unified Germany has so far merely transferred the bulk of West German political and economic institutions into East Germany. Although this has brought political stability to East Germany, it has also saddled East German firms with regulations and laws meant for modern, productive firms.

Looking at the present state of the East German economy, it is hard to imagine that it was once considered a socialist version of the "German economic miracle." There were some compelling reasons to believe that. The economy of the GDR produced the highest per capita GNP of any socialist country in the world. In fact, the GDR had the eighth-largest per capita GNP in the world, actually putting it ahead of Britain and Italy in 1979.

But the lofty position of the GDR's per capita GNP in international comparison did not tell us much about the quality of the goods that were produced, or about the actual distribution of social and economic amenities in the GDR. When we compare the standard of living of East Germans before unification with that of Western Europeans, and look at the competitiveness of GDR products on the world market, then the East German economic miracle quickly begins to lose its luster.

As several authors have pointed out in their chapters, the paramount political factor in determining the nature of the development of East German institutions during the unification year was the Alliance for Germany's victory in the March 1990 elections. The Alliance had run on a platform of reforming the East German economy in the spirit of Ludwig Erhard, the creator of the West German economic miracle, and the promise of speedy unification. In other words, the Alliance presented a platform that argued that by adopting the West German economic model, East Germany would also become a prosperous society. It was this hope of a rapid attainment of the wealth of their West German compatriots that attracted East German voters to the Alliance. As the GDR economy worsened and then collapsed following monetary union, the calls for the immediate adoption of West German institutions from the CDU-led East German government became more urgent.

With political union on October 3, 1990, East Germany effectively transferred the majority of West German law and regulations into its territory. Yet many of West Germany's institutions have proven an unbearable burden to East German businesses.

Two sets of West German institutions particularly trouble East German firms: The first is economic regulation, and the second is environmental regulation. Combined, they have added significantly to the problem of attracting investment into East Germany. Economic regulations have dissuaded potential investors from eastern Germany because they do not want to incur the costs of bringing East German firms up to the standards set for West German firms. These include standards for safety, working hours, and product specifications. Many East German firms had seen only minor improvements since they had been inherited from the Nazis in 1945. To suddenly burden them with regulations meant for efficient and technologically advanced West German firms means that a huge amount of capital would be needed to bring East German firms up to those levels.

The most costly set of institutions transferred from the West into the East are environmental regulations. The East German environment is in a dismal state. Forty years of environmental neglect have left East Germany with severely polluted water, soil, and air (see Chapter 10). The situation has improved somewhat since 1990, mostly due to the closing of many polluting East German firms. West German investors are strapped when they buy an East German firm because they take on its environmental liabilities. The antiquated technology and lack of environmental measures taken by East German firms mean that many of them have accumulated very substantial environmental liabilities, making them very unappealing investment prospects. The costs of modernizing firms that employ technology from the turn of the century—something that is not uncommon in East Germany—is enormous.

Developing institutions for the recreation of private property rights in East Germany has also proven to be an immensely complicated task. There were actually three sets of property rights issues involved in East Germany. The first set of property rights claims came from those who had their property confiscated by the Nazis. The second set of property rights issues concerned property confiscated by the Soviets during the early period of the occupation. The third set of property rights issues centered on property expropriated by the East German state. The first two sets of issues were quickly settled by disallowing claims against properties confiscated by the Nazis or by the Soviets. The claims of the victims of the Nazis were refused because it was felt they had already been compensated. The Soviets objected vehemently to any claims on their expropriated property, and, since Soviet acquiescence to unification was crucial, the West and East German governments dropped the issue. But the issue of restoring private property rights from what had been East German state property remained a major problem.

Instead of compensating the former owners of confiscated East German property, the German government decided to restitute the property to their owners. This decision to find the original owners of properties has created a huge bottleneck in attempting to set up secure property rights. It has also created an atmosphere of great economic uncertainty, which has been a major source of investors' unwillingness to invest in eastern Germany. More than a million claims were filed for property in the GDR in 1990 alone, many of them conflicting and exceedingly difficult to verify. One out of every four properties in the former GDR is now the subject of a claim.

The major organization charged with privatizing former East German state properties is the *Treuhandanstalt*. Originally established by the East German government to hold state property, it is a holding company that has the enormous task of trying to sell former East German firms. To date, it has been surprisingly successful. It privatized the whole subset of service and trade firms of the former GDR. However, it has had much less success with East German industry. As of December 1992, the *Treuhandanstalt* had sold a full half of East German industrial firms. But the crucial factor is *how* the East German firms are being sold. They are often sold in pieces rather than as whole productive units (*Kombinate*). West German firms have so far typically bought parts of the East German firms to produce components or selected lines rather than the full range of goods. The *Treuhandanstalt* is thus left with the unattractive parts of firms, which it must then try to sell. Consequently, it ends up subsidizing those divisions of firms it has little hope of selling. As each firm is broken up and sold, new firms are created to be sold, with no end to the process in sight.

Although the institutions of economic and environmental regulation have been transferred into the eastern *Länder,* the institutions of West German corporatism have not been recreated in East Germany (see Chapter 9). West German organizations of labor and capital have replaced their eastern counterparts, but these organizations have much different resources in the East. The comparative strength of East German trade unions vis-à-vis East German industry has meant that East German wages have soared after 1990 as unions have become more aggressive in their attempts to achieve wages that match those in West Germany. Wages in East Germany have risen 60 percent since unification, while productivity has fallen dramatically. This has meant that East German firms have become even less competitive and have had to let more workers go. The official unemployment rate in the eastern part of Germany stood at 14 percent in late 1992. But when part-time workers and those in retraining schemes are included, the rate actually approaches 25 percent. In industry, the unemployment rate rose to 50 percent by 1993.

Encouraged by their West German union leaders, who have been fighting for wage increases higher than the rate of inflation, East German workers have shown little willingness to moderate their wage demands to give East German industry a chance to build an economic base. In West Germany, unions have become more aggressive, breaking with their pattern of moderate wage demands of the 1980s. The threat of a strike in the steel industry was avoided only at the last minute. But the most dramatic demonstration of West German labor's newfound assertiveness were the strikes by public sector unions in April and May 1992. These were the first strikes by public sector unions since 1974, and many questioned whether Germany's corporatist arrangements were fraying.

Surprisingly, the German government initially did little to mediate the conflicts between labor and capital in East and West Germany. But realizing that continued conflict between labor and capital threatened to undermine his policies for economic recovery in the East, Kohl took the initiative by calling for a "Solidarity Pact" between labor, capital, and the state on September 9, 1992. The proposal met with a cool response from labor, which argues that its wage claims are not the cause of Germany's economic problems. They lay the blame with the Bundesbank and its tight monetary policy as well as the Kohl government's miscalculation of the costs of unification.

The huge cost of reconstructing the East German economy had initially been meant to be self-financed (see Chapter 6). The initial annual cost of resource transfers from West Germany to East Germany was supposed to be DM 35 billion and was to be financed by private investment and the sale of East German firms by the *Treuhandanstalt*. As the expected private investment did not materialize and the *Treuhand* had serious difficulties selling East German firms, the cost of German unification began to become obvious. Instead, since 1990 the Kohl government has had to pump an average of 160 billion D-Marks a year (approximately US $100 billion) into East Germany in the form of subsidies and unemployment compensation. The result of these enormous aid transfers has been a growing budget deficit, which is expected to reach DM 125 billion in 1993. Kohl was forced to confront economic reality. This meant that higher taxes were included in the federal budget in March 1991 because the aid transfer for 1991 was DM 140 billion instead of the DM 35 billion predicted. The tax

hikes consisted of a temporary, one-year 7.5 percent income and corporation surcharge starting July 1, 1991; a tax increase of 25 *Pfennig* per liter of
gasoline; and tax increases on tobacco and insurance premiums. The federal government further decided in November 1991 that a 25 percent with-
holding tax on investment income, with exceptions for personal savings,
would be necessary. In light of the growing budget deficit, new tax laws
were passed in February 1992 (to go into effect in January 1993) in order to
make up for the loss of revenue after the termination of the temporary surcharge on incomes. The VAT was also increased from 14 percent to 15 percent. It remains to be seen whether these tax increases will cover the rising
costs of reconstructing the East German economy.

Aside from straining the German budget, the huge aid transfers to the
eastern *Länder* have exacerbated inflationary pressures. The Bundesbank
has reacted to the threat of inflation in customary fashion. Karl-Otto Pöhl,
the Bundesbank president, had warned in early 1990 that monetary union
would not only destroy the East German economy, but that it would threat-
en price stability as well. When he was ignored and came under increasing
political pressure because of the soaring costs of unification, Pöhl decided
to resign on May 16, 1991. He was replaced by Helmut Schlesinger, a
career Bundesbank official well known for his strict monetarist views.
Schlesinger immediately moved to warn the German government and the
unions that increased wage demands and subsidization of East German
firms would bring added inflation, which would threaten the East German
economic recovery. When the Bundesbank saw no movement toward its
position from the government or the unions, it turned to a very tight monetary policy. The Bundesbank's monetary target for 1992 was an inflation
rate of 2 percent, but the actual inflation rate was double that figure. This
led the Bundesbank to hike interest rates to 8.75 percent, the highest interest rate in Germany since the 1930s. With East German inflation reaching
14 percent, there was little likelihood that the Bundesbank would relax its
monetary policy substantially in the near future.

The effects of this tight monetary policy have been decried in East and
West Germany. Critics of the Bundesbank's monetary policy warn that
continued monetary contraction will stifle the potential for growth in the
eastern *Länder*. But the East German *Länder* have begun to show some
encouraging signs of economic recovery. Some claim that East German
economic decline bottomed out in 1992 and that they expect a growth rate
of 10 percent per annum for the next several years. The outlook for western
Germany is not as optimistic. The five German economic institutes reported in late 1992 that no economic growth should be expected in West
Germany for 1993. Many economists now envision the costs of unification
leading to recession in West Germany for the next several years.

Elections and Public Opinion After Unification

Economic conditions and economic reconstruction in the East have also played a major role in the electoral arena following unification. Almost immediately after the December 1990 election and the Kohl government's resounding defeat of the opposition, the euphoria of electoral victory started to wear off and the costs of governing began to accumulate. Only five months into the new year, protest rallies were already being held against rising unemployment and the economic crisis in the East. Especially in the new *Länder*, Kohl's public opinion approval ratings plummeted. His first post-1990 election visit to eastern Germany was on April 7, 1992, to the city of Erfurt, where he was taunted and pelted with eggs by several hundred protesters. In February of 1990, enthusiastic crowds of over 100,000 had cheered him on his last visit there.

The electoral picture was not much better for Kohl in 1991 and 1992. The CDU lost or did not do particularly well in all five *Land* elections held in western *Länder* after unification. Instead, there appeared to be a distinct move by voters to the far right and toward the SPD. Only one month after the national election, in the January 1991 election in Hesse, the incumbent CDU-FDP coalition lost its majority. As a consequence, the SPD and Greens formed a new government under the premiership of the former mayor of Kassel, Hans Eichel (SPD). Three months later, in April 1991, Kohl's most stinging post-1990 defeat came in his own home state of Rhineland-Palatinate, where he had been premier before going to Bonn in 1976. In this election, the CDU lost power for the first time since the founding of the Federal Republic in 1949! The symbolic importance of this defeat is difficult to miss. As a result of these two elections, the SPD was now in power in ten of the sixteen German *Länder* and in eight of the ten western *Länder*. But an end to voters' frustration with the Kohl government was not yet in sight. In June 1991, the Social Democrats regained an absolute majority of seats in the elections to the Hamburg Senate. The *Land* elections in Bremen (the smallest *Land*) in September 1991 brought the first loss to the SPD after the December 1990 elections. However, a small right-wing party, not the CDU, gained from the SPD's misfortune.

The CDU's electoral fortunes did not improve during 1992 in any significant way. In *Land* elections held in April of 1992 in Baden-Württemberg and Schleswig-Holstein, the Christian Democrats lost their absolute majority in Baden-Württemberg, while the SPD was able to maintain an absolute majority in Schleswig-Holstein. In Baden-Württemberg, the CDU held on to the premiership under Erwin Teufel, but only in a Grand Coalition with the SPD. Both campaigns were dominated by the question of the influx of asylum-seekers. In both *Länder*, right-wing parties performed well; in Baden-Württemberg the Republikaner got 10.9 percent of the vote, whereas in Schleswig-Holstein the German People's Union (DVU) got 6.3 percent. In these *Länder* right-wing parties became the third-strongest parties in the state legislatures.

Although not too much should be made of these *Land* election results, it appears evident that the financial costs of unification that have mainly been borne by the western part of the country, as well as the frustration with the slowness of economic progress, have taken their political toll. It is well-established political lore that *Land* elections and elections to the European Parliament serve an important barometer function. Viewed from that perspective, it is clear that Kohl's government lost favor with the general public starting almost immediately after its inauguration. It should be pointed out that all these elections were held in the West, where the economic situation was far from precarious. Had these elections been held in the East, it is doubtful that the CDU would even have done as well. However, it is also important to note that the CDU's losses were greatest when the election campaigns focused directly on Kohl, his achievements in office, and the promises he made during the 1990 national election campaign. The election in Rhineland-Palatinate is a case in point. Not only was there a good deal of symbolic value attached to this *Land* election because Kohl had been the premier of this *Land* before going to Bonn, but Rhineland-Palatinate—together with Bavaria and Baden-Württemberg—has traditionally been one of the most pro-CDU *Länder* in West Germany's postwar history. The *Land*-SPD under the leadership of Rudolf Scharping made a concerted effort to turn the election into a referendum on Kohl's pledge that a tax increase would not be necessary to pay for the economic restructuring of the East German economy—a pledge that was reminiscent of George Bush's "Read my lips—no new taxes" pledge. As mentioned earlier, the federal government's new budget, which was submitted in March 1991 shortly before the election, included substantial and regressive tax hikes. In the immediate post-1990 period, the Rhineland-Palatinate *Land* elections were probably the first clear barometer election, turning on Kohl's tax hikes and the economy in general. Obviously, the SPD's strategy of telling people to send a message to Kohl and his government worked.[1]

The consistent focus of Germans in East and West on the economy is not new and therefore not surprising. It resembles the voting behavior of East Germans in the three elections in 1990 (GDR elections in March, *Land* elections in October, and national elections in December), when they based their evaluations of the parties and the candidates on the prospect of economic prosperity under CDU-led governments. The East German public has been reacting negatively as the prospects of prosperity appear to be slipping away. The decline in Kohl's popularity in the East is likely to correlate highly with rates of unemployment. Moreover, West Germans are reacting negatively to the broken promises of an intense national election campaign. What is interesting to note, however, is the fact that voters were well aware all along that unification would probably bring increased taxes in the West (see Chapter 2).

After these election results, it became more difficult for Kohl and his coalition to govern in Bonn because these elections changed the composition of the Bundesrat, the upper house of parliament; an SPD majority could now block important pieces of legislation, or at least exert increased pressure on the Kohl government. Moreover, as important postunification pieces of legislation necessitate changes in the country's constitution, the CDU is dependent on SPD support in the Bundestag because such changes require passage by two-thirds of the parliament.

Postunification Party Politics

Aside from these currents of political popularity and the electoral fortunes of the Kohl government, several substantial changes took place after the 1990 deluge that have altered the faces of Germany's political parties and have changed, and are still changing, the German party system. Broadly speaking, there has been a process of revival and rejuvenation within the parties on the one hand. On the other hand, there was a clear and conscious movement by the SPD toward the political center while the CDU/CSU tried to placate political conservatives.

A new generation of leadership appears to be taking over the reigns of political responsibility in the big three parties, the CDU/CSU, the SPD, and the FDP, as the post-1990 period allowed them to replace some key officials with younger politicians. The most prominent examples within the CDU are Wolfgang Schäuble and Volker Rühe. The leader of the CDU in the Bundestag, Alfred Dregger, was replaced by the (then) interior minister, Schäuble. This essentially made Schäuble the party's number-two man. Volker Rühe, a Bundestag deputy from Hamburg, and one of Kohl's most ardent supporters who had been the general-secretary of the party after Kohl's falling-out with Heiner Geißler, became defense minister after Gerhard Stoltenberg resigned. Stoltenberg, who was also a former premier of Schleswig-Holstein and minister of finance under Kohl, represented to many the old guard in the CDU. Rühe's successor as general-secretary of the party was also a younger Bundestag member, Peter Hintze. Even though Kohl is still the undisputed leader of his party at the time of this writing, he has clearly turned some leadership responsibility from the old guard over to his two "crown-princes," Schäuble and Rühe.

As Peter Lösche points out in Chapter 3, the West German parties did not take over the East German organizations. Unlike the SPD, the CDU has had to deal with the problem of what to do with the eastern part of the party; there has been a good deal of intraparty quarreling over the course of

East-West integration of the party and the role of politicians from the East. In fact, Kohl's strategy appears to have been to remove those eastern politicians who posed a potential embarrassment to the party and his government. Thus, he exerted, through the then general-secretary of the CDU, Volker Rühe, a good deal of pressure on the last prime minister of the GDR, Lothar de Maizière, to resign from party and other political offices after repeated allegations had surfaced that de Maizière had been an informer for the East German security police. Because of the eastern CDU's collaboration with the Communist regime, de Maizière has not been the only case of political embarrassment for the eastern CDU. A number of deputies of East German *Landtage,* and even a couple of eastern *Land* premiers, have had to resign following allegations of improper coziness with the Communist regime. The CDU made efforts to overcome the tarnished image of the old bloc party in the East by promising to transfer all East German (bloc) CDU assets to the *Treuhandanstalt.* However, there have been considerable delays.

It is safe to say, then, that the national CDU party organization and even the eastern *Land* parties are firmly under the control of the western party establishment. In fact, the CDU imported a number of old party stalwarts to take key positions in the East, such as the premierships in Saxony, Thuringia, Saxony-Anhalt, Mecklenburg–West Pomerania, or party chairmanships as in the *Land* of Brandenburg. In terms of East-West integration, the top leadership of the CDU thus mainly represents the western party elite, with a few East Germans serving to provide some balance.

Major changes were not really anticipated in the CDU's sister party, the CSU, because the most radical shifts of power within the CSU had already taken place before unification due to the death of Franz-Josef Strauss, the premier of Bavaria. The CSU's top leadership responsibilities are now essentially split between Max Streibl, who succeeded Strauss in the post of Bavarian premier, and Theo Waigel, the federal finance minister, who was elected party chairman after Strauss's death.

Major changes also took place within the SPD following the clear election defeat in December 1990. Oskar Lafontaine, the SPD's candidate for chancellor, declared after the 1990 election that he intended to remain premier of the Saarland instead of going to Bonn as the opposition leader (something Helmut Kohl had done in 1976 after he had lost the election to Helmut Schmidt). Consequently, the SPD presidium nominated Björn Engholm, the premier of Schleswig-Holstein, to succeed Hans-Jochen Vogel as party chair in May 1991. Engholm's image stands in marked contrast to that of the feisty and at times almost bohemian Lafontaine. Engholm is a centrist and pragmatist by nature, and he is typically identified with the moderate wing of the party that Helmut Schmidt, a fellow northerner, represented as well. In fact, Engholm had been education minister in Schmidt's last cabinet. At the party convention held May 28–31,

1991, in Bremen, 97.4 percent of the delegates elected Engholm chairman of the SPD. With Engholm a new leadership team and a new leadership style moved into the SPD headquarters in Bonn. Engholm decided that the party needed a manager and gave the post to Karl-Heinz Blessing, a young and capable union official. Moreover, in November 1991, the party also elected Hans-Ulrich Klose, a former lord mayor of Hamburg, to lead the SPD Bundestag delegation. Thus, both the CDU/CSU (Schäuble) and the SPD (Klose) had new leaders in the Bundestag.

In addition to these personnel changes at the top of the SPD came substantive changes. Under Engholm's leadership there has been a clear move by the party leadership toward the political center. The motivation for this policy move was mainly based on electoral and power considerations. As Engholm declared at a party conference in November 1992: "We want to govern this country as soon as possible." At the Bremen party convention, the delegates agreed in principle to German participation in UN peacekeeping efforts; in August 1992 the SPD's party leadership decided that it was time to modify the party's opposition to a change in the Basic Law dealing with the right to asylum, a position that had been advocated by the CDU/CSU. As Gerard Braunthal points out in Chapter 5, Germany has been swamped with an increasing number of asylum-seekers, refugees, and ethnic Germans after the collapse of the Soviet empire. It came to a point where communities and *Länder* were no longer able to accommodate them. Engholm declared that the immigration had to be "braked and controlled"; thus, he took a significant step toward the political center by essentially stating that not everyone was welcome. The CDU/CSU had been trying to paint the SPD as soft on the asylum issue by declaring that if the party was against changing the letter of the Basic Law, it was essentially defending and promoting increased numbers of foreigners pouring into Germany. At a conference, the party leadership under Engholm decided to agree in principle to a change of the Basic Law, which would presumably facilitate the stemming of the flood of asylum-seekers by streamlining the application process for foreigners seeking to stay in Germany. Even though polls showed that over 70 percent of the German population supported such a strategy, a number of the SPD's local branch organizations rejected any proposals for changes of the Basic Law. At a special party conference in Bonn in November 1992 the SPD rank and file endorsed the SPD's and Engholm's "turnaround" (*Wende*) on the asylum issue. In January 1993 the Kohl government introduced legislation to streamline the processing of applying for political asylum, formulated on the basis of a compromise with the SPD. However, in May 1993 Engholm resigned as SPD party chair because he had lied to a special investigative committee of the Scheswig-Holstein *Landtag*, thus leaving the SPD in disarray little more than a year before the next Bundestag election.

The SPD and the CDU/CSU were not the only parties replacing some of their key officials and party functionaries. The most significant development within the FDP was the meteoric rise of Klaus Kinkel, a protégé of Hans-Dietrich Genscher's and a former chief of the West German intelligence service who had become justice minister under Kohl. When Hans-Dietrich Genscher resigned for health reasons in April 1992, after eighteen years as foreign minister, the FDP chose to replace him with Kinkel. Even though the FDP leadership had originally favored Irmgard Adam-Schwätzer, also a protégé of Genscher's, the party's parliamentary group in the Bundestag rejected this proposal and nominated Kinkel for the post. Kinkel is also scheduled to take over the party's chairmanship in summer 1993 after his main (potential) rival for the party chairmanship, Jürgen Möllemann, had to resign from his post as minister of economics in January 1993 because of improper use of his office.

After the stunning election results that left the West German Greens unrepresented in the Bundestag, the party started to reexamine its basic strategy. As a result, a group of radical ecologists split from the party under the leadership of Jutta Ditfurth, a former Bundestag deputy, to form the Ecological Left/Alternative List in December 1991 in Frankfurt. It is probably safe to say that most party faithful and political pundits saw the December 1990 election result more as an accident than the beginning of the decline of the Greens. In fact, the electoral successes of the Greens at the *Land* level after 1990 seem to support this view as well. In four of the five *Land* elections after the national election, the Greens even managed to increase their share of the vote compared to the previous elections in these *Länder*. After much intraparty debate, the confederation of East German citizen's groups, Bündnis90, and the Green Party decided to merge in May 1993 in order to be able to contest the 1994 election as a united party.

Internal party politics, however, are not the only phenomena of change in the new German party system. The party system itself is likely to undergo some change as well. The SPD's move toward the center and toward voters that may have been suspicious of the SPD's and Engholm's electability constitutes one major example of such changes. Given the country's electoral laws, it is unlikely that the PDS will be represented in the next Bundestag, to be elected in 1994. Since the PDS is essentially an East German phenomenon, it will be very difficult for the party to climb the uniform 5 percent threshold that will be applied in all of Germany, unless the party finds a credible partner in the West. At the time of this writing, this is an unlikely scenario, especially as the party's attraction in the East is fading as well. One vehicle that has been supported by the PDS in the East has been the so-called committees for justice, which were founded in July 1992 as a cross-party movement to represent the interests of East Germans. The main advocates of these committees have been Peter-Michael Diestel (CDU), the last interior minister of the GDR and former CDU chair in the *Land* of Brandenburg; and Gregor Gysi, chairman of the PDS. Committees for justice were to be set up at the grass-roots level. However, there appeared to be little enthusiasm for the project among the citizens.

The likely prospects of the Republikaner and other right-wing parties are difficult to gauge. It is clear that they hit on a political gold mine with the asylum issue. They also benefited from the worsening economic conditions, which only added to a general feeling of discontent with politics as usual among many voters. However, it is questionable whether these parties are anything more than single-issue parties or convenient vehicles for voters to register protest. As Germany comes to grips with the question of immigration and the right to asylum, and as the economy improves—in particular in the East—the electoral success of the Republikaner and others like them can be expected to recede.

Overall, then, two main processes have shaped the way political parties operate in the new Germany: The election of a new generation of party leaders and the temporary disruption of the party system. There are clear signs that there has been a changing of the guard, in particular at the top of the parties. Even though Helmut Kohl still heads the CDU, a number of top officials in his and the other parties were replaced by younger ones. Most significantly, the SPD elected Björn Engholm to lead the party into the next legislative cycle, and Engholm lost no time in moving the party toward the political center and possibly toward eventual participation in the government.

Although the West German party system of the 1980s—consisting of the CDU/CSU, the SPD, the FDP, and the Greens—has been disrupted by the failure of the western Greens to make it into the Bundestag in 1990, the representation of the PDS in the first all-German Bundestag, and the success of right-wing parties in a number of *Land* and local elections, it appears safe to speculate that the system will move back toward something of an equilibrium after 1994. The PDS will probably fail to overcome a nationwide 5 percent threshold in 1994, whereas the Greens are likely to reenter the Bundestag then. To a great extent, the potential success of the right-wing parties will depend on the way the traditional parties deal with the question of immigration and whether the government is able to deal with the profound economic problems in the East.

Coping with the Past and the Present

As we mentioned above, much of the current domestic politics of Germany can be understood through the dual lens of the economy and the legacy of Germany's past. However, it needs to be pointed out that Germany is in fact dealing with three separate pasts. One is the legacy of the GDR and the Communist regime. Another is the legacy of the old Federal Republic, its history and self-image. And the third is the legacy of Nazi Germany—a legacy that is shared by both parts of the new country. As Gerhard Lehmbruch and Wolfgang Seibel point out in Chapters 1 and 6, respectively, while it may seem to some, especially in the western part of the country, that dealing with the past and adjusting to the new reality of German politics means dealing with the East German and the Nazi past, it is clear that the West Germany that existed prior to 1990 has disappeared as well.

The handling of the East German past has obviously captured the public agenda and media interest to a great extent. Newspapers are filled with stories about East German politicians' alleged collaboration with the SED regime, accounts of trials of the Communist leadership and trials of border guards who shot to kill those who tried to flee East Germany, and investigations into the practices of corruption among elites and the surveillance of the population by the secret police.

A prominent example of an eastern politician who supposedly informed the secret police (Stasi) on fellow citizens was Lothar De Maizière. De Maizière (CDU) was the last prime minister of the GDR, and he led the negotiations that led to the signing of the unification and the monetary union treaties with the Federal Republic. After allegations surfaced that de Maizière, who had been a lawyer defending regime critics in East Berlin before the revolution, had informed the Stasi about his clients, he resigned as minister without portfolio in Kohl's cabinet and as deputy leader of the CDU on December 17, 1990, while still keeping his seat in the Bundestag. But the rumors did not die down. He finally retired entirely from political life by resigning his posts in the CDU, the Bundestag, and in his home state of Brandenburg on September 11, 1991.

But de Maizière was not the only case of alleged collaboration with the old regime among the new office holders from the East. In fact, the process of regime change in the East was far from complete after a new government came to power in 1990. Of the five premiers of the eastern *Länder* who were in power after December 1990, only two are still holding office at the time of this writing (Manfred Stolpe and Kurt Biedenkopf), and only one is actually a genuine East German (Stolpe).[2] In July 1991 the Saxony-Anhalt premier, Gerd Gies (CDU), resigned and was replaced by the former finance minister (a West German), Werner Münch. On January 23, 1992, Josef Duchac (CDU), premier of Thuringia, resigned because of connections with the Communist regime before unification. He was replaced by Bernhard Vogel, the former premier of Rhineland-Palatinate, who had been in semi-retirement as the head of the CDU party think tank, the Konrad-Adenauer-Stiftung. On March 16, 1992, Alfred Gomolka (CDU), premier of Mecklenburg–West Pomerania, resigned and was replaced by Berndt Seite (CDU), the CDU *Land* party's general-secretary who is also a West German.

The case of Manfred Stolpe, a former church official in the GDR and currently premier of the *Land* of Brandenburg, is a telling example. As a representative of the Protestant church in the GDR, his job required him to have contacts with the state apparatus because the church played an enormously important role in East German society as the only non-Communist official institution tolerated by the regime. Stolpe admitted that he had had regular contacts with the Stasi. The fundamental question is, however, how much contact was too much, or, what level and what kind of interaction with the Communist state disqualifies an individual like Stolpe from holding high office in the new democracy.

Old Communists have also been the focus of much attention. A number of them have been charged with election fraud, misappropriation of funds, or simply corruption. While these may be significant issues to some, among the most important trials dealing with the legacy of the old Communist state are those of border guards who shot to kill and those who gave the orders for such a policy. Willi Stoph, a former chairman of the East German Council of Ministers; Heinz Kessler, a former minister of national defense; as well as Fritz Streletz and Hans Albrecht, former members of the East German Defense Council, were all put on trial for incitement to manslaughter. The most important trial of all, however, started in November 1992, when Erich Honecker, the leader of the East German state for more than twenty years, was charged with forty-nine cases of manslaughter and with misappropriation of state funds. Honecker had fled to the Soviet Union in March 1991 and sought refuge in the Chilean embassy on December 12, 1991. He was returned to Germany on July 29, 1992. After the trial started in Berlin in November 1992, the Supreme Court of the *Land* of Berlin held on January 12, 1993, that the trial against Honecker should not be continued. Since Honecker, who was 80 years old at the start of the trial, and, doctors attested, near death (he had incurable cancer) and would probably not survive until the end of the trial, the judges found that continuation of the trial violated Honecker's constitutional right to "human dignity." This is all the more remarkable as Honecker's regime was one that had for decades shown no respect for its own people's dignity.

The breakdown of the Communist regime also provided the West German part of the new society with an opportunity to deal with an important aspect of its own past: the terrorism of the Red Army Faction (RAF), which had been active in West Germany since the early 1970s. In 1990 a number of ex-RAF terrorists were arrested in East Germany. It turned out that these individuals had been given new identities and been helped in various other ways by the Communist regime in the East. While the RAF continues to commit heinous crimes, such as the murder of the *Treuhand* chief, Detlev Rohwedder, a considerable number of RAF terrorists have been put on trial and sentenced by German courts.

Maybe the most important legacy that Germans in East and West are dealing with today is the powerful combination of the history of two authoritarian regimes (the Nazi regime and the Communist regime) coupled with the desperate economic situation in the East. As Gerard Braunthal points out in Chapter 5, right-wing extremism and racist violence have been on the rise since unification, in particular, but not exclusively, in the East. In the first eight months of 1991 alone, four people were killed and 169 injured in attacks on foreigners by neo-Nazis and other right-wingers. On October 5, 1991, two days after the first anniversary of unification, the tomb of Konrad Adenauer, West Germany's first chancellor, was painted with swastikas. Over the weekend of February 8–9, 1992, alone there were two separate attacks in which fifteen people (including eight children) died. From August 22 to 26, 1992, five nights of riots took place in Rostock where several hundred skinheads and neo-Nazis rioted at a reception center for asylum-seekers. One newspaper reported that "Rioters gave the Nazi salute and shouted slogans such as 'Sieg Heil,' 'Foreigners out!,' and 'Germany for the Germans.' They were in many cases cheered on by local bystanders." On November 23, 1992, in an arson attack near Hamburg, a Turkish woman and two Turkish children died.

Initially, some East German politicians, such as the interior minister of Mecklenburg, Lothar Kupfer (CDU), expressed "a certain understanding" for the rioters. Politicians and state authorities appeared unable or unwilling to quell the violence, and it took the federal government and Helmut Kohl in particular a long time—too long, some feared—to speak out publicly and forcefully against the violence. However, at the beginning of November 1992, a massive public outcry against racist violence started to form, manifesting itself in large mass demonstrations against neo-Nazis and violence and for living in peace with foreigners. Thus, while it took the state and its officials quite some time to react forcefully and with élan, a general consensus appeared to develop in the German population that something needed to be done about the violence as well as the question of asylum-seekers. In 1990 there were 270 attacks by extreme right-wing militants. In 1991 this number had grown to 1,219; 92 percent of these attacks targeted foreigners.

As mentioned before, the "undigested" legacies of German history have had enormous effects on the post-1990 domestic politics: Violence against non-Germans and the campaign to discover who collaborated with the Communist regime dominate much of the political agenda. Right-wing parties such as the Republikaner have benefited at the polls, and the Social Democrats have made efforts to move toward the ideological center on the asylum issue and on Germany's role in the international arena. At the same time, the CDU has been caught in the middle because it has been eager to keep its traditionally conservative voters in line while at the same time being charged with leading the state's response against violence.

Creating a New Polity

Even though the name of the unified German state is still "The Federal Republic of Germany," the old Federal Republic is no more. Yet many of the basic institutional structures are still in place and they frequently do not function differently than they did before the East German revolution. However, it is also clear that the new Germany is not only larger than the old Federal Republic; the Germans who live in this new Federal Republic are also a somewhat different people than the population of the old West Germany. Germany is not only considerably more Protestant and more oriented toward the East, it is also a country whose citizens have to come to grips with the new and different makeup of their own state. Because of the dominance of the old West Germany in the unification process, it is easy to forget that sixteen million of the eighty million people who live in the new Germany never had any experience with the democratic political process prior to 1990.

Building a new Germany is not simply a question of integrating the citizens of the former GDR into the old FRG. The old FRG has been forced to change by the process as well. Yet quite a bit of confusion remains. The public debate surrounding the move of the Bundestag from Bonn to Berlin is a case in point. Important symbolic and practical considerations played a role in the decision to make Berlin once again the capital of a democratic Germany. And this process of adjustment is far from complete. As if to demonstrate Germans' uneasiness with the realities of the postunification era, the parliament's upper house, the Bundesrat, voted to remain in Bonn, while the lower house voted to move to Berlin.

Other, more fundamental, issues that were once believed to have been settled have taken center stage on the political agenda again, such as the writing of a constitution or the question of abortion (see Chapter 7). A constitutional commission was even established to consider possible changes to the Basic Law, such as an extension of *Länder* powers, the right to political asylum, abortion, and whether a referendum should be held on the changes. Moreover, Germans debate whether their country should once again—after all that has happened in this century—take any significant responsibility in the international arena.

It is not just the system of formal political institutions that has Germans wondering aloud these days whether unification can be mastered as planned or as originally envisioned. For those used to orderly political and economic processes or "managed democracy," the domestic politics of German unification must be very unsettling. For those who are willing to take the responsibility for participating in the creation of a new German polity, unification has opened up opportunities that were inconceivable only a few years ago.

Bonn was not Weimar. And the new Berlin is not the old Berlin. But unification has changed and will continue to change the parameters of German domestic politics, and will challenge Germans to reflect on and question anew their national identity for many years to come.

Notes

1. However, it should be noted as well that there were important regional and local factors that led to the suboptimal performance of the CDU in a number of the *Land* elections. Such factors were the disarray within the CDU in Rhineland-Palatinate and the scandal that forced Baden-Württemberg's CDU Premier Lothar Späth to resign in 1991. There was also the general discomfort with the growing influx of asylum-seekers, refugees, and ethnic Germans, in particular in economically depressed areas such as Bremerhaven, a part of Bremen where the right-wing DVU did particularly well.

2. The only exception was Kurt Biedenkopf, a CDU politician from North Rhine–Westphalia, who was an exchange professor in Saxony at the time of unification and who subsequently became the premier of Saxony.

About the Contributors ——

Christopher Anderson is assistant professor of political science at Rice University.

Gerard Braunthal is professor of political science at the University of Massachusetts, Amherst.

Arthur B. Gunlicks is professor of political science at the University of Richmond.

M. Donald Hancock is professor of political science at Vanderbilt University.

Max Kaase is professor of political science at the University of Mannheim.

Karl Kaltenthaler teaches in the Department of Political Science at Washington University in St. Louis.

Donald P. Kommers is professor of government at the University of Notre Dame.

Gerhard Lehmbruch is professor of political science at the University of Konstanz.

Peter Lösche is professor of political science at the University of Göttingen.

Wolfgang Luthardt is associate professor of political science at the Free University Berlin.

Lutz Reuter is professor of political science at the Bundeswehr University, Hamburg.

Wolfgang Seibel is professor of political science at the University of Konstanz.

Index

About the Book

Prominent German and U.S. scholars examine the domestic political events that led to the unification of the two German states. The authors analyze the breakdown of the East German regime, the electoral politics of the unification year, political parties and their strategies, political elites, and the rise of right-wing extremism. They also investigate the challenges and problems caused by the unexpectedly rapid unification process.